"Daniel Smith is a great American with an extraordinary story. Son of a man born into slavery, he has seen the struggle for a multiracial democracy from a multitude of perspectives--and he is still pushing the arc of the moral universe toward justice in 2022. Most of all, he has lived a life of uncommon decency and dignity, a life that should push us all toward the better angels of our nature."

— Martin Dobrow, Author and Professor at Springfield College, Mass.

"America owes a debt of gratitude to Dan Smith, who has worked non-stop throughout his life to make America live up to its ideals. From out-running racists night riders—yelling "PULL OVER NIGGER" and "YOU BLACK COON"—along a dark, rural highway in 1960s Alabama to fighting microaggressions and blatant racism during his career as a federal employee, Dan has been a courageous leader—as he demonstrated during difficult days working in a federally funded anti-poverty program and at the National Institutes of Health. Government executives can learn from his leadership in the federal workplace and his determination to make Washington work for all America.

—Joe Davidson, *Washington Post* "Federal Insider" Columnist

To my parents, family, friends, and colleagues
both Black and white
who have shared this journey with me

*October 19, 2022*
*Daniel R. Smith died in the Capital Caring hospice at*
*Sibley Memorial Hospital, Washington D.C.*

# Contents

# Why My Story Matters

Most Americans think that the Civil War is distant history. But that history lives on in me, quite literally. My very own father, Abram (A.B.) Smith, was born enslaved in 1863 on a plantation in Virginia, part of the Confederate South. He was still effectively enslaved as a child laborer in 1870, five years after the 13th Amendment to the Constitution abolished slavery. He eventually moved north, where he worked as a janitor, had three wives and many children of whom I am the last still living.

My father was 70 years old when I was born in 1932. I am now 90 years old and have reason to believe that I am likely the last descendent of a man born into slavery in the United States. My father had terrible stories to tell about what he and his people were forced to endure, but he also had great strength of character and he taught his children to be proud of our heritage. Despite the hardships he endured, he would never let any of us speak badly of our country.

As for me, I have lived through a lot of America's history during my long life. Although knocked down again and again because of the color of my skin, I learned early in life from my father and Bambi (a film I adored as a child) that when you are knocked down, you must always get back

*Abram (A.B.) Smith (1863-1938), date of photo unknown.*

up. I also learned to believe that hard work and good principles would help me succeed.

In emphasizing my father and telling my life stories, I want to show and stress to those who believe the Civil War is distant history that it was truly not so long ago. The cruelties that whites inflicted on Blacks in our country for nearly 250 years under slavery, starting in 1619, continued during and after Reconstruction. Fostered by the Ku Klux Klan (KKK), these atrocities grew in the Jim Crow era of the early 1900s and were unrelenting for decades afterwards. They came to a head during the battles for civil rights in the 1950s and 1960s and resurfaced with a vengeance with the murder of George Floyd in Minneapolis, Minn., on May 25, 2020, and the attack on the U.S. Capitol on January 6, 2021.

I lived this history -- in my childhood, youth, adulthood, and even now, in my twilight years. I hope that the stories of my life can give readers insight into the depth of the problems Black Americans face. I have never forgotten the words my father said, and what I have tried to live by: "Dan you're the son of A.B. Smith. We survived the ships. You are strong, and don't ever forget it!"

People today who continue to allow racist evils to fester are just as guilty as those who started them hundreds of years ago. My story, however, does not stem from anger for the racial struggles that I personally experienced. Indeed, I was lucky to have been born in the North, which had racial discrimination but not as much pervasive and overt segregation as in the South. I had and still have many white friends.

As for me, while I encountered discrimination, I do not remember facing instances of overt white supremacy in my younger years in Connecticut, nor in my Army service as a medic during the Korean War, nor in the predominately white Springfield College that I attended and where I was even elected student body president. However, it was always lurking there below the surface, and it popped up not infrequently. I later faced it head on as a Black social worker in a mostly white mental health facility in Connecticut and more so as director of an anti-poverty program in Alabama during the height of the civil rights movement in the 1960s, even almost losing my life to KKK-inspired night riders. And again, I encountered it when trying to buy a house in Bethesda, Maryland, a largely white suburb of Washington, D.C.

Worst of all, I had to combat white supremacy in implementing a major new federal government program at the National Institutes of Health (NIH), where I was initially denied the help I needed to develop and implement the national Area Health Education Centers (AHEC) for which I had been appointed Director. It grew worse when my leadership was later attacked by white superiors who tried to demote me. In many cases of discrimination, when employees seek help, they are advised to relocate to another division or department, or to move on, rather than to "fight the system" for their rights.

I preferred to do battle for my rights as a full-fledged government employee entitled to the same treatment, respect, and rewards as non-minorities. Fortunately, I received pro bono help from a high-level law firm (Wilmer, Cutler, & Pickering, now known as WilmerHale) and in the process received numerous accolades from medical leaders throughout the country acknowledging my accomplishments.

That said, I feel I have had a very good life with many adventures and chances to meet interesting, indeed important, people. They include Rev. Martin Luther King, Jr., and Representative John Lewis, and much later, when I served as Head Usher at the Washington National Cathedral, I met and interacted with Presidents Bush (both of them), Clinton, and Obama, and with Supreme Court Justice Sandra Day O'Conner. I also treasure the memories of my friendships with Bishop John Walker, the first Black Episcopal bishop of the Washington Diocese, and Desmond Tutu, the first Black Anglican Archbishop of South Africa.

Because of all the intersections I've had with important historical events and famous people, I've been called the "Black Forrest Gump." I do believe that much of the success in my life and, frankly, anyone else's, is due not only to good luck – and I have fortunately had lots of it, – but also being at the right place at the right time. More important is knowing oneself enough to seize a moment of opportunity and make things happen. Success requires a willingness to take a risk and try something new. Plus, for Black Americans, we must outsmart and outwork competitors, regardless of their race or color. Most of all, I attribute success not only to hard work but also to astute foresight and a strong belief that regardless of one's parentage, we must strive and persevere in whatever we do.

I hope that readers will find inspiration in my story of how I was able to turn the inherited shame and stigma of slavery into a source of pride and strength. How I used hard work, self-discipline and self-belief as a way of enduring the abuse, injustice and unfairness of a system that was stacked against people like me. How I tried to prevent indignities from festering into anger, how I used the many opportunities that living in America presented me with, and how I did my best through action and industry to try to change things politically and to direct my future personally.

I am still acting on these values today as we publish this book. I hope you will find it both enjoyable and inspirational, regardless of your age, gender, ethnicity, or race. We have much to learn from each other.

And please remember my view on life, taken from the words of Edward Everett Hale: **"I am only one, but I am one. I cannot do everything, but I can do something. And what I can do, I ought to do. And what I ought to do, by the grace of God, I shall do."***

*Daniel Smith (upper right) with siblings Jenny, Abe, Marion and Hennie at Marion's 80th birthday party, Hartford Conn., December 2003. Missing is Dan's sister Margaret, who died in 1963. Photo by Loretta Neumann*

---

* Edward Everett Hale (1822-1909), American author, historian and Unitarian clergyman. *https://www.goodreads.com/author/quotes/8183.Edward_Everett_Hale*

# SON *of a* SLAVE

*A Black Man's Journey in White America*

## CHAPTER 1

# The Beginning: Virginia to Connecticut

Like many Black Americans, my family has little documentary information about the personal lives of our ancestors, enslaved families who
were dragged out of Africa and then sold hither and thither without written evidence of who they were or where they came from. Most enslaved
people were not allowed to be educated and could not read or write. Even
slave owners did not always refer to enslaved persons by full names or describe them in detail, except to list them on property accounts for sales and
estates. What we know about the ancestors of my father and mother are
mostly derived from federal census records starting after the Civil War
and, where available, from marriage and death certificates.

Hence, we know little about the early days of my father, Abram
(A.B.) Smith, sometimes also referred to as Abraham. Based on census
records, we know that he was born into slavery in 1863 during the middle
of the Civil War, the son of William and Augusta Smith. They lived in
bondage in the Massies Mill district of Virginia, a bucolic, unincorporated
community in Nelson County. Located in the foothills of the rolling Blue
Ridge Mountains, the region had been settled by white Europeans beginning in the late 1600s.

In 1796, a large section of land in the area was purchased by Maj.
Thomas Massie, a Continental Army veteran. He built his home, named
"Level Green," and enlarged a gristmill that became Massie's Mill. He
gave land to his youngest son William, whose slaves built a substantial

house and plantation that he named "Pharsalia" after the tragic poetic history of the Roman civil wars by Lucan.[1] Other smaller farms were also cultivated in the area. Most had slaves, although the number varied depending on the size and affluence of the own- ers. By 1860, 45 percent of Nelson

*Massies Mill, VA. 2014.*
*Photo by Loretta Neumann.*

County's population consisted of Blacks, most of whom were enslaved.[2] At that time, Virginia had more slaves, 490,865, than any other Southern state.[3]

## My Father's Family

Research has shown that my great grandparents on my father's side likely were Daniel and Elvira Smith.[4] They were apparently the slaves of Robert T. Hubard who, in 1860, owned 76 slaves in Buckingham County, and 104 in Nelson County, Va.[5] My grandfather William's wife Augusta (1847-1914), was the daughter of Mary Carey (1819-1870) and Spotswood Jones. Mary was the daughter of a Mr. Carey born in 1798.

This genealogy has been very exciting news for us, because before I began writing my book, I never knew the names and locations of any of my ancestors except for my father's parents, and I only found them while taking a genealogical class at the National Archives in Washington, D.C. To know that we can trace our family back to the late 18th century is enormously gratifying. Hopefully, we will learn more as further research is conducted.

According to the 1870 census,[6] by then my grandfather, William Smith, was 33 years old, living in Massies Mill, and married to "Agusta" Smith, age 23. My father, Abram, was listed as seven years old, Black and a "Farm Laborer." That was not unusual, as it has been noted that after the Civil War ended in 1865 and despite emancipation, a large core of former slaves had stayed in the area to work as farm laborers.[7] Also listed in the 1870 census in the William Smith household were my father's brothers, Nelson Smith, age 3, and Spotswood (no age given; probably under one year.)

The 1880 census provided more information about my grandfather. It said William Smith, age 34, was born in 1846, and his race was identified as Black. He was married to Augusta, age 33, born in 1847 and identified as "mulatto." At that time, they were living in Scottsville Va., about 40 miles east of Massies Mill. My father was not listed in the household. He would have been around age 17 and was likely living elsewhere.

The 1890 Census was burned by a fire in the Commerce Department Building in January 1921. However, from the 1900 census, we learned some of what probably happened with my father after 1870. We found that he had an early marriage around 1890 to a Virginia-born woman, whose first name we do not know. They moved to Iowa and had a son named Carl, born in 1891.[*] We do not know about my father's life in Iowa, but I recall family lore that at some point he had gone "out West."

By 1900, however, my father was living in North East, a town in Dutchess County, N.Y. We have no information about how or why he moved there. North East contains the village of Millerton and several hamlets. My father and his wife must have moved there several years earlier, as their daughter Mary was born in Millerton on January 31, 1893.[†]

---

[*] Carl Smith, my half-brother, later moved to Philadelphia, where he died Feb. 1, 1966. He was described as mulatto; his wife's name was Gracella.

[†] Mary, my half-sister (we called her "Sister Mary"), married Julius Johnson, and they lived in Bridgeport, Conn. She had two sons and a daughter. She died on September 3, 1998, at age 105, and I attended her funeral.

Abram's wife, mother of Carl and Mary, evidently died during the 1890s. There was a cholera epidemic in the region during that time, and death in childbirth was also frequent.

In the 1910 census, we found my father working as a self-employed day laborer, still in the town of North East, N.Y., living with his family on Spencer Corner Road. He and his then-wife Jane B. (whom he married in 1901) lived in a house that he owned. A story in our family was that my father owned property in Millerton but was swindled by an unscrupulous lawyer and lost it.

### My Mother

The birth certificate of my mother, Clara Wheeler, states that she was born on June 10, 1908, in Sharon, Conn. Her father was listed as John Wheeler, a laborer, and his color was noted as white. His residence was listed as Po'keepsie, NY. Clara's mother was Annie Garrison, age 23, also described as white. Her residence was given as Sharon, Conn. Unstated was the fact that my mother

*Clara Wheeler Smith,
portrait date unknown.*

was born white. Although we were later told that she was part Native American and Scots Irish, we have no documentation for that.

The 1910 census reveals that Clara was living with her grandparents, Charles and Mary Potter, on Spencer Corner Road in the town of North East in Duchess County, N.Y., about 17 miles from Canaan, Conn. As noted earlier, my father's household was also in North East at that time, on the same road. In 1920 the census states that Clara W. Smith had attended school and was able to read and write. Her race was given as "mulatto" instead of white, likely because the other household members included my father Abram and Jennie B. Smith, who were Black.

At some point after that, my father's wife Jennie (listed as Jane in the 1910 census) apparently died. The 1930 census for the Abraham Smith household shows him married to Clara Wheeler and living in Winchester (which includes the town of Winsted) in Litchfield County, Conn. It states that his home was rented, that he had not attended school, but that he was able to read and write. His occupation was given as janitor at a clock factory. The listed household members were Abraham B Smith, age 68; Clara W, 26; Marion, 6; Abraham, 4; Jennie, 2; and Henrietta, 0.

I was born on March 11, 1932, in Winsted, Conn. My birth certificate lists my father Abram Smith as colored, age 70 years old; my mother Clara Wheeler is now also listed as colored and much younger, only age 23.

The 1940 census for Clara Smith lists her age as 33; race, Negro; marital status, widowed; address 423 Main St., Winsted, Litchfield, Conn.; house rented; occupation, housework. Household members: Marion, age 16; Abraham, 14; Jennie, 12; Henrietta, 10; Daniel, 8; and Margaret, 4.

## EARLY LIFE IN WINSTED

Winsted was a small New England town with a population of about 10,000, of which only a handful of residents were Black. It is located about 28 miles west of Hartford, the capital of Connecticut and a city rich in history and culture. Hartford is known for Daniel Webster, Harriet Beecher Stowe, Mark Twain, and the Bushnell Memorial Performing Arts Center. One of my first experiences at the Bushnell was seeing and hearing

Tchaikovsky's Swan Lake Ballet. Indeed, the Bushnell played an influential role in my interest in classical music and the arts, offering opportunities to me that were not always available at the time for other Black children throughout America.

I was raised in a Protestant Christian home, a combination of Southern and

*Map of Winsted and environs.*

Northern Baptist, Congregational, Episcopalian and AME Zion religions. We were very poor, but there were firm "House Rules," developed by both parents and strictly enforced by my mother before and after my father's death. The rules included no men or boys wearing hats in the house and no hats at the dinner table, unless outside for a picnic. (I still require this in my home). Also, no smoking, drinking liquor, swearing, dancing, or playing of cards were allowed in the house.

At the same time, we always found it amusing that as poor as were, living from hand to mouth, our father never allowed us to play with poor kids. Hence, we had to learn to associate and play with what my parents viewed as middle-class kids (mostly Italian, but white, of course). I look back at those days, and the families we associated with were, for the most part, all poor. But because they had telephones and were not on a party line, did not live in a so-called tenement dwelling, and had a bathtub or shower in their home, they were considered rich. They certainly had more material items than we did, but they were still poor.

Our home was on the second floor of a dilapidated tenement located on the west side of Main Street in Winsted. The bathroom was on a porch in the back that overlooked the Mad River. We could stand on the porch and look down at the big sewer rats running around on the edge of the riverbank when the river was low. During the summer huge fish, probably carp, could be seen swimming in the deep center of the river.

One summer morning, the neighborhood gang called for us to come out to play. We could enter the river from an alley off Main Street, and kids often used that entrance to throw rocks at the rats on the other side. My sister Hennie was upstairs and had not yet come out. Someone in the group decided to construct a raft, which we all participated in building, using old boards that were scattered here and there. We carried the raft down to the river.

I can't remember how I ended up being tied to the raft and pushed out into the river, but the kids did it. I screamed for help because they left me and just walked away to play someplace else for another adventure. I slowly floated closer to the deep center part of the river. Farther down, there was a dam, and although the river had receded, the sides were somewhat rocky and muddy. My raft was headed for the deeper part of the water. Fortunately, Hennie came out of the house to play and heard me screaming. She ran down the alley and saw me tied to the raft. She waded into the river, stepped on exposed dry rocks, and grabbed the raft before it went into the deep part of the river. I know she saved my life.

## Little Copper

Despite our poverty, I feel I had a happy childhood. My parents did their best to help us, my brother was tolerant, and my sisters doted on me. All mostly supported my wants and needs. One of my favorite memories from early childhood occurred when my father was still alive. Near where we lived was an elderly school crossing guard. Every morning, dressed in a policeman's uniform, he would be at the corner of Main and Elm Streets controlling traffic to provide safety for the children going to Central School. He seemed old to us, and we called him Grandpa Dartis. I wanted to be a policeman and help him.

My sister Henny insisted that I needed to have a proper police uniform. So, she saved some coins and presented them to my mother and father one night and begged them to get it for me. She said it could be purchased at the local Sears Roebuck store. My parents agreed, and I finally received my policeman's uniform at Christmas. I was overjoyed. It consisted of a child's policeman's cap and jacket with a badge, cross and strap belt with

pants, toy handcuffs, billy club, and small crossing guard stop-and-go shield. (The photograph of it is the only one I have of me at that early age.)

Each school morning my mother would help me get dressed, and I would run down to the corner to meet Grandpa Dartis and help him control the traffic in the street for the children crossing both ways. This was a big honor, and it made the family proud that I was working as a crossing guard.

*Daniel Smith (a.k.a., "Little Copper,"), about 5 years old. Hereinafter in captions, just "Dan."*

## The Spanking

My mother had a profound influence on my life. When I was young, she was a strict disciplinarian. It was important to behave and not cross her. Any infraction of her rules or talking back or being disrespectful would call for a spanking. Now this was not what we called a "white folks' spanking." She would bend you over her knee – and don't you dare run – and spank you with a wooden spoon or the "spanking board" until she felt you had learned your lesson. Then she would slam you down on a chair.

"Now, sit there and cry," she would say. I watched her do this to my brother and three older sisters. I learned very quickly to observe what type of behavior she expected.

Of course, one day my turn arrived. I was about four years old, which I know because I was not old enough to attend kindergarten class until age five. It must have been on a Monday, because we had gone to church the day before, and I was home while my older siblings had gone to school. My mother accused me of taking something from the kitchen while she was cooking and not returning it to the table. I told her that I had not taken anything, but she said I did. I said again that I had not done it.

Oops, big mistake! She grabbed me and pulled me over her knee and gave me a sound spanking. Then she slammed my behind down on the chair, repeating her famous words, "Now sit there and cry. Sit there and cry." I remained seated.

"I ain't gonna cry!" I exclaimed. At this point she returned and picked me up, spanked me much harder, and slammed me back down on the chair.

"Now, sit there and cry!" She exclaimed.

"I ain't gonna cry," I responded again. It was hard, however, as the third spanking truly hurt. But I was determined not even to whimper. Finally, she turned to me.

"You are different from the other kids," she said. I thought to myself, "Yes, and I always will be different."

It was at this point that I determined I would be my own self. I would not let people accuse me of something I did not do and let them receive a reward for it. I still don't know why I came to that conclusion at such a young age, but I do know that I was keenly aware of how my older siblings reacted to our parents' decisions on their lives. My mother was right. I was different. And I would go my own way.

There was a considerable amount of discussion at the dinner table that evening about my not crying from mother's spanking.

## MEMORIES OF MY FATHER

I do not personally remember much about my father. My oldest sibling, my sister Marion, told me much later that he was a short, small man.

"We're all short," she said, "with medium skin. Mother was very fair." She said that when she was growing up, he had a gun in the top dresser drawer. I recall it too. We all did, but we never dared to explore what was in that drawer.

"Once a big river rat was behind our couch," Marion said. "Daddy got the gun and shot at it. The rat came back out, and he shot again three times until he got it."

Our father was employed as a janitor at the Winsted Gilbert Clock Company on North Main Street in Winsted, Conn. I've been told that he was a hard worker. He also had all the necessary equipment to make shoes and belts; indeed, we often called him "Dad the shoemaker." Mother talked about how "crafty" he was, creating things out of wood and even making his own wine.

Father worked at the clock company from 7 a.m. to 6 p.m., which meant he had to arise very early to ensure enough time to walk a half hour or more to his job. Because of his schedule, I didn't get to see him very often. He left before I got up, and I went to bed shortly after he returned home.

I vividly remember when he left for work one winter morning. I was

*Gilbert Clock Factory Winsted CT where Dan's father worked as a janitor. National Register of Historic Places.*

awake and saw him pad himself with newspaper for insulation before putting on his coat to protect himself from the cold. In New England, the winter weather can be frigid, and the streets and sidewalks extremely hazardous, especially if they are not plowed or shoveled.

At the time, I marveled at the way my father conducted himself. Although a janitor, he was dignified, religious, well respected, and stern but gentle. On Sundays, he always dressed as a gentleman, wearing a jacket and tie, with a pocket watch and looping chain across his chest. He also made certain that the family was well dressed for Sunday service at the First Congregational Church. When we arrived at church or when walking through town, we could hear people sometimes whisper, "That's the A.B. Smith family." We stood out among the few other colored families in Winsted.

After church, he would take us kids for a long Sunday walk. It was his opportunity to have quality time with us, and it also gave our mother a break. She needed time to herself. During the walks he would chat with various people and barter with them to obtain things for his family.

"You really don't need that, do you?" he might say. "My child could use a nice chair like that." According to my mother, he was just bartering, and they would often exchange things with him that he would take home to us.

When returning home, we always had great Sunday dinners, just a step down from a dinner with all the extra trimmings that a family has on holidays. I looked forward to Sundays as a day when the whole family was together. Indeed, my father was a good family provider. When he was alive, we never went hungry! I do not know how he and my mother managed on his meager income of only $16 per week.

*Dan's father, A.B. Smith, with older son Abe and youngest daughter Margaret, ca. 1936.*

"YOU MAY BE POOR, BUT YOU CAN STILL BE CLEAN AND REFINED," my parents drilled into me and my siblings. "GOOD MANNERS WILL GET YOU FARTHER THAN MONEY!"

They stressed that it was important to act well. We were poor as church mice, but we felt that we were better because my father said so.

"Life has no meaning unless you help others," he often told us, stressing that we should be kind and, when we do something for other people, we should not expect something equal in return. Instead, we should hope that they will benefit from us and help others who are less fortunate.

Either because my father was not in the house all day or was not inclined to be a strict disciplinarian, he seldom severely punished us children. I do recall once he got upset with me when I was very young. I was crying and whining over something I now don't remember. He didn't hit me but took me by the shoulders with his big hands and shook me hard.

"You have nothing to cry about!" he exclaimed. "Remember, you are the son of A.B. Smith! We survived the ships. You come from the strongest of the strong!" I immediately stopped crying. To this day, I have never forgotten his words.

Father also respected the police. "When you go out of town and if you get into trouble, go to the police station," he told us.

"It's a free country," I remember my parents both saying. "YOU CAN DO ANYTHING YOU WANT AND BE ANYTHING YOU WANT." And they believed it. Indeed, after all my father had endured during his life, he nevertheless spoke well of America and defended our country.

## STORIES ABOUT SLAVERY

On Saturday evenings after dinner my siblings would gather in my parents' bedroom and listen to our father's stories from the past. Although I was considered too young to participate, I would sneak out of my bed, crawl on the floor into the room, and put my head on the corner of the bed to hear him speak.

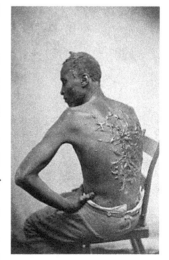

Although he was only two years old when the Civil War was over and the enslaved were legally emancipated, he remembered what his parents had told him about slavery. One thing that brought tears to his eyes and to ours was the story his parents told him of how, because enslaved people did not have their own homes and were frequently moved, they lost precious memorabilia, such as old pictures and family artifacts.

*This famous photo of the back of an enslaved man, always reminds Dan of his father's story of the Whipping Post.*

Several stories that I vividly recall involved the whipping post, the hanging tree, and the wagon wheel:

- **Whipping Post.** There was a "whipping post" out in the field to which slaves were tied and beaten for various infractions during the day. They also called it the "whipping and crying post," because people heard the moans and groans of the slaves being whipped. "It always brought a hush over the other slaves," my father recounted.

- **Hanging Tree.** Another story involved two slaves who, for some reason, were chained together at their wrists and tried to run away. They were found by some vicious dogs under a tree, where they were then hanged together at the same time.

- **Wagon Wheel.** The most egregious story was of a slave accused of lying about something to his owner, a charge the slave denied. It was during a very cold winter. The owner had the slave's family come outside barefoot in the snow to watch. He said the slave had not told the truth, and the owner forced him to put his tongue on a frozen metal wagon wheel, where it stuck. When the slave tried to remove it, half of his tongue came off.

I remember my father's tears as he recalled the stories that he had been told so long ago. Today they still bring tears to my eyes, too.

"For our parents to talk about the past was painful," my sister Marion told me later. When our brother Abe asked our father about something about it, he was admonished. "You don't need to know." Marion said that those early days for our father's family were so bad in Virginia that he and others went west to get away.

"I think people came and recruited them," she told me. "A lot of former slaves were in upstate New York, bordering Connecticut – Sharon, Cornwall, and Kent. People would bring freed slaves up the river to work on their farms."

When asked about Blacks being free in New England, Marion responded sadly. "You were free in a way, but you weren't free. There was slavery in Connecticut. In downtown Hartford, you can see graves of slaves. They were called 'household servants."

## MY FATHER'S DEATH

It was December 22, 1938, a typical snowy New England day. Christmas was in the air, and we knew my father would be home early that evening. He left work, taking the shortest route home. He walked south on North Main Street, then turned right on Elm Street, walking down the right side of Elm, then across to the other side. There he would be able to pass the Central Elementary School where the sidewalks in front of the school were always shoveled. As he crossed Gay Street to the shoveled Central School side, he was hit by an unknown vehicle. We did not know how long it was before he was discovered lying in the road by three teenagers and was transported to the Litchfield County Hospital on Hinsdale Avenue.

I recall that it was dark outside when police arrived and informed my family about the accident. My mother secured a ride from someone to

17

take her to the hospital. Meanwhile, there was panic in our home. Everyone had speculations as to what could have happened. For example, was he purposely hit and killed by one or another of the local Blacks with whom he didn't get along because they thought my father and our family were too uppity? Or was he hit by the local drunk who was always getting arrested? Did someone owe him money and didn't want to repay him? In any event, I remember the crying and wailing in our home.

White and Black men of the cloth showed up to offer condolences. People I had never seen before brought money, food, and other goodies that were put in the pantry and quickly consumed by family and visitors. I saw one of my resourceful sisters sneak a brightly colored package of food and put it in her favorite hiding place. When it came time for the funeral, I was not allowed to go because they said I was too young to attend. (I was only six years old.)

On my father's meager $16 weekly income as a janitor, he had no savings nor any health or life insurance. He died with only his few possessions. He owned the revolver, which my older siblings made certain was quickly removed from the house and given either to a family friend or the local police department. He also had a prized mantel clock, a metal statue of an Indian horse rider being attacked by a lion, and his 50-year-old collection of assorted birds' eggshells. These remain in my possession, and I greatly treasure them.

Also, at some point after my father died, I remember my mother being very distraught one day, and she tore up a large picture of him that was hanging on the wall.

"WHY DID HE DIE AND LEAVE ME WITH ALL THESE KIDS?" she wailed. I saved the pieces but, unfortunately, they got lost along the way as I grew older.

*Winsted Citizen, Dec. 27, 1938.*

CHAPTER 2

# Aftermath: Surviving

It was a bleak time after my father's death. My mother and our family went through a series of challenging stages for several months. In addition to being economically stressed, my mother was left responsible for six children, ranging in age from four to 16. She was determined to keep us all together, although there was pressure on her by female friends to give her children away or let us be adopted. She rebuffed them all and, instead, kept us as a family. (Unfortunately, we were so poor, we had no camera and hence no photos of those early days.)

At first, people arrived from the AME Zion Church and the Salvation Army to provide help. Other "do-gooders" seemed to come out of the woodwork. They also enjoyed the meals my mother made from the food donations we had received. Soon, however, there was very little – often nothing – left to eat in the house.

For Easter that year, mother took our family to the church service. When we returned home, she placed six drinking glasses on the dining room table. She half-filled them with water and crumpled stale bread into them. Then

*Dan's mother, Clara Wheeler Smith, date unknown.*

she poured evaporated milk on top and sprinkled the bread with sugar. Mother gave each of us a glass. That was our family's 1939 Easter dinner. So different from the bountiful holiday meals when my father was alive!

## Commodities

Our struggle to survive continued. This was especially true while we were waiting for my mother to obtain help from the state and be approved for Aid to Dependent Children, a U.S. Government-supported program. I believe it was administered through the Department of Agriculture to the states for distribution to those entitled and approved for such support. When the program was finally approved for my mother, my sister Hennie and I made biweekly trips to the town hall to collect our commodities.

It was always a humiliating experience – that is until we learned to make a game about the redheaded commodity distributor, Ms. Jones. She, like everyone else in Winsted, knew the names of the few Black families that lived there. However, when we arrived for our commodities, she would always ask us, "Now, let me see, what family are you from?" Then she would proceed to count and give out the eggs.

"One egg for Marion," she would say, "and one egg for Jennie, one egg for Henrietta, one egg for Danny, one egg for Margaret, and two eggs for Clara." Clara was our mother, and this would almost send my sister and me into a rage, because no one outside her friends and adults in the family was allowed to call my mother by her first name. She always demanded that she be addressed by her surname, Mrs. Smith. This was significant because white America, for the most part at the time, always addressed Black Americans by their first name rather than their surname. We were in a rage internally because we needed those commodities but could not say anything.

Ms. Jones would proceed with the same approach for every commodity she gave us: butter, powdered milk, beans, flour, and sugar. Also, a package with a solid pound of vegetable oil that contained a small amount of yellow food coloring; mixed together, it resembled butter, but it tasted like margarine. We also were given a one-pound bag of cornmeal. Cornmeal and flour were staples in our house.

One day, my sister Henny and I picked up the commodities, and then we wanted to see our brother Abe. It was summer but a little misty rain fell as we walked past our house to the YMCA where Abe was now staying. Near the entrance to his building, the cornmeal bag sprang a leak, and a trail of cornmeal spilled all the way from there up the stairs to Abe's room. Abe was embarrassed because all his friends and other tenants kidded him about his poor family.

Ms. Jones always ended her distribution with a little speech.

"Remember how lucky you are to receive commodities," she would admonish us. "Hard-working people had to pay their taxes to provide food for poor people like you." We always noted that she never said hard-working white people, but we assumed she was implying that white America had contributed the money through taxes and that she felt it did not come from Black Americans.

## ABE TO THE RESCUE

After my father died, my older brother Abram ("Abe") stepped up to the plate to help keep the family from starving. He became the man of the house, putting food on the table. Without him, we would have been in total disaster. Those were memorable days but not necessarily happy times.

We learned to be creative. For example, Abe had only one pair of shoes, both with holes in them. He would stuff cardboard and paper in

*Dan has no photos of his brother Abe when young, but loves this one of him in his 90s with his great grand children, Giovanni and Lelia Vazquez, Feb 2019. Photo by their mother, Dr. Ebonie Vazquez.*

them to protect his feet from the cold. Later I was pleased when the shoes were passed down to me. I wore those shoes with pride. The bottoms of his socks were non-existent, so he taped the top of his socks to the bottom of his feet to give the appearance when walking that he had socks on. This worked well until gym class when playing sports such as basketball, because jumping revealed that Abe was wearing socks with no bottoms.

Abe moved into the YMCA. In high school, after classes he had a part-time job at the local bowling alley setting up the pins. Abe was one of the few Blacks who worked there. As he later explained it to me, Joe Gatto from Hartford and his family had set up shop in Winsted. Joe had five sons, and Abe worked for them in the bowling alley, which was located down the street from our home on Main Street.

"If I remember right, they paid us about 13 cents an hour," Abe later told me. "We would all go down to Joe's place. He owned the bowling alley, and his brother had the restaurant, which included a bakery. So, we would go there and get something to eat. Then we would get some pin bags." Pin bags were the unsold daily baked goods that were put into small bags filled with donuts, twisted cinnamon bread, and the round centers from the donuts. Abe would not finish work until sometime late in the evening. Afterwards, he would pass by our house on his bicycle headed back to the YMCA. We would wait up in the evening until Abe came by with the famous pin bags. I still do not understand why we never got diabetes from eating and surviving on the many sweet goodies from the bakery.

## MOTHER'S REMARRIAGE

After my father died, our family stayed for a couple years in the rented house on Main Street, initially subsidized by many good people, churches, and the Salvation Army. Meanwhile, urged on by her friends to get a man to help her raise the children, mother met and married George Smith, no relation to my father and quite the opposite in character. George, also known for some reason as "Monk," was an alcoholic and a philanderer, mean natured and a poor provider. We children – the entire A.B. Smith family – rejected him. And when mother gave birth to two sons, George (we called him Georgie) and then Edward (Eddie), we rejected them too. The only one who didn't was my sister Hennie.

Mother's husband George would go away for long stretches of time. One weekend he returned, having been gone for several weeks. He was drunk and angry. Mother and George were in the kitchen, where one white light bulb hung down in the center of the ceiling. My sister Marion and I were sitting next to the sink and stove when our mother and George began a shouting argument. It quickly escalated to a wife-beating scene. He was slapping my mother and she was screaming and trying to defend herself.

Suddenly, Marion – usually a very quiet and serious girl – sprang from her chair like a lioness. She grabbed a little tin measuring cup in her right hand and pounced upon his back. With her left hand wrapped around his throat, she pounded his head with the tin cup.

"Don't you hit my mother!" she screamed over and over as she pounded his head seven or eight times. I was startled. This spectacle was to me beyond belief as I saw the rescue of my mother by my usually calm sister, who was crying and hanging onto the tin measuring cup. Because of the commotion, neighbors came out of their apartments into the hall outside our apartment. Someone called the police and the preacher from the local AME Zion Church, which we attended at that time. A neighbor separated the three of them and told Marion and me to stay in the hall until the preacher arrived.

I recall the hall was dim, with only a dusty screen window that enabled us to look out to Main Street. While she cried, Marion was leaning on the dusty screen window, her forehead pushing against it. At that time, screens were made with a very thin, wire, checkered mesh. Marion was light skinned, so when she moved away from the window her forehead appeared with small black square checkmarks. At that moment I could not understand how all the little checkered squares got on her forehead. However, it soon became clear to me when I placed my damp hand against the screen and came away with the same small square checkmarks like those on my sister.

Soon two women preachers from the church arrived. They were followed by two white policeman who were instructed by the preachers to leave. The preachers said that this was a family issue and did not involve the police department. The preachers also directed their conversations at Marion, who was told that as a young girl, she should not get involved in her parents' arguments. Their intervention and advice were certainly not what my mother or Marion needed or wanted to hear, but times were different back then.

*AME Zion Church, Winsted, Conn.*

Afterward, George left again and soon my mother was once more left destitute. Because she had no money and the white community would often only rent to a Black if there was another home next door rented to a Black, she could not find anyone willing to rent to her. That summer, the AME Zion Church on Gay Street (also known in Winsted as the "Nigger Church") let us live in the parsonage rent free. Our accommodations consisted of one room that was partitioned with curtains for separation. We had no running water (people brought us water in buckets), no kitchen facilities (people brought us food), and no bathroom (we used a "slop pot" instead). This was when my brother Abe moved out of our house and into the YMCA, and my sister Marion went to work as a live-in housekeeper for a white doctor's family. It was an extremely hard time for all of us, not having a "real" home.

One good thing I remember was that the church was next to a horse stable. The men who worked there were expert horse and dog trainers, and they shared with me some of the fundamentals of dealing with animals. I was especially interested in the dogs and went fox hunting with them and their fox hounds. Their instructions helped lead me later to learn more and to become one of only a few Black dog trainers. And, as a result, I have had a lifelong love of dogs.

## LIVING IN MOOREVILLE

The following September, Mother was able to move us to Mooreville, a small, rural community on the outskirts of Winsted. By then I was about 9 years old. Our home was really a ramshackle barn that had been somewhat remade into a house. It should have been condemned. It had no inside plumbing, just an outside privy, and no running water except from a well up the hill. The property was owned by the Vernazies, an Italian family who lived in front of our house next to the driveway. The mother of the family, who owned the property, would often walk over to visit our home and chat with my mother.

The only monies that came into our home were from mother working as a housekeeper and taking care of foster children and from my brother Abe who provided funds from his job at the bowling alley in Winsted. He lived with us in Mooreville for a while before joining the Army during World War II. I remember that Abe often had to close the bowling establishment, count the money, and return it the next day to the manager. It was quite an honor for him, as a Black, to be so trusted by the white owner. This was also significant because my brother at the time had no car, only his bicycle. Living in Mooreville on the outskirts of Winsted, he had to bike to our home in pitch blackness on a dirt road with a great deal of money in his pockets. Although Abe never encountered any incidents, he remained fearful because he was the son of an "uppity Black."

Afterward, when Abe was in the military service, he sent money home to mother. His war bonds also arrived monthly to her for safekeeping and were used to help us. Nevertheless, this was still a bleak time for the family. Winter presented special challenges for us, as the house was drafty and cold. There was little food in it, and we lived on my hunting skills, using Abe's one-shot Remington 22 rifle that he had left home before going into the military service. I had graduated from my faithful Red Ryder BB gun. I remember once I was able to bring home two squirrels, a partridge, a rabbit, and a deer – all in one lucky day!

The next month our cupboards were back at the bare-bones level. Up the hill was an orchard with Macintosh apple trees. The apples would drop off the trees, get buried in the snow and freeze. One winter day mother sent my sister Hennie and me to get some frozen apples, with which she was going to make an apple stew. Hennie and I walked up to the orchard and started digging for apples in the two feet of crusted snow. It was amazing how quiet the area was. As we looked up, however, four deer stood only a few yards from us. One big 10-point buck and three smaller deer. They looked at us as we looked at them. They stomped their feet. We stomped our feet. They got closer. We kept stomping and yelling until they backed off.

I stood guard while Hennie dug and groped for the frozen apples. She then stood guard while I took my turn scavenging for buried apples. We were fully aware that we were competing with the deer for food. I was extremely nervous, thinking they might attack us. It took about 45 minutes to fill a peach basket with the frozen apples. As soon as the basket was full, we ran back down the hill to our house. The big buck moved directly to where we had been digging, and the other deer pounced ahead, searching for apples. We looked out the window of our house and saw the deer looking directly at us. Then my mother made a delicious meal for us with spices, herbs, and, of course, lots of previously frozen apples.

*Well Water and the Snake*

Even getting water could be a hassle, as our source was a well located up the hill near the apple orchard. One summer, because the weather had been so hot, the well had gotten low to the point that water would not flow into the farmhouse. Hence, mother instructed Hennie and I to go up and get some water from the well. Normally the pump on top of the well could be used to bring water from the bottom to the top and into the buckets. However, the well water was so low that the pump pipe did not reach it.

*Dan has no photos of himself and his sister Hennie when they were young. This one is from 2012, when Hennie was 82. Photo by Loretta Neumann.*

Consequently, Hennie and I tied a rope to the pail, and dropped the pail upside down to the water. We then pulled the filled pail back to the surface. Because the water was so low, we had to drop the bucket almost halfway down into the circular stone well. Then we encountered a snake that lived among the rocks of the well. Every time we went down, there was the snake circling around in the stone well.

Hennie and I took turns, starting on one side of the well and banging on it to get the snake to move to the opposite side. When the snake moved to the other side, one of us dropped the pail into the water, which caused another loud bang, scaring the snake. Once the pail was filled with water, we banged on the side for the snake to move and then dropped the pail back into the water and, pulling on the rope, we retrieved it, filled with water.

This was a harrowing experience, especially since the snake looked like a garter snake but was larger, probably four or five feet long. Of course, its big black tongue stuck out. After the ordeal of getting the water from the well, we would run down the hill as fast as we could carrying four buckets of water.

## Dora Adams – Learning Kindness

Despite our abject poverty, mother gave us love and taught us kindness. A prime example was with a very elderly Black woman, Dora Adams, who lived a stone's throw from us in Mooreville. Her dwelling was worse than ours. Her companions were her eight cats, to which she was devoted. We never socialized with her, but Mother always insisted that we save some of our meager food to take over to Miss Dora's home. I remember my sister Hennie and me bringing a portion of our apple soup and baked rabbit to her.

"Never be ashamed of being kind," Mother admonished us.

The same was true for Mayday on May 1. I did not know why we celebrated it, but every year at that time Hennie and I would find wild-flowers and make bouquets using gill-over-the-ground (an evergreen creeper of the mint family) as a base. We gave one to Mother and one to Miss Dora. It made us very happy, before we ran off to play in the fields.

Another occasion came at Christmas. Mother worked cleaning houses, and when she came home, she would tell us about a flower vase that she cherished in one of the homes. Around Christmas time, she showed us the flower vase that a woman she worked for gave her as a present. Mother was so happy and proud, until she walked by the window and saw Dora Adams' house. She stopped and began walking as if in a trance from the window to the table with her new vase. She never said a word, just walked back and forth, window to table. Suddenly, Mother got some Christmas wrapping paper and wrapped the vase.

"Now, you put on your coats and take this over to Miss Dora as a gift from the Smiths," she said to my sister Hennie and me. We were startled but said nothing. The vase meant so much to our mother. But we walked over, knocked on Miss Dora's door, and gave her the present. We could see how pleased she was. It was a good lesson for us, and it made us feel good too.

"Life has no meaning unless you help others," Mother stressed to us a few days later.

### *"Our Lives May Depend on You"*

When I was in the third grade in the Greenwood School in Winsted, the principal was Mrs. Enrico, a gray-haired, indomitable woman who drove a Model T Ford. She was so revered that when she drove down the hill to our school, the students playing outdoors would stop and stand at attention.

I had been appointed to be the class door guard, which meant if there was a fire drill, I was allowed to leave my seat without permission from the teacher and go out and hold the front door open for the other students to leave. One day, the fire alarm went off, and I followed the procedure. As I held the door and the kids filed out, suddenly Mrs. Enrico came down with a group of students, stopped, and looked at me.

"Danny," she said in a loud voice. "Danny Smith! Our lives may depend on you one day!" Well, my chest went up. I was so proud she even knew my name. It gave me an enormous sense of responsibility and a confidence in my ability to help people and not be afraid to step out in front. It was especially important to me, as the only Black student in the school, that she would respect me that much.

*Trying to Save a Dog*

Starting from when I was very young, I loved dogs. I had an early encounter with one that has moved me all my life. As I recall, we were living in Mooreville, and I was about 10 years old. The schools were closed that day because of sleet and rain and the need to get the roads in town salted and plowed. Since I was homebound, it was a great day to go walking in the woods. I bundled up and set out by myself. Ice shingles hung from the tree branches. The temperature must have been about 32 degrees Fahrenheit, because the rain had crusted the snow, so I was able to walk on top of the snow without breaking through.

I ended up at the old Trussle Bridge. Below me was a 3- to 5-foot-deep stream. It was where I had learned to swim with other kids in the summer. I would dive upstream, so that the water flow would carry me back down past the Big Center Boulder to the other side. The water under the stream was always flowing even when the top was frozen over.

That winter, as I walked along the edge of the stream, I saw a dog in the middle. He had tried to cross to the other side but fell through. He was hanging on to the ice with his two front legs, trying to get out of the cold water. I started across the stream to rescue him, but about midway I too broke through the ice into the frigid water and started to be washed downstream underneath.

Fortunately, there was an air pocket, a small space of air between the water and the ice above. I used it to suck air ("burning" my lips on the ice) until I hit the Big Center Boulder in the middle of the stream. The water flowing on the north side of the boulder did not freeze. I believe that, because the boulder parted the flow of the stream, I was able to break through the ice and crawl on my belly to safety onto the snow-covered land. Meantime, the dog somehow escaped the frigid water, and I saw him running away.

I was soaking wet as I walked almost a mile back to our house. My clothing was as stiff as a board. As soon as I arrived, my mother made me change clothes and bring in more firewood for the stove.

I have spent many hours in classes in the Boy Scouts, high school, college, emergency management training, and the Army in South Korea learning the dangers of water in severe cold weather. I still cannot understand why that day I survived and did not get hypothermia. Perhaps it was because the sun was high and shining on the crusted snow below, and there was no wind to further chill me. Or perhaps I was just lucky.

*Eddie Caine*

My best childhood friend was Edward (Eddie) Caine, a white student of Irish descent. We attended Central School, later named Isabelle M. Pearson Middle School. Our first encounter was when we were about 11 or 12 years old. One day, we were scolded by our teacher because we had not returned to her class after recess. A male Collie had wandered on the school grounds, and as dog lovers we wanted to play with him. At the time, neither of us owned a dog.

Subsequently, we joined Boy Scout Troop 18, and we discussed having a dog kennel where we would breed, board, and train dogs. We both got dogs that were mutts. They were our companions and were with us nearly all the time we were not in school. We were working to become Eagle Scouts. Although we never achieved that rank, we had a lot of fun together.

Eddie and I enjoyed hunting, camping, and fishing in the mountains and streams of the area. One time in the late fall, Eddie and I were in the woods at dusk. We ended up on the opposite sides of an icy stream, afraid that the water was too deep to try to wade across. It was getting darker and darker. Eddie, who had more brush and trees on his side of the stream, bent a tall, slim tree, and it reached my side. I was able to grab it and come across the chest-deep water. We laughed and trudged back home.

## CHAPTER 3

# Moving On, Facing Racism

Mother's life took another turn when her second husband George returned to our house in Mooreville one day, again in a violent, drunken, wife-beating rage. He attacked her, and she called the police. I saw them come and take him away to the city jail. I don't know how long he was there.

"He's not coming back," mother told us later. She said she had been informed by the police that he died by hanging himself. My siblings and I felt no remorse for his passing. He had never been a part of our lives, and we had often seen how badly he treated our mother. Most of all, we felt he did not have the good character that our father had.

## BACK TO WINSTED

In 1944, when I was a little over 12 years old, we moved back into the heart of downtown Winsted, on Chestnut Street, just east of Main Street, on the third floor of another dilapidated tenement house. It was an Italian and Polish neighborhood, and we were the only colored family on the block. We felt fortunate to be there. While we were still very poor, we were closer to our church and schools and friends. Mother had more opportunities to earn money for doing housekeeping and my brother Abe, still in the Army, was continuing to send funds for the family. And as her children grew older, I feel that mother grew also, becoming even more independent and less reliant on outsiders.

SON OF A SLAVE

*Protecting Our Home*

The standard practice of the time was that whenever a colored person was passing through Winsted, since there were no hotel accommodations for them to stay at overnight, they generally depended on relatives or friends who lived in town. On one particularly hot summer afternoon, our Italian neighbors across the street were sitting on their front porches with their doors open. (No air conditioning back then.) A Black man whom someone in the community did not recognize had been seen walking up Main Street. So, the police were called. It was customary in those days for police to contact the colored families who lived scattered around the town, to find out if they had a Black guest in their home.

I was in my bedroom which, like our other three bedrooms, opened into the kitchen/dining room. I heard a loud clunk, clunk, clunk, like someone was coming up the outside stairs. When I came out of my room, I saw a policeman at the front screen door. Of course, as in most poor people's homes, the screen had a rip in it. When he saw me, he took his billy club, pushed the door open, and entered the kitchen.

"Hello, sonny," he said, looking around our apartment. At the same time my mother came out of her bedroom on the opposite side of the kitchen. She stood at her bedroom door as the policeman entered the kitchen.

"I am officer John Jones* from the police department," he said. "We received a report that a colored man was seen walking up the street, and we want to know if he is staying with you." My mother looked at him and then spoke to me. She never took her eyes off him.

"Danny," she asked, "did you invite this man into my house?" Before I could say anything, he answered back.

---

* Fictitious name.

"I saw this young boy, and I came in to find out if a colored man is visiting here." My mother never said a word. She just kept looking at him. I knew exactly where she was going and what her next action would be.

"Danny," she repeated, "did you invite this man in the house?"

Before I could respond, the policeman looked at her and, in a very authoritarian, stern voice said, "You are Mrs. Smith, aren't you? I am Officer Jones. Now, Mrs. Smith, I'm the law. You can answer these questions here, or you can come down and answer them at the police station."

My mother never took her eyes off him. She was still standing by her bedroom door. She reached her right hand behind her. Next to the door she had her old, faithful, protective broomstick. She brought that broomstick up and grasped it with both her hands.

"In this house," she exclaimed, "Clara Wheeler Smith is the law!" Then she cracked the broom handle down on the left side of his head. Blood spurted out. He put his hand up to his forehead, and she smacked again. He rushed to get to the door. She followed him out the door, beating him all the way down the stairs.

"Don't you ever come back!" She yelled. Our neighbors on their porches across the street were all looking at my mother. She looked around at them.

"He's not coming back here anymore," she said.

It should be noted that my mother was well respected in Winsted because she had what they called a "Christian house." She was refined, always went to church on Sunday, and did day's work housekeeping. The community knew she had six kids to look after. So, she was quite highly regarded. However, everyone also knew that she had a temper.

Mother would defend what she thought was right and took nothing from anyone in the house or the neighborhood or the town. The small police department knew it too. We later learned that the officer who came that day was new to Winsted and new on the job. They deliberately sent him to our house, most likely because no one else wanted to confront my mother. Today I am sure the police would react quite differently!

## Learning from the Movies

Mother had two main outlets for her enjoyment in Winsted, both located on Main Street. One was the St. James Episcopal Church, where I recall her singing in the choir and playing the piano. The other was The Strand Theater, which showed movies. She would take me there on occasion when she could afford it and when I pestered her enough.

One movie that taught me a lifelong lesson was Walt Disney's *Bambi*, which came out in the early 1940s. The story was about a young white-tailed male fawn who fell while running away from a forest fire. He had been badly hurt.

"GET UP, BAMBI," his father, the big buck who was the Prince of the Forest, yelled at him. "GET UP!" Bambi struggled, and his father called again, "YOU MUST GET UP! GET UP!" Bambi did, and he strode off with his father. His life was saved, and he grew up to become the next Prince of the Forest.

There have been times in my life that I have felt the same – down and out, almost defeated, but then I remembered the call, "YOU MUST GET UP!" Bambi's father reminded me of mine. Over the years, his words have gotten me through some very dark times.

## Love from Mother and a Dog

Mother was also instrumental in my getting my first dog, my preteen canine companion Wolf. He taught me more about love and devotion than all the psychology classes and books I was required to study in college. We had just moved to our home on Chestnut Street, where we lived on the third floor of a tenement house. A Polish family lived on the second floor below us.

It was in mid-fall with drizzling rain outside. My room's window backed up to an old horse

*Dan's first dog, Wolf.*

barn, and outside of it was a sort of doghouse that leaked. A mixed German Shepherd was chained to the doghouse without a swivel in the chain. When the dog moved around, the chain would bunch up and the dog could not enter the so-called doghouse.

I looked out my window and saw this poor animal with big ears and huge eyes looking up at me and whining. He could not reach the doghouse because of the twisted chain, and there was no other covering for him. The rain was pouring down, and the temperature was at freezing. The dog and I looked at each other, and I could see that he was begging for help. It was not my dog, however, so I could not do anything. It began to rain harder, with snowflakes starting to accumulate.

I was in near panic. It upset me so much that I yelled to my mother, who was in the far room. I kept frantically running back and forth from the window to my mother, crying and pleading for her to come and see the dog's predicament. Mother was a strong-willed woman and a no-nonsense parent, but she was very compassionate. I begged her to go tell the owners to bring the dog into their house.

Mother threw on a jacket and ran downstairs to the Polish apartment. She pounded on the neighbor's door, and Mrs. Flotat appeared at the entrance.

"If you don't give that dog to Danny, I'm going to get a chain and tie you out there with it!" Mother screamed.

"We would be glad to give the dog to Danny," Mrs. Flotat immediately said. "We didn't know he liked dogs. You can have him right now, Mrs. Smith." My mother called me, and I ran outside, untangled the dog, and he became mine.

Wolf was the first dog who really bonded with me. He responded to any type of training I introduced him to. We were constant companions. When we later moved to a different house on Gregory Street, I used to win bets with my buddies that Wolf could jump from the ground into my twelve-foot-high bedroom window and that he could also jump back from the window to the ground. I put Wolf on the "stay" about 30 feet from the base of the house. I would bend down next to the house, and he would jump from the ground onto my back up to the window. In reverse, he would jump from the 12-foot window down to my back onto the ground. Everyone was amazed! Wolf was with me for about three years until he came down with an illness and passed away.

## FIRST JOBS – THE JOY OF WORK

Throughout my life, I have held many different jobs, starting with non-professional employment. When I was young, I did not consider it a chore. There was a certain joy in working. I found it both enlightening and educational, and I got self-satisfaction out of the challenges. I learned new skills, had fun, made new friends, and received income for my labors that was much needed for our family.

*Hauling Garbage*

It was summer, and I was 12 years old, living on Chestnut Street with my mother and three strong-willed sisters. I was coming into my pre-teenage growth, but still very much a "runt." I had to obey or take a licking from those in the house who were older and stronger than me. I was determined to get away from the household of women, who always had some form of drama in their lives. I asked my mother if I could work for our local garbage man. She agreed but reminded me that I would have to remove my clothing on the outside porch each day before I entered the house.

The garbage man was named Perry, but my mother insisted that I address him as Mr. Perry as a show of respect for his age. He was white, very unkempt with no teeth, smelly, wore shoes with no socks, and was always swearing. In those days, they did not call him a "sanitation engineer." He drove an ancient, non-dump truck with cardboard and plywood-like siding.

Mr. Perry agreed to take me under his wing. I would wake up early, and he picked me up at 9 a.m. and returned at 3 p.m., Monday through Friday. He paid me a "big 50 cents a week." Not much, but I felt it was my choice, and it would give me some freedom from the house.

In those days, they had no plastic bags or recycle tubs. All trash and food, fresh or otherwise, were thrown into a large 10-gallon galvanized tub by the household. I had to retrieve the barrels, carry them from the back porch of houses or apartments (many times from the third floor), haul them into the truck, empty them, and return the barrels from where I got them. Emptying the barrel was scary, because bees and large river rats would lay their eggs and have their young in the barrels – and scatter all over when the barrel was emptied. Some rats jumped off the truck back into the street sewers.

One summer day, we were driving down Main Street around 1 p.m. on the way to the town dump, which was located past Forestview Cemetery and Tiffany's Picket Lumberyard on the outskirts of town going to Torrington. I was always embarrassed and hoped that no schoolmate would see me riding in the cab with Mr. Perry. One day in the middle of Main Street, the truck broke down and just stopped. In addition, one of the plywood sides came apart, spilling the load of trash all over the road. Rats were running for cover. Some women walking to stores started screaming and they ran too. Of course, several of my schoolmates saw me and started laughing. I looked for a hole to crawl into and hide.

On another occasion, a woman who lived on the second floor of an apartment house placed a small desk-type record player (Victor) on her trash barrel to be taken to the dump. I asked Mr. Perry if I could keep it. He agreed and said to throw some rugs over it to protect it from the other trash on the truck.

It was Friday and "payday." We returned to my house, and I placed the record player on the sidewalk and went back to Mr. Perry for my pay.

"I can't give you the record player and 50 cents, too." Mr. Perry said.

So, I opted for the record player. I took it to the back porch, cleaned it so that it shined, cut the head off a common pin, and used it for the record player's needle. I sold the player for five dollars, turning a negative into a positive, instead of feeling sorry for not getting my weekly pay of 50 cents. The joy of work!

## SETTING PINS AT THE BOWLING ALLEY

Thanks to my brother Abe, after he joined the Army I was able to work off and on in the evenings as a pin boy at the bowling alley in Winsted. Our bowling alley used Duck Pin balls, about one pound each and the size of a large grapefruit with no holes. There were no automatic pin-setting machines, so pins that were knocked down had to be reset manually in the wooden pits. This was a hazardous location for the pin setter because the balls rolled down the alley at a speed estimated at 40 or more miles per hour. We pin boys sat between two alleys on a narrow wooden bench and retrieved the pins that were knocked down. We would then reset the pins that had a female hole in the bottom to the male metal knob which protruded from the floor and would fit into the bottom of the female hole.

Often there were league nights, an even more dangerous event for the pin boys. With 20 alleys in activity at the same time, pins and balls were flying around. We never knew which one was headed our way. I learned to hold three pins in each hand between my fingers at the same time to speed up the process of resetting the pins. Perhaps this was one reason why, as I grew older, people used to remark about my big hands and fingers.

### Picking Tobacco

In 1946 I got a summer job as a picker for the Consolidated Cigar Company, which required boys to be at least 14 years old before they would permit us to be employed. Based in Glastonbury, Conn., Consolidated became the nation's biggest cigar maker. It grew what is called Connecticut Shade Tobacco, grown to make high-quality cigar wrappers. The tobacco plants grew under poles with netting resting on the top of wires and along the sides of a series of wires on probably a 40- or 50-acre spread of land.

Picking tobacco was absolutely dirty work. In late spring we had to stoop on our knees to pick the young plant's tobacco leaves. By midsummer, the plants had grown taller (and the sun got hotter) as we stood up to pick the higher up tobacco leaves. Temperatures under the white netting could often reach over 110 degrees, and the sticky sap from the plants would drip down onto our hair and clothing. At the end of the day, the trucks would arrive around 5 p.m. and return us to the morning pick-up

*Workers tying Connecticut shade plants, Windsor Historical Society.*

site. We were paid on a piecemeal basis of several dollars per day or a certain number of dollars per bin. I found it fun and was pleased to have the income.

I later learned that a couple years earlier, the Cullman Brothers cigar company, through a subcontract with Consolidated, had an arrangement with Morehouse College in Georgia and some other southern Black schools to provide lodging and meals for the students to work in their tobacco fields. Martin Luther King, Jr., (then using the name of Michael King) was one of the students who came up from the south during the summer to work in the fields around Simsbury, Conn. On the weekends they would ride on integrated buses to go to Hartford and other locations and view Connecticut's integrated towns and cities.

Hence, at a young age, Martin Luther King, Jr., had a good introduction to northern social society. He saw the stark contrast when returning to Atlanta,

*Tobacco barn in Simsbury, Conn. where Martin Luther King worked in 1944 and 1947.*

writing later in his autobiography: "I could never adjust to the separate waiting rooms, separate eating places, separate rest rooms, partly because the separate was always unequal and partly because the very idea of separation did something to my sense of dignity and self-respect."

I never saw Martin Luther King, Jr., when he was in Connecticut – our times working in the tobacco fields were two years apart – but I now feel that his being so close to where I was at that time and doing the same kind of work, was a harbinger of what was yet to come. As young Blacks growing up in a white world, both of our lives were irrevocably altered by our experiences in Connecticut, enriched in ways that we would never have known by living solely in the south.

## RACISM IN CONNECTICUT

I don't recall when I realized that I was Black and that being so meant that many white people looked down on me, even in Connecticut, which was historically progressive about racial issues. Indeed, the state was home to abolitionists in the 1800s, including the infamous John Brown, hero of the raid on Harpers Ferry before the Civil War. He was born in Torrington, Conn, less than 10 miles from Winsted. But even in Connecticut, we could not get away from racial discrimination and the hateful words that went with it. I first encountered it when I was about five or six years old, walking with my mother on Main Street. A boy about my age was walking with his mother and saw us.

"Look at those niggers coming down the street," he blurted out.

Hearing that statement, my mother went after the child, and he ran behind his mother. There was a struggle, but the woman protected her child. This commotion resulted in a small crowd of about 10 people gathering around us. It was interesting that most of the crowd supported my mother and frowned upon the other woman for allowing her son to use such hurtful language to Mrs. Smith.

I believe that everyone benefited from that experience. The young boy was wide-eyed and forced to apologize in front of a crowd, and my mother's image of a dignified woman remained intact. But when I think of it, the little boy was really addressing that term to me because mother was very light skinned, and I had a darker hue than her.

Another instance occurred in November one year while I was still very young. My mother and I went to the grocery store to purchase items for Thanksgiving. It was a large, mom-and-pop type Italian store. As my mother and I were walking up and down the aisle, the salesman came around the corner. My mother was looking at the nuts because I had said I wanted some for Thanksgiving.

"Here are all these nigger toes," the salesman said to her. (They were Brazilian nuts.) She just looked at him. He said it again. "We have all these nigger toes."

"If I hear you say nigger again," mother said, "I'll take this bag of nuts and crack you over the head!" The salesman was startled, but he just walked away. He did not want to bother my mother.

*Pickaninny*

When we were growing up, there was always a parade down Main Street on May 30. It included a procession of pets, homemade floats often pulled by an old John Deere tractor, and a marching band from local schools, followed by State Police horses, other horses, and antique cars.

Mr. Nolan, a local businessman, was also an amateur music teacher who taught the flute and had his own fife and drum band that played in the parade. His young girl students wore colorful costumes, and with their flutes they marched down Main Street as a group. My young sister Margaret loved to play the flute and had practiced with a girlfriend her age. Born two years after me, she was light-skinned and spunky, better known as "Apple" because she was cute, and one of our neighbors had called her an apple. Everyone liked her.

Apple wanted very much to be a part of Mr. Nolan's band and participate in the parade. Mother inquired of

*Dan's sister, Margaret ("Apple").*

Mr. Nolan if Margaret could take lessons from him and join his band.

"I'm not going to have any Black pickaninny walking in my group," he bluntly said. Hence, my sister was not able to participate, which really hurt her. To me, that was not just discrimination but overt racism, especially since the group consisted of several of her white friends about the same age.

So, on May 30 our family was upset as we watched the parade pass by without Apple in it. Of course, the only ones affected by the situation were us. The remainder of the people watching the parade did not know what had happened, and they went about their daily business unaware of Mr. Nolan's brainwashed racism. The memory of it still haunts me as an example of Blacks being within a white community but still not really being a real part of that community.

## Hennie's Views on Slavery and Race

Those days, there weren't enough books for the students, so teachers often read to them. When my sister Hennie was in eighth grade, her teacher

47

read to the class *Uncle Tom's Cabin* by Harriet Beecher Stowe. It dwells on the issues of slavery, the conditions enslaved people endured, and how some escaped through the Underground Railroad.

The teacher was on the last chapter, and the students were listening intently. Hennie was the only Black in the class. She had fair skin, but she knew she was Black. When the teacher finished reading the story, there was silence in the room. The teacher thought she had gotten across to the class how bad slavery was.

"Now, class, why don't you raise your hand and tell me what you think of slavery?" she asked. One hand went up, and it was my sister Hennie's. She was a spirited young lady and always had something to say when it came to issues being discussed.

"Yes, I would like slavery today," she exclaimed, "but I want white slaves, and I would treat them the same way as whites treated Blacks!"

A different class involved Hennie's music teacher, Mrs. Sonia, a circuit rider who taught basic music theory and how to read music. At the end of her classes, she would ask students if they would like to sing a particular song. Very few Blacks were in the whole school, but for the most part white students understood that Blacks did not like Stephen Foster's songs that were demeaning to us.

One day Mrs. Sonia asked if there was something they would like to sing. Hennie was sitting in front of the room, and a new kid who sat in the back raised his hand.

"Yes, "he said, "I want to sing Old Black Joe." That was one of the Stephen Foster songs that were offensive to Blacks. Hennie turned her head around, glared at him, and shook her head. As soon as the singing ended, the boy bolted for the door with Hennie in hot pursuit. The boy ran outdoors because recess was just starting. Hennie followed and chased him all around the yard. She finally caught up with him.

"Please don't hit me," he cried. "Don't, don't beat me up! I didn't know we shouldn't sing that song."

"Well, okay," Hennie replied. "I'm not going to beat you up this time, but if I ever hear you ask for that song again, I'm going to beat you up. Do you understand?" The kid sighed with relief.

"Yes, I'll never asked for that song again." Then Hennie beat him up anyway. That was my sister Henrietta!

## *Marion – "Slave Labor"*

My oldest sister, Marion, because of her drive to become a professional nurse, gave me insights and a goal to complete my education and strive to improve myself. But Marion had her own struggles growing up with discrimination and racism, even in Connecticut. For example, while she and my other sisters were tolerated by schoolmates in Winsted, they really had no close white friends as I did, nor were they invited to parties with the white students. And Marion was once offered an insulting job cleaning toilets at a local institution, which my mother would not allow her to accept.

Following the death of our father, Marion obtained a live-in position with a local doctor and his wife. The unwritten agreement was that she would have her own room and provide service as the housekeeper. She would receive a weekly allowance of five dollars, and the balance of the money would be retained and given to Marion when she left.

With the onslaught of World War II in the early 1940s, the defense plant in Hartford, Conn., needed workers. Marion decided to relocate to Hartford, work during the day, and complete her high-school education taking evening classes. She discussed her plans with the doctor and his wife. They said they had to deduct money she used for electricity, water, and heat for her room along with other things that she used while living with them. They presented her with a $100 check for her three years of service. Marion was shocked. Even when she was in her 90s, if this issue was discussed, she became angry and teared up.

"Less than one dollar a week for all that service is slave labor!" she exclaimed.

Not to be deterred, however, Marion persisted. She was determined to get more education. After graduation from high school, she attended Hampton University, a historically Black college in Virginia. She was very unhappy there because of the racism outside the school.

"I wasn't used to the segregation in the South," Marion explained. "Life was okay on campus, but very difficult outside. Black women could not even try on clothes or shoes or hats in the stores. I left after one year."

Her goal was to become a nurse. She learned about the Lincoln School for Nurses in New York City, founded in 1898 in the Bronx to train Black women to become nurses. It was the first school of its type in the United States. Marion was accepted, and after three years she received her Bachelor of Science in Nursing degree in 1951. Meanwhile, she also gained a social education.

*Dan's sister, nurse Marion.*

"At Lincoln, they taught us not to be narrow minded," she said. "Every week, two or three of us would get tickets to go to the opera, ballet, a play, or something. We heard Marion Anderson sing. I saw South Pacific three times with Ezio Pinza and Mary Martin. Afterwards we would eat dinner, then take the subway back to Lincoln. We were never afraid."

While in New York, Marion went to Bellevue Hospital for three months and studied psychiatry. She then applied for a federal grant to study psychiatric nursing in Boston and was one of four nurses to be accepted. She stayed a semester and a summer at the Massachusetts Mental Health Center. She also went to hear the Boston Pops, under Arthur Fiedler, at Faneuil Hall. Marion later went to work in Chicago and then returned to Hartford where she got married, had a son, Philip, and continued a successful career as a health educator in the Hartford school system. She also taught at Hartford's Institute of Living, a prestigious private psychiatric institution for the rich and famous. In short, Marion never let discrimination get in her way!

## Racial Myths

There have always been myths about Black Americans, embedded in the minds of both whites and Blacks. This is often a subtle form of racism. As psychologists have said, if you repeat something enough times, it can become believable in the mind of the listener. Such was the case as we grew up. Some examples of myths that we heard: Black men are more endowed than white men; Blacks can tolerate pain, are immune to common illnesses, and/or have good healing powers; Blacks are dirty, lazy, and intellectually inferior; Black men are not smart enough to be NFL quarterbacks; Black women are loose.

An unusual myth was revealed on Highland Lake, located above Winsted. Circled by cabins and some wealthy homes, the lake had a spillway for water runoff. On one side of the spillway, kids from the area would frolic and swim in the summer. One afternoon, our gang from Chestnut Street went there to swim. A corner of the spillway had a patch of poison ivy that we all avoided. A discussion came up about staying away from poison ivy. My sister Hennie quickly called the white kids scaredy cats and sissies. She walked over to the poison ivy and, while still dripping wet, grabbed some of it and rubbed it all over her body.

"It won't hurt me!" Hennie exclaimed. "I'm Black, and we don't get poison ivy!" She continued playing in the water.

The next day, Hennie, who was light skinned, had the worst case of poison ivy that the doctor had ever seen. She had believed the myth that Blacks were immune to such things. She certainly learned her lesson.

## CHAPTER 4

# Navigating the White World

When I was in high school, my brother Abe, who had moved to Chicago for college and earned money "flipping" houses that he had bought and renovated, purchased a home for our mother in Winsted. I remember him coming back with a contract and a five-hundred-dollar bill in his hand. He described the house he was buying for her. Mother's response shocked us all.

"All that education and no common sense," she exclaimed. "I can't have that house. It's nicer than some of the homes owned by the people I clean for!"

To me, this was a prime example of how brainwashed Blacks had become. She was a strong woman who could beat off a police officer, but she could not see herself owning a nice house. Abe subsequently bought another one, a two-story Victorian on Gregory Street. It was not as fine as the first one, but it was quite adequate, with a living and dining room and kitchen on the first floor, and three bedrooms and a full bathroom on the second floor, a basement, and an attic. It was what mother had always said she wanted, and compared to what we had lived in before, it was great!

*Dan's brother, Abram ("Abe") Wilson Smith ca. 1951.*

Fondly called "Granny's House," it was large enough to hold many people. I lived there while visiting from college. as did many other family members from time to time. Also, my sister Hennie, then my niece Gail (Hennie's oldest daughter), and my half-brothers Georgie and Eddie. My younger sister Margaret and her husband Clarence Parks stayed there when they were first married, until after they had their two sons, Clarence, Jr. (Bitzer) and Michael and moved to their home on Royer Street.

The agreement was that her children would pitch in to help pay the monthly mortgage. I was determined to help, and I always worked hard to earn enough money to contribute my share. I also dedicated my labor to fixing and maintaining the house. One summer, Hennie and I decided that we would reroof the house. So, we got shingles and tarpaper and climbed up on top. Not easy! From the tip of the roof to the foundation was probably 30 or more feet. However, because the house was located on a hillside, if you fell off the roof, you would probably fall almost 50 feet into the brush and rocks below. As we were putting tarpaper around in preparation for the shingles, I started sliding down toward the gutter. I

*"Granny's House" on Gregory Street, Winsted,*
*Conn, 2019. Photo by Loretta Neumann.*

knew I would not be able to stop. I yelled up for Hennie. Just as I was about to reach the gutter, she grabbed me.

"Gotcha," Hennie smiled. "You didn't catch the rope guard we made." She pulled me up. Hennie saved my life again.

The next weekend we scraped, primed, and painted every inch of the house. Unfortunately, we never painted the shutters. Nevertheless, Hennie and I were pleased with the results but unhappy that our siblings did not help. They did, however, show up for our family's midsummer get-together and cookout, and they marveled at the appearance of Mother's painted home. And the roof never leaked after our repairs.

## WORKING

Throughout high school, I had several jobs, both during the school year and in the summers. With my brother Abe gone, I felt an even stronger obligation to bring in money to support our family and to help pay for mother's mortgage. I also saved so that I could have things that I needed.

My main job was working as a kennel boy for Dr. Raymond B. Church, a local veterinarian in Winsted. I would arise at 6 a.m. and arrive at Dr. Church's veterinary hospital by 7 a.m. to run the dogs and clean the kennels. Then I went to school at 8:30 a.m. until school let out at 1:30 p.m. A half hour later I was back at Dr. Church's kennel and stayed there working full time, taking care of the dogs until 10:30 or 11 p.m. That was about 10 hours of work. Then I would go home and study. The next day at Gilbert I would often fall asleep at my desk. I did that for about three years of high school. I made only 75 cents an hour. It rounded out to less than $8 for the day.

Every other Saturday I needed a haircut, but in Winsted during the 1940s, most barber shops would not cut the kinky hair of colored people.

They claimed that they did not know how to cut it. I think they just did not want me to be seen sitting in the barber's chair because of the stereotype that Blacks were dirty. On occasion, one of the barber's helpers, a man named Joe, would come to my house and cut my hair in the kitchen. Joe had served time in prison and, while incarcerated, he had cut Blacks' hair.

Usually, however, I had to take a bus to Hartford, about a 30-mile drive, to get my hair cut from a colored barber. That required me to get up early to go to the kennels and take care of the dogs. Then I would catch the bus to get to Hartford then a cab to the barbershop, a trip totaling more than $6. Then I would wait my turn for about two hours for the barber, who charged a couple of dollars. Then I had to reverse my travel, paying the same amount to return to Winsted, where I went back to work at the kennels until about 10 p.m.

Hence, I had no recreational time for two Saturdays a month. Plus, those excursions to get my haircut cost me $15 or more, yet I only earned $8 for my day's work. But I felt it was necessary for me to look appropriate throughout the week, especially since I was in the school glee club, and we often had to be ready for music concerts in other communities. And, despite the cost and inconvenience, I enjoyed the Hartford barber shop as it had many interesting customers. Saturday morning was always packed with Blacks from different groups, including ministers, teachers, day workers, physicians, one or two Hispanics, and sometimes an elected official. All forms of conversation took place. I once saw a business transaction where someone sold a new car to a customer with only a 25-cent down payment.

As I grew older, I learned to appreciate what a Black barber shop has to offer and looked forward to getting my biweekly haircut. I have been patronizing Ronnie Mitchell's barbershop in Takoma Park, Md., for the past 50-odd years and have made many friends. I took my young son there for his first 3-year-old haircut. However, I never allowed Ronnie to use a razor on my son's head to shape the style, until my son was seven years old. I never had my own hair razor styled, never got a "conk" hairstyle, nor wore the bush that was popular in the 1960s. Instead, I found a hairstyle that I liked and never had it changed.

*Dan with his lifetime friend, Alfred Youmatz,*
*Winsted Conn. 2018. Photo by Loretta Neumann.*

## Poultry Farm & Alfred

During the summers, my high school best friend Alfred Youmatz and I worked at a local chicken and turkey farm owned by "Smitty," a white man who had been a combat engineer in World War II. Smitty had been stationed in the Far East and spoke a couple of Arab languages. He smoked a smelly cigar and always had tobacco juice streaming down the side of his jaw. But he was an accomplished builder and an excellent teacher to us two "crazy kids." His farm, a large complex with about 20 two-story buildings, supplied the local grocery stores with poultry.

Among our routine jobs was to pick up the chicken eggs, weigh them for size, candle them for determining the sex, then sort and pack them for the grocery stores. A "cardinal rule" for workers on poultry farms is that you do not deliberately break eggs. If you do, the chickens will eat them, then peck at other eggs in the nest, and start eating their own eggs

One day I arrived at the chicken farm before Alfred. So, I got my metal egg basket, went around and picked up the chicken eggs in my coop. About a half-hour later, I saw Alfred walking up to the building. When he came in, he had to open the door slowly, so as not to scare the chickens. I took my basket and hit him with eggs. One smacked him in the head and another on his shoulder. Then I ran and hid among bales of chicken feed. Alfred was very mad. He grabbed his basket of eggs and started looking for me.

"I'll get you, Smith," he yelled, "I'll get you, Smith, I'll get you, Smith!" He looked all over for me. But where I was hiding in the feed bin, I could see everything, but no one could see me. Then suddenly Alfred saw a door open slowly. He got his eggs and threw them because he thought it was me. Oops, it was Smitty, the owner! Alfred smashed him with eggs. Of course, Smitty got angry. He went into a frenzy, screaming and hollering.

"Danny," he yelled. "Get down here! I know you started this!"

Meanwhile, two large feed trucks arrived, loaded with several 100-pound bags of chicken feed. They needed to be unloaded, a big undertaking. To top it off, it was 4 p.m. on Friday, and we were getting paid that night. Then we were going to go to a dance at the YMCA. Smitty told Alfred and another student who worked with us to unload one of the feed trucks.

"Danny," he said, "I know this mess was your doing. So, you have the whole other truck for yourself to unload in building number two."

Alfred and Don each carried their 100-pound sacks of feed one at a time, unloading their truck. However, I was not going to be outdone by them. I took 100 pounds of feed under one arm, 100 pounds on my left shoulder, and 100 pounds of feed under my right arm, and climbed up three flights of stairs to unload my truck. I unloaded before they did – 300 pounds of feed at a time!

At the end of our work, we all got paid, went home, washed up, changed clothes, made it to the YMCA dance, had fun, and my white friend Alfred and I have remained best friends throughout our lives.

## HIGH SCHOOL

The Gilbert School is a private school that serves as the public high school for the towns of Hartland and Winchester (including Winsted, which is inside Winchester). The school was founded in 1895 from a bequest of William L. Gilbert who, in his will, left funds for the "establishment and maintenance of an institution of learning to be known as The Gilbert School." He directed that the school give instruction "for the improvement of mankind by affording such assistance and means of educating the

*Dan, teenager at Gilbert Highschool, early 1950s.*

young as will help them to become good citizens." Beginning in September 2011, Gilbert became a six-year, comprehensive, middle and high school.[8]

I attended Gilbert and graduated in 1952. My brother Abe had attended before me, but I was the only Black student throughout my years there. Although this was before the landmark 1954 case of the Supreme

Court in which the justices ruled unanimously that racial segregation of children in public schools was unconstitutional, Connecticut schools and other public facilities were not segregated. Certainly in Winsted, with so few Black families, there were no alternative schools for Black children.

My older sisters Jenny and Hennie had attended Gilbert before me, but. it was difficult for them to make friends, as they were the only Black girls there at the time. Afterwards, Jenny went on to receive a three-year certificate in dressmaking and fashion design from Hartford Technical School and worked as a seamstress for two department stores. Later she took courses in early childhood education at St. Joseph's College and earned an associate degree in English literature from Hartford College for Women. She became a nursery schoolteacher, a substitute teacher in elementary schools, and an English as a second language teacher in adult education. She was active in her church and also wrote poetry.

I was an active student at Gilbert, and elected vice president of my class. But it wasn't always easy. While I had many friends, all white of course, I still often felt alone. I was friendly with a girl named Barbara, who was crippled and confined to a wheel chair. She was otherwise attractive and seemed to be doted on by our classmates. One day while I was wheeling her down the hall, we talked about an upcoming social event that neither of us had been invited to.

"You and I are just alike," she said. "We can both quickly become invisible when our classmates make plans for themselves."

I was struck by her words. This was the first time I realized that discrimination could be based not just on the color of one's skin. She was white, but she experienced it too.

*Lessons in Music*

Although our family was poor, we had an old, out-of-tune, upright piano. Mother played well, and we children would often gather around the piano on Sundays and sing songs of the day, especially movie tunes, religious gospel songs, and Christmas carols. Mother had sheet music from George Gershwin, Cole Porter, and John Newton's song, "Amazing Grace." That is how I learned to sing and carry a tune.

Mother really voiced serious concerns when they jazzed up gospel music in the late 1940s and early 1950s. And she especially did not like Elvis Presley.

"Doing all that foolishness," she complained.

Singing was reinforced in elementary and high school by a circuit-rider music teacher, Miss Sonia. She would spend time with the class teaching us the Do Re Mi basics of music. She also spent time with the class teaching a bit of music appreciation (Handel, Bach, Mozart, etc.). My interest in music expanded in high school. I sang in the glee club and was elected president of it. We traveled throughout New England competing with other high schools. In addition, we had an outside quartet called the "4 Roses," which included class heartthrob Ernie Plude, Faud Francis, me, and another student.

Often in school when a student is elected to a sought-after position, he or she is viewed by other students as someone who is omnipotent in the subject. I found myself in that situation, once elected president of the glee club. One night, at a glee club practice, Miss Sonia was discussing the great historical composers (Bach, Liszt, Mozart, and Wagner). She asked me a question about the German composer Richard Wagner. I fumbled through with the correct response, as the other students clung to my every word. But I was shaken, because I really had no clue what Wagner had written besides the Ring Cycle. I was determined to learn.

For the next several days during recess, I visited the school's library and went through the old faithful card catalogs looking for Wagner, spelled with a V. No luck. On the fourth day, Mrs. Schaffer, the librarian saw me with a bewildered look on my face. She walked over to my table.

"Can I help you find what you are looking for?" she asked. When I spelled out "Vagner," she gave me a quick education that while his name was pronounced as a "V" in German, it was spelled with a "W." I quickly located Richard "Wagner" on the shelf – and I found a new home in the library.

## Racism in Class

As usual, I was the only Black in the class at Gilbert in which the baseball coach, Carl Coleman, was an instructor for many years, teaching a class on the environment and agriculture. Coleman was good at teaching and was respected for his baseball coaching. Winsted, however, was a small town, and it always had a lot of gossip. Such was the case with Coleman. The buzz in the community was that none of his four children had ever graduated from Gilbert.

Coleman enjoyed telling off-color jokes, especially about Negros. For example, he would talk about the Jewish actor Al Jolson, who blackened his face portraying a Black man. Coleman would brag that Al Jolson was the best thing that happened to the Negros. We Blacks, in turn, hated Al Jolson's character because we saw it as insulting to our race. In any event, "Carmen Jones," a movie based on Bizet's opera "Carmen," was playing at the Strand, the only theater in town. Calypso singer Harry Belafonte and gorgeous actress Dorothy Dandridge, both Black, had the lead roles. The movie was discussed in Coleman's class.

"Danny, how can you tell a good-looking colored woman?" Coleman asked me. I was surprised and irritated, so I lashed back.

"If you don't know at your age, you'll never learn," I exclaimed. "And coach, how many of your children have finished high school at Gilbert?"

Coleman glared at me and left his position at the front of the class. He was fuming and his face was beet red. He waddled his 6-foot frame after me and chased me around the desks in the room, but I eluded him and ran out the rear door to safety. I did not enter his class again for a whole week.

## Interracial Dating

Although I enjoyed a good social life with my high-school classmates, as a young Black man I did not, however, experience the usual type of dating. Indeed, I was often not invited to parties in the girls' homes and was not encouraged to dance with them at school functions. The YMCA's Friday-night social functions, however, provided more opportunities. The YMCA played current music of the day (Johnny Mathis, Tony Bennett, Brook Benton, and Frank Sinatra) and couple dancing was acceptable, along with square dancing by a caller.

I observed early in high school that boys bragged – especially about their conquests – while girls gossiped. But I never bragged or gossiped, and I always showed great respect for girls, which made them feel very comfortable with me. I did have some romantic interactions. The girls, all white of course, understood as I did the unwritten social norms related to interracial dating. They knew they must initiate the relationship. They often did this by a brief phone call or by talking to me during recess in the high-school hallways.

Fortunately, I had a part-time job and a car of my own. A girl would suggest we meet somewhere or ask that I give her a ride to a school function. I do not remember ever calling a girl and asking her out. Nor did I pick up a girl at her home specifically for a date. There was always another excuse. A girl and I usually arranged a meeting time and place out of the view of her family or the public. We looked for somewhere it would appear that we were having a chance meeting. Sometimes she asked for a ride home after school. Or she requested a ride to the Wednesday night glee club rehearsal.

For the glee club, once we had an agreement for me to provide a ride, she offered the opportunity to a few of her friends. Then I would pick her up first. She would sit next to the passenger's door in the wide front seat. (That was before bucket seats limited it to just two people.) The second girl I picked up would get in and sit next to her, so my girl could move over closer to me. Then we picked up additional passengers who would sit in the back seat.

After glee club, I dropped off my classmates in reverse order, leaving my girl next to me as the last person in the car. We spent some personal time together before I drove her home. As a result, no one was the wiser and no explanation was needed to her family or friends as to why she was alone in the car at night with me. In short, we had a date!

*Silent Treatment*

Despite my best efforts, however, sometimes others found out about my dates with white girls. There was an incident one morning at school when I was walking down the hallway.

"Hi," I said to a group of my male friends. They all just looked at the ceiling and said nothing. I did not catch the message at first and walked by a second group. The same thing happened. They did not say a word. Later I saw my friend Alfred Youmatz and told him what had happened.

"Well, Dan," he chuckled, "they're giving you the silent treatment."

"What's that?" I asked.

"They discovered that you went out the other evening with one of the most sought-after girls." We both smiled. Then the bell rang, and we went to class. Two days later, life at Gilbert was back to normal.

### First Date with a Girl of Color

My older sisters had a problem with my interracial dating, of which they heard snippets. My sisters then lived in Hartford. They arranged several blind dates for me there. My first date was with Barbara Jean Barrow, an attractive, slim contralto who sang in the church choir. I told my buddies about it beforehand, and they roasted me about the passionate Black men and women, especially with respect to the Mandingo (West African) type of man and the Black Jezebel women. Apparently, Barbara's girlfriends said similar things to her.

When Barbara and I finally met each other, we were both very hesitant and never even held hands. Of course, I had to visit with her parents and be given guidance on her curfew. I had purchased tickets to a movie and paid for supper that evening. When we separately returned to our respective schools, we were the center of questioning about the date.

Barbara was not the only girl of color that I dated. There were others I met in neighboring towns and through musical meetings that I found of interest.

### Special Lessons

While my grades were not the best because of the long hours I chose to work every day, I nevertheless learned a great deal that has served me well throughout my life, not only from books and instruction but also from leadership opportunities and other experiences. I especially thank Mr. Mosely, the principal and stern headmaster of Gilbert. I spent much time in his office being admonished because of my poor study habits.

"Dan, you are doing a lot of outside work, and sometimes you are not awake in class," he said. But he encouraged me, saying he knew I could do better. "I think you should decide whether you want to make a living with the benefit of academics or just do some other type of work." I never forgot his advice.

He also taught me the riddle of the Sphinx, a creature in Sophocles' play *Oedipus the King*. The Sphinx was a creature with the body of a winged lion and face of a woman that destroyed travelers on the road to Thebes who failed to solve the riddle: What walks on four feet in the morning, two in the afternoon and three at night? Answer: It's man, who crawls on all fours as a baby, walks upright in the middle of life and uses a cane when elderly. Mr. Mosely said riddles like this help lead to critical thinking. Another lesson I never forgot.

## Graduation

The high-school yearbook stated under my photograph: "Known for his big friendly grin, Danny is liked by all. That booming bass of his is certainly an asset to the glee club. He's reliable and extremely considerate."

I vividly recall graduation night. My friend Pete Aldridge, the girls' heartthrob, and I went from party to party in the new car that Dr. Church, the veterinarian, had loaned me. When we arrived at one party, a highly sought-after girl ran out to the car, which I was driving.

"I'm French kissing all the senior boys!" Betsy exclaimed. She ran to the driver's side where I was sitting with the window rolled down. She looked at me but did not kiss me. Instead, she ran around to the passenger side, gave Pete a prolonged kiss, then ran back to the party.

About 15 years later at a class reunion, my wife Sandy and I arrived at the hotel ballroom where it was being held. Even before we took our coats off, Betsy ran across the room and planted a kiss on my lips – much to the dismay of my wife. I viewed it as Betsy's apology. Many years after that, especially after President Obama was elected and after I myself started getting media attention, I received several cards and emails from women who had been classmates of mine at Gilbert. They apologized for not having invited me to their parties or danced with me at the school and YMCA socials.

**DANIEL R. SMITH**

March 11, 1932          "Danny"

7 Gregory St.          General

Known for his big friendly grin, Danny is liked by all. That booming bass of his is certainly an asset to the Glee Club. He's reliable and extremely considerate.

*Dan's graduation yearbook photo, 1952.*

## WHITE MALE MENTORS

I was very fortunate to have several surrogate fathers as mentors when I was in high school. Three stand out, and all were white: Dr. Raymond B. Church, Jonathan Ells, and James P. McCabe. I do think they helped me become the man I am today.

*Dr. Raymond B. Church with Dan, 1996.*

## *Dr. Raymond B. Church*

Dr. Church was one of two local veterinarians in the Winsted area. His office was located on Torringford Road. A graduate of University of Pennsylvania Veterinary School, Dr Church was a solid Methodist who lived and practiced his religion. He and his wife Ruth had two active daughters, who often interfered with my mowing the lawn by running back and forth around the mower. As I mentioned earlier, I worked as a kennel boy for Dr. Church during my high-school years. He had a busy and lucrative small and large animal practice and instilled and reinforced my interest in dogs. At the same time, he taught me many medical skills that I was able to use later as a medic in the Army in Korea. He worked with me and encouraged me to become a veterinarian. I cannot speak highly enough about his mentoring while I was in high school.

At one point, there was a major event at the Kiwanis Club when the members invited guests to their dinner. Dr. Church invited me to attend with him, and I was pleased to go. However, the entertainment speaker at the dinner was a bigot who told racist and other off-color (Jewish, Polish, and Chinese) jokes. Dr. Church stood and berated the leadership of the club as well as the speaker for the offensive entertainment. I stood up too, and we were applauded. Driving away from the club, we discussed the issues of racism.

Dr. Church demonstrated other acts of humanity. When my brother and I were trying to purchase a house in Winsted for my mother, Dr. Church worked diligently and successfully with an attorney, Jon Ells, to help us locate a home to purchase. And when it was graduation night from high school, Dr. Church loaned me his new car so that I could ride to the various school parties. Years later, Dr. Church served heroically as a veterinarian providing medical services during the historic 1955 flood in Winsted.

Yet even a good man can be flawed. During my sophomore year at Springfield College, I came home on Christmas break and swung by Dr. Church's office to say hello. He was upset over his plight with the city fathers. The state was planning to build a new highway through Winsted and was using eminent domain to buy up homes that were in its path. Dr. Church's property was one of those. To replace it, he wanted to buy a property on Main Street, but the city fathers objected to a veterinary practice in the middle of town. They told him that he should move it to the outskirts of town, where they thought veterinary practices should be located.

Dr. Church told me that he was thinking about going down to a Waterbury, Conn., community, which at the time was predominately Black, to find a Black woman and pay her to come to Winsted with a baby carriage and children, walking back and forth in front of the property he wanted to purchase on Main Street. Dr. Church knew the town fathers would rather have a veterinary hospital there than have a Black family live on the property. That is what I call blatant racism. Hence, I discussed it with him. I said I felt that although he was a good practicing Christian, this was a classic example of how people have been brainwashed by the American system to support the original sins of slavery and racial separation.

"Americans for the most part," I said, "do not know whether or not they are racists until they are confronted with a problem that directly affects them." Dr. Church subsequently re-established his practice on the outskirts of Winsted.

When I graduated from college in 1960, I had tickets for the graduation, and gave one to Dr. Church to attend. He was pleased and asked for the ticket for his wife Ruth (he called her "Mother"). I replied that "Mother" was not coming to my graduation. She and I never got along. She was always peeking in the windows to see what I was doing. Once she accused me of stealing drugs from the office because I was always tired. Of course, I was working at the kennel 10 hours a day while attending high school. One morning, Dr. Church had me sit and roll up my sleeves to check my arms. There were no needle marks. That was why "Mother" never received a ticket to my graduation.

The postscript to this is the fact that I classify people as my friends not for the money or title they have, nor their celebrity status, but because I feel we are on the same wave length and they are decent people. I can get along with someone, but not feel obligated to love their entire family. Indeed, I am still friends with and in communication with Dr. Church's only living child, Connie Lasik of Florida.

*Jonathan Ells*

Another major mentor was Jonathan (Jon) Ells. He was a graduate of Yale University and one of several attorneys in Winsted. He was also a member of the Kiwanis Club, which sponsored Troop 18 Boy Scouts, to which I belonged. He was a fine, upright Christian man who was a mentor to me during my pre-teen and high-school days.

When it came time to purchase a house for my mother, he was extremely instrumental in making sure we received a fair deal. In fact, he even assisted with the initial down payment of the property. He further worked out a system by which my mother's children were collectively able to contribute to paying the monthly mortgage. He brought another attorney, Albert Manchester, the probate judge in Winsted, to assist him with various legal documents.

I sadly remember when Jon Ells came down with pneumonia. He was home and ill for three days. He was sent to the hospital and died on the fifth day. I lost another good friend.

## James P. McCabe

When I was a pre-teen and our family lived in Mooreville, one of my neighborhood friends was Donald Bleur (white, of course). He was my age and had just become a member of Winsted Boy Scout Troop 18. So, I joined too. The troop leader was James P. (Jim) McCabe, office manager

*James P. McCabe with daughters Ginny and Pat.*

of the Connecticut Light and Power Company. He and his wife Frances had two elementary school daughters, Ginny and Pat. Mr. McCabe and I bonded. He lived the Christian life and was one of the finest and most ethical people I have ever met.

Occasionally, Mr. McCabe invited me to his home after supper and he would help me with my homework. One night, we were at his white-tableclothed kitchen table, and he asked if I wanted something to drink. I requested my favorite drink, hot chocolate. His wife made some and brought it to me not in a mug, but in a nice cup with a saucer. As I went to pick the cocoa up to drink, I spilled some in the saucer, which, of course, I dribbled on the white tablecloth. I did that about four times. Although my mother had instilled in her children the basic foundations of manners in her home, I was totally unaware of the mess I was making with my hot chocolate. Neither Mr. McCabe nor his wife commented on my poor manners.

Off to school the next morning, I went into the school library where Mrs. Schaffer, the librarian, was working on the faithful old card catalogue. As I was walking down the library aisle, I dropped my pencil. When I stood up after retrieving it, I found I was in the section on etiquette. I opened a book entitled, "Elinor Ames' Book of Modern Etiquette," and was shocked to read a section that described a "boorish" person just like me who dribbled coffee and beer all over a tablecloth. I read other sections of the book and suddenly realized that I was not aware of my lack of social graces. I then read other books on etiquette in the library, such as the Vogue Book of Etiquette and Amy Vanderbilt Complete Book of Etiquette. Those types of books (some of which I still retain), gave me even more of an understanding of white American thinking along with the social graces. I was, and still am, keenly aware that there were no etiquette books written by people of color in the library.

## SCOUTING

As for the Boy Scouts, I had great experiences with Mr. McCabe. Scouting was in its glory days back then. It was both educational and great fun, affording me the opportunity for comradery with the other boys and to enjoy the forest world while camping, hunting, fishing, and studying about animals. A master at leadership, Mr. McCabe was an expert in teaching young boys about being responsible citizens and leaders. We scouts would hang on every word when he spoke of survival, kindness, and helping others. He assisted me with becoming a leader and learning to be a rugged gentleman.

One event I vividly recall was when the Boy Scout Council had a "Father's Night" dinner. At our troop meeting prior to it, Mr. McCabe suggested that each scout inform his father and encourage him to attend. Of course, I had no father to inform, since he had died when I was six years old. I discussed the situation with my mother and sisters, none of whom thought I should ask any of the eight or 10 men of color in town, not even the minister, to represent our family. However, Mr. McCabe must have shared the information about the dinner with his wife Frances, as he later called me on the phone and asked if I would go to "Father's Night" with him. My family and I were all surprised but very pleased. I was the only Black person at the dinner, but I had a wonderful time.

The highlight of my Boy Scout days occurred in 1950, when I was working toward the Eagle Scout badge. I had served as senior patrol leader of Troop 18 and was surprised to be honored at a candlelight ceremony at the Methodist Church by being promoted to the post of Assistant Scoutmaster. I was doubly honored when it was also announced that my fellow troop members had voted to select me to represent them the next July at the Boy Scout Jamboree in Valley Forge, Pennsylvania. My mother attended the ceremony, and I was overwhelmed by the attention everyone gave me.

Afterward, I was featured in an article in the *Winsted Evening Citizen* newspaper.* It was extremely rare at the time for most mainstream media to publish positive articles about people of color. The article quoted the chairman of the troop committee, Jonathan Ells, who said about me that Danny was practically "turning himself inside out getting through Gilbert school, working afternoons and Saturdays on a nearby chicken farm to help out his mother in supporting the family, looking after his scouting laurels, and taking an extremely active part in dog training and obedience work."[9]

Our family was then living on Chestnut Street, and mother rented our home from an unfriendly, racist landlady. On the Sunday afternoon after the article appeared, she stood outside the tenement with our Italian neighbors. Someone must have commented on my story in the newspaper.

"I don't care what the paper said about Danny Smith," she proclaimed in a loud, boisterous voice. "He will always be a nigger to me!" Nevertheless, our other neighbors were excited for my accomplishments.

In turn, I thoroughly enjoyed my trip to the Jamboree, which was truly exciting. Scouts from other troops in Connecticut rode together on the bus to Valley Forge. For many, including me, it was our first trip far from home. Once at Valley Forge, we pitched our tents. I sensed that it might rain, so I dug a trench around mine and, sure enough, later I remained dry when others got soaked.

We were encamped on the actual parade grounds and former sites of the 18th century brigades of the original Valley Forge encampment. Over the next week, I met many interesting scouts from all over the country. Organized geographically, we shared stories about scouting and traded goods that we had brought. I was glad to meet a few other Black scouts. And I learned more about crowd control and how to maneuver people when necessary, abilities that came in handy later in my life.

Years afterward, I learned that the 1950 Jamboree was only the second one ever held by the Boy Scouts of America. The first was in 1937, but World War II subsequently intervened. Ours was held from June 30-July 6, 1950, with over 45,000 in attendance. President Harry Truman and General Dwight Eisenhower both spoke to us, Truman at the opening and Eisenhower on July 4. It was the week after North Korean forces crossed the 38th parallel (June 25, 1950), which started the Korean War. Truman did not mention Korea but spoke against racism and advocated international fellowship and human brotherhood. Eisenhower damned the invasion and hinted at U.S. intervention.[10] I recall that President Truman spoke at night to the scouts, and sternly admonished us to turn off our camera lights. Most of all, to this day, I still thank Mr. McCabe, Mr. Ells, and the members of Troop 18 for making my attendance possible.

## CHAPTER 5

# Learning from Dogs

Before, during, and long after high school, I was very engaged with dogs, both as a trainer and as an owner. While training dogs, I also learned how much they taught me – about friendship and the joy of simply being alive. I have heard it said that dogs are racist, but from my experience that is far from the truth. Dogs biologically are color blind and see colors differently from humans. Most will love anyone who loves them, regardless of our pigmentation. They just need our help – e.g., training – to maneuver successfully in a human-dominated world. In turn, we often need them to be our friends when no one else is there for us. I know for sure that has been the case for me. When I was young, I always found that if I was depressed or if something stupid was done to me and I could not share my problems with anyone, I would take my dog and head up into the woods, lay in the field, and talk it over with my dogs. That may seem odd, but at critical times throughout my life, each one of my dogs gave me the comfort and attention that I needed very much. Indeed, dogs have been so much a part of my life, that I strongly feel the need to devote a chapter to them.

## BECOMING A DOG TRAINER

I first learned about the biology and psychology of dogs from Dr. Church, the veterinarian for whom I worked in high school. I also benefited greatly from the Litchfield County Dog Obedience Training Club, which met

*Dogs in the Litchfield County Dog Obedience Training Club
where Dan was a trainer, 1950.*

monthly at the Burrville Volunteer Fire Department, located midway between Winsted and Torrington, Conn. The club taught owners how to train their dogs. I was introduced to it and attended my first meeting in the summer after elementary school. Because this was a "working man's" community, most of the training club's members could not afford the recreational luxury of having the time or money for a dog just to "show." Instead, in those days dogs were used for guarding homes or property, and some police departments were just starting to learn about the value of dogs in their work.

Through the tutelage of several seasoned animal trainers, I progressed in dog training to a point that I became one of the lead trainers in Litchfield County, along with Duke Perkins from Waterbury. He and I took turns operating the training club. Most of the members were somewhat ordinary people, older and without purebred dogs. A few were high-school age. I remember Beth Law from Bloomfield, Conn., who trained at the club with her smart Border Collie. She and I became close friends.

Dog training was coming into vogue at that time. The New York event of the American Kennel Club (AKC) was held annually in Madison Square Garden. With an entrance fee, it was mostly an activity for rich white people who hired dog handlers to show their dogs and parade them around the ring to be "judged." The dogs were grouped by breed and examined by specific judges in an effort to win the title Best Dog in Show. I was usually the only Black trainer there.

Few books were written then about dog training. I remember obtaining a copy of Blanche Saunders' book *Training You to Train Your Dog,*[11] which we called the bible. In particular, on page 82, "The Training Class Director," it explains, in good detail, how a training director should conduct classes. It served me well. I was able to be guided by the book, along with a couple of seasoned dog and horse trainers. I went on fox hunts with the stable owners and their trainers and observed the behavior skills they demonstrated in the field. Later, someone gave me a book, *Follow Your Leader: Guide Dogs for the Blind*, a program initiated in Morristown, N.J.. It was one of the dog books I collected and read often, which broadened my knowledge about training and teaching in general.

Then I discovered in the Gilbert School library *Dogs at War*, a book by Clayton G. Going concerning dogs used during World War II.[12] I was especially struck when I learned about a mixed-breed German Shepherd-Collie-Husky named Chips, who was the first American dog "hero" in the war. In July 1943, Allied forces launched the invasion of Sicily. Chips and his handler, Private John P. Rowell, were unexpectedly attacked by a machine gun squad on a Sicilian beach. Chips broke loose and charged the machine gun nest. Soon an enemy soldier came out of the machine gun nest location with Chips at his throat, followed by three other enemy soldiers. One of them shot his revolver and grazed Chips' scalp, but the dog was quickly patched up. Later that day Chip helped capture 10 enemy soldiers. As described in the book: "In a few brief and dangerous seconds, this American dog singlehanded and at great risk of his own life eliminated an enemy machine-gun position and saved the lives of many of his comrades. His bravery enabled the inland advance to continue."[13]

Chips became the only dog to be given a Silver Medal for his heroic actions. Later, he and Private Rowell took part in the Battle of Salerno. Subsequently, General Dwight D. Eisenhower, the Supreme Commander of Allied Forces, came to congratulate the unit. He bent down to pet Chips, but apparently did not know that only the handler could touch their war dogs. So, Chips responded as he was trained: he bit the general! According to the book, Eisenhower was "a man of infinite patience and good humor and must have thought that the army had trained this trigger-tempered warrior well."[14]

## *Facing Up to a German Shepherd*

Training at the Litchfield dog club one night, I experienced a harrowing incident that I have never forgotten. A young married couple came to the club with their beautiful pure-bred, untrained, 12-month-old German Shepherd. They had kept their pup on a "wire chain run" during the day, which allowed it to run back and forth attached to a chain collar. The dog stayed in the house at night, thereby not socializing with other dogs and people or giving it an opportunity to adjust to the real world.

When they entered the club, I observed that their Shepherd was so happy to see all these other funny-looking dogs. He was laughing and trying to play and make friends. I never saw a happier dog, but he was pulling his owner all over, and she could not control him. He and a boxer nearly got into a fight over turf. In this type of situation with a new, untrained dog and handler, the trainer will often take the dog from the owner and walk it through an exercise along with other owners and their dogs. Usually, the dog will settle down and be returned to the owner, who then continues the training. Not this time! With leash in hand, I gave the class the command "about face" (turn around and go in the circle the other way). When I led the "about face," the Shepherd did not follow me, but remained at the spot where I was. I gave him a hard jerk on the leash and kept walking, expecting him to come to my left side.

The Shepherd suddenly realized that he did not know me, and he started coming after me. People began yelling and screaming. I turned around, gathered the leash, and pulled him toward me, lifting the dog's feet off the floor. I was choking the dog. Normally, once the dog is lowered and his feet touch the floor, he calms down and begins to obey commands. Again, not this time! As soon as the Shepherd's feet touched the floor, he lunged up to my face. I gathered the leash and pulled him up again in front of me until his feet were off the floor. But he was still trying to get at my face, yelping at me. He was so close to my face that I could smell his breath.

Mind you, holding a 100-pound fighting dog off the floor for a second time is not an easy task. My arms were getting tired. I lowered the pup until his feet touched the floor. Fortunately, I was able to talk to him, calm him down, and pet him like we were old friends. The episode ended, but I was so shaken that I had to go out and sit in my car for some time. That was an experience I never wanted to go through again.

The evolution of dog training has changed since the 1940s and 1950s. The military and police departments have played a major role in training dogs. Using a choke collar and abusing the dog if it did not respond to the trainer was never a good training method.

# MY DOGS

I have owned many different breeds of dogs, which I now wish to describe for other dog lovers. Each had a special, often important, role in my life. "Wolf," the mixed Shepherd that I wrote about earlier, taught me more about love and devotion than any books. "Mark," a Doberman, was my devoted companion for 12 years. "Thor" was a protective Great Dane. "Mikey," a dynamic Dachshund that was really my son Rob's dog. And "Gallant Rex of Fairfax," an intelligent and beloved Airedale.

## *Mark (Otto Von Bismarck III)*

Mark, a Doberman Pinscher, was my devoted companion for 12 years. I had read about how the Marines trained and used Dobermans in Guadalcanal, Bougainville, and other Pacific islands. They called them "Devil Dogs" because they were so fearless and effective in smelling out the enemy and exposing ambushes. They saved many Marines by being the "point dog" when they went with their handlers on patrol. A War Dog Training Company was organized at Camp Lejeune, North Carolina, and the Doberman Pinscher Club of America undertook recruiting Dobermans, which became the official Marine combat dog.

As a boy, I longed to have a Doberman, but I was too young and could not afford to buy one. At the dog training club, I met Joe and Dorothy Quinlan, a middle-aged Irish-German couple from Winsted who came to the club with a female Doberman named Renie, whom I fell in love with. Although she was always distant from me, I became enamored of her. The Quinlans and I quickly bonded, and we became good friends. Their dog Renie was subsequently bred to Barron and produced six pups: Hanzi, Guy, Mark, Lady, Jet, and Shy Freda. The Quinlans offered me the pick of the litter. I chose Mark, and he and I became inseparable. A great companion!

I named him Mark because I was studying European history and became a great admirer of Otto Von Bismarck. The Doberman was developed by a German named Louis Doberman in Germany around 1820 and was a cross between the Rottweiler, the black and

*Dan with his Doberman Mark, early 1950s.*

tan Terrier Shepherd, the Schnauzer, and the Otterhound.

Joe and Dorothy had no children, and their dogs became their children. The Quinlans were ineffective in getting them to obey, so I trained all of them in obedience. I recall that when it came time for them to receive their immunization shots from the local veterinarian Dr. Church, the Quinlans wanted to take them three or four at a time in their four-door sedan. However, that required their windows to be rolled up, and the dogs bounced from the front to the back seats, barking at other dogs or anything that was strange to them. Hence, I was asked to take them for their shots.

I had my old faithful 1938 Terraplane (Hudson) car, in which I put their five dogs in the back seat and my dog Mark in the front seat. I rolled all the windows halfway down and ordered the dogs on "Stay and Quiet." Then I proceeded down and back to the veterinarian without a bark from the now year-old pups. In short, they understood me as sort of the Alpha Leader.

Mark was a very devoted, protective, smart dog. I enjoyed showing off with him and demonstrating how I never needed a collar or a leash in public because I trained him with hand signals. I could have him do things just by the glance of my fingers and hands and related body language. When I went to obedience dog shows with Mark, there were usually only a couple of Black trainers, mainly Harold Park from Hartford, who owned a female Doberman named Donna, and myself. The other people putting dogs through the paces were always white. Nevertheless, I became extremely popular at shows because of my connections with my dogs, which people admired.

*Dan made friends with dogs even in Korea, 1954.*

When it was time for me to enter the Army during the Korean War, I left my dog Mark in the care of the Quinlans. They had purchased a plot of land up on Platt Hill Road just past an old brick schoolhouse cabin that had an interesting history. I was told that in years back, a German Nazi had lived there and only left on occasion to go to town to buy groceries. I rented the cabin before college and the Quinlans moved their dogs to their newly purchased property from the barn at their home by

Highland Lake. Ironically, at one point I could have accepted an offer to purchase the old cabin school with the 17-acre property – which I loved – but I did not because in my brainwashed mind I felt I should not be going to college and at the same time buying property. Ever since then, I have regretted that decision.

I was in the military for two years, and Mark became a devoted companion to the Quinlans until I returned and walked into their house. He then immediately came to me and had nothing to do with them. When I returned, I was also surprised at first when people came up to me at dog shows and said, "Hi, Dan," addressing me by my name although I did not know them. I soon realized that many people knew me because I was only one of two Blacks in the circuit. I realized much later that I did not have to remember the names of new white social acquaintances, because they knew mine and I did not have to know theirs – a flaw in my social thinking.

## Thor

My next dog was Thor, a Great Dane with one ear that always flopped half-way down because of a botched ear job. I had two children with my wife Sandy, and Thor loved our children. As he grew from a puppy to a 150-pound Great Dane, he became a constant companion to April and Rob and to our cat Cleo. When we were living in Alabama, Thor was with us and was a great comfort to the family when I joined the civil rights movement. My wife always felt safe with Thor at home. We had a fence around our property, in which he stayed during the day in the summer. Although there was a doghouse, if it rained hard, we would bring him inside our home.

When we moved to Bethesda, Md., in 1968, Thor came with us. One Sunday, a woman neighbor was out walking her dog, and he was off leash as all the dogs were at that time. Her dog spotted our cat Cleo and ran up the bank to get her. Cleo initially stood her ground but then bolted up a tree. As our neighbor walked by, she smiled.

"My dog is king of the neighborhood," she said. This was the first week we had moved into the house, and Thor had been at a boarding kennel until the fence for the backyard was built by Sears. A couple of Sundays later when we had bought Thor home from the kennel, our neighbor was walking her dog again, and the dog ran after Cleo. Thor tore into the dog and chased him down the block. I smiled.

"I guess we have a new king of the neighborhood," I said.

Later we decided that because we had a small house and not what I thought was adequate land for his exercise, we gave Thor to a white gentleman from Alabama who had always admired him. The man and his wife drove all the way up from Alabama to retrieve him. However, I subsequently agonized that they may have used Thor to hunt wild boar or other large animals, including bears.

## Mikey

Mikey, a brown Dachshund, was really my son Rob's dog. Neighbors used to call him the "Smith's hotdog." There are several things I always remembered about Mikey, besides his ripping up mail from the mail slot. We lived on a cul-de-sac, and in the summer, Mikey would go out and lay on his back in the middle of the road and fall fast asleep. Cars would back up and toot and toot their horns until we came out and removed him from the road.

Another thing we remember about Mikey was his sixth sense about ice cream. When subsequently we relocated to Fairfax Road in Bethesda, Md., we lived in a three-story home with a basement where we enjoyed watching TV. My son Rob had his bedroom on the third floor. My wife Sandy and I could be in the basement watching TV, and Mikey could be sleeping on the third floor with Rob. However, as soon as one of us "decided" we would like some ice cream and headed up to the kitchen, no matter how quiet we were, we would hear Mikey tripping down the stairs. He would wait at the refrigerator not for food or doggie treats, but only for his share of ice cream. We never could figure out how Mikey knew that we were coming upstairs to get some ice cream.

*April and Rob with their Dachshung, Mikey (a.k.a. Mike, Mooshy, The Moosh, and Fosco). Early 1970s.*

Also, Mikey was always getting into fights. He and the other dogs in the neighborhood were usually out playing off leash with the kids, a group of children around the ages of 9 and 10. Danny was a Shetland sheep dog owned by the Marino family who lived diagonally across from us. One day Danny must have thought that Mikey was violating his turf and was too close to his family. Danny tore Mikey up, ripping Mike's right side. Blood was pouring from the wound. We took Mikey to the vet, where he stayed for two weeks. We returned him home and kept him in the house or on a leash for a week. Then on the next Sunday there was another neighborhood gathering of kids. Mikey went out and started a fight with Danny and got torn up again. So back he went to the vet (Dr. Benson) for another veterinary bill.

## *Gallant Rex of Fairfax*

My last dog was Gallant Rex of Fairfax, what is called a Giant Airedale. Although he was my dog, he became a new companion for my children, who were both at the time in Bethesda Elementary School. I obtained him while we were living on a corner lot on Fairfax Road. It was summer, and my daughter April and son Rob were outside our house with Rex, playing in the front yard. Another dog came down the street, from the opposite side of the road, and stood there barking at Rex. Rex suddenly bolted across the street, just as an elderly woman driver was passing. She hit and ran over Rex and kept going.

April and Rob started screaming and hollering, and I rushed down the stairs from the third floor. My daughter, who was named "the fastest runner" in the elementary school, sprinted after the elderly lady, who had left the scene. She pounded on the car for her to stop and got her name and other information. Hence, another veterinarian bill, but a good recovery.

Subsequently, Rex and I joined Dogs East, a search and rescue organization. We trained our dogs to go into the woods to find a lost child or other victims. Rex would go out, off leash, locate the victim, return to me, the handler, and then take me to the victim. The Dogs East group was required to have all the paraphernalia necessary to survive away from home, even in a winter wooded area, for three days. I enjoyed that time very much, because survival training generally took place on the

*Dan with daughter April, son Rob, and dog Rex, mid 1980s.*

weekends, which allowed me to be alone with my dog. And I loved the woods and the wilderness.

Unfortunately, one evening I took Rex for his run, right next to the Marriott office complex and Walter Johnson High School on Rockledge Drive in Bethesda. Rex was a very obedient and well-trained dog, but he was off leash at my left side, and it was pitch black. We were walking back to the car when a white-tailed rabbit dashed within two feet of us. Rex instinctively took off after him, and before I could open my mouth to give the command "down," he crossed the service road, at which time a Metrobus hit and crushed him.

I was distraught. This was already an extremely difficult period of my life. I was having a racially motivated battle with the government, my wife had just left the family, we were losing our home because we now had only one income earner, and I was searching for funds for my children's' college education. The loss of my faithful companion was devastating. I think that was the only time my children saw me cry.

## CHAPTER 6

# Korean War, Becoming a Man

In 1952, a few months after I graduated from high school, I was drafted into the Army. This was during the height of the Korean War (June 1950 to July 27, 1953). Many of my friends received the same letter ordering us to report to Fort Devens, Mass., where we got processed. Some of them literally cried, fearing that they were being sent to be killed. I thought of it more like going off to summer camp. Of course, I found out differently after I was there. Korea really turned me from a boy into a man. So many experiences shaped my future in ways that I never would have anticipated.

Indeed, I had already had an extremely sad experience about the war in Korea involving my dear friend Eddie Caine. When he was just 16 years old, Eddie had been pressured by one of Winsted's dredges (my term for a "low life") to quit school and join the Connecticut National Guard. That was in 1948. Eddie, who was white, was first stationed in Germany for two years, and then for a year was an instructor training recruits at Fort Benning, Georgia.

In 1950, President Truman signed the Selective Service Extension Act, which extended the draft and au- thorized the call up of the National

*Private Daniel R. Smith, U.S. Army, 1952 – 1954.*

Guard to go to Korea. Eddie came home to visit on furlough in May. My mother gave up a ticket to my younger sister Margaret's eighth-grade graduation so Eddie and I could attend together. On the day of her graduation, Eddie changed into his new Army dress uniform. He looked splendid, and we had a great time.

This was the last time we saw each other. In late 1951, Eddie was sent to Korea. He had risen through the ranks to become, at age 21, a master sergeant, and he led a platoon with direct responsibility of up to 50 men. On April 5, 1952, his unit was attacked by the North Koreans. He courageously fought off the enemy troops, sending his men further back to safety, but in the process, he was killed.

Eddie was posthumously awarded a Silver Star, the nation's third highest decoration for gallantry in action. His citation noted how he "laid down such a devastating hail of fire that numerous casualties were inflicted, and the foe was forced to withdraw." When the enemy tried to charge again, he left his machine gun to help a wounded comrade. "Taking the weapon of the wounded man, he fearlessly dashed over the fire-swept terrain to a position where he could fire most effectively on the assaulting foe. Although this position was completely exposed to the hostile fire, he undauntedly remained, firing with such devastating accuracy that the enemy was forced to flee in disorder. Seeing the enemy assault repulsed, he proceeded

*M. Sgt. Edward Caine*

to leave his hazardous position, but in doing so he was mortally wounded by an enemy mortar blast."

When Eddie's mother received his body, she asked me to be one of his pallbearers. The funeral was held at the New Hartford Episcopal Church with burial at the Winsted Forest View Cemetery. I attended the memorial services with his

*Edward (Eddie) Caine grave, Winsted CT, 2019. Photo by Loretta Neumann*

mother. Of course, she was devastated, as was I. She never got over the loss of her son. She was pleased, however, that we were able to spend our time together, and I still retain the thank you note in a letter she sent to me after he died.

Prior to his death, when the Korean hostilities intensified, Eddie and I had agreed to stay in touch with the other's mother in the event one of us died. Subsequently, after Eddie's death, I annually sent flowers or a card to his mother for Mother's Day, Easter, and her birthday until she died at age 98. Fast forward to 1995 and the celebration of the opening, on the Washington Mall, of the Korean War Veterans Memorial. As I was one of the leaders for the celebration by the Korean War Veterans Association, I invited and arranged for Eddie Caine's sister and her daughter to attend the banquet and to be seated at my table. And in my presentation at the Washington National Cathedral's special memorial service for the assembled Korean Veterans, I spoke of Eddie, our growing up as youths together, and his courage.

I still grieve for Eddie Caine. He was a good friend who served his country well and never lived to have a family as I did. I feel very strongly that as an American, we should not forget those who sacrificed their lives for this country. I often think of how lucky I have been despite the racial discrimination of America. Although I faced many challenges along the way, I was alive, went to college, married, had two beautiful children, and led a productive life. Eddie may have been white, but he never had those opportunities.

## DISCRIMINATION IN THE MILITARY

The Korean War had a major impact on my life. It began in June and prior to that, in 1948 by executive order, President Harry Truman desegregated all the U.S. military. This was a big deal, since before then all military troops led separate white and Black lives. There was segregation and discrimination in assignments and deployment before the order, but in fact it continued after that. Troops in all branches of the service were generally under the sole leadership, direction, and authority of white officers.

Most of the top leadership, like Generals Marshall, MacArthur, and Patton had gone to a service academy like West Point, Virginia Military Institute, or South Carolina's Citadel. Many were from the South. I believe that they came with segregation and discrimination in their hearts and in their minds. The white academy soldiers received the bulk of the promotions. Black officers, who you could count on one hand, who had gone through Officers Candidate School or came from the National Guard, were not given the same respect as those from the military academies.

My brother Abe, who served in the Army during World War II, suffered from the discrimination that was common at that time. When the United States entered World War II, Abe was in high school and, like many young Americans, he left school to join the military. First, he tried the Marine Corps, but was rejected because he could not play a musical instrument, which the recruitment staff said he needed to keep calm if he got pinned down by enemy fire. So, Abe went home and with lots of practice learned to play the harmonica. When he went back to the recruitment office and demonstrated to them that he could play it, they admitted that they were not taking Negros into the Marines.

Next, because he loved airplanes and knew a lot about them, he tried the Army Air Force. But nope, they too had a racist excuse for not accepting Blacks. Finally, Abe was drafted into the regular U.S. Army. He was sent to Keesler Air Force Base, located within the city limits of Biloxi, Miss., on the Gulf Coast. Mississippi was (and remains) one of the most racist states in the South and racial separation was the norm.

Abe was assigned to an all-Black unit with white officers as leaders. One night, the whistle blew for Abe's platoon to fall out and line up by squad. Abe was light skinned, as were the soldiers to his right and left side. The company commander brought with him an aide, the town sheriff, a young white woman in her late twenties, and her brother. That group went up and down the line looking at each soldier. The woman stopped in front of my brother and stared at the three other light-skinned Black men. She pointed at the soldier on Abe's left.

"That's the man who raped me!" she screamed.

The unit was dismissed, and the accused was taken to the office of the Commander, who called for the medical officer to examine him. The soldier was required to remove every stitch of his clothing in front of the group. He had, however, three days previously been circumcised, and the stiches were plainly visible. Hence, it was impossible for him to have had intercourse with anyone at the time the rape was supposed to have happened.

The frightening thing is that had she accused my brother, he would have been taken by the sheriff to jail. Given Mississippi's reputation for lynchings, who knows what might have happened to him. Instead, Abe went on to serve like many drafted Black soldiers, assigned to positions that did not utilize his abilities. Abe was very intelligent and had many skills, but he was assigned to more menial tasks such as garbage detail, picking up trash. He would lift 50-gallon cans of refuse and manually dump them into the trash trucks. As a result, he ended up with three hernias. But he still felt proud to be part of the Army at that very difficult time. And the fact that he wasn't sent overseas to battle probably saved his life.

## BASIC TRAINING & TRIP TO KOREA

After I was drafted into the U.S. Army in 1952, I was sent from Connecticut to Camp Pickett near Blackstone, Va., for basic training. I traveled there with white friends who were also from New England, an integrated group. When we arrived at the camp in Virginia, I found that many of the Black southern troops were unfamiliar with interacting with white Americans. Later in Korea, some of the southern Blacks who had been at the camp in Virginia, who got to know me as a friend, told me that they had not initially liked me because they thought I was spending too much time with the white guys whom I came down with.

At Camp Pickett, we were given opportunities to state what we would like to do in the Army. Because of my experience training dogs, I applied for the canine corps. But despite President Truman's Executive Order integrating the Armed Services, I was told that they weren't taking "coloreds" into the canine corps. I was given a similar response when, because of my swimming expertise, I asked to be part of the Underwater Demolition Team (UDT). Given that both jobs were extremely dangerous, I was probably better off just doing what other draftees did – learn how to kill people.

I remember vividly our drill sergeant teaching us to use the bayonet. He was an older man, and I thought he was always going to fall over when he came out in front of the troops to train us. But he kept us alert.

"Rape! Kill! Plunder!" Those were the words he always used when we went through bayonet training.

After six weeks, the basic training was over. We had a week off (furlough) before we took a train to San Francisco to board the troop ship to take us to Korea. When we arrived at San Francisco, the situation was rather chaotic because all the troops were piled into one compound. There was no military leadership for us privates, and no one above our grade to give directions. It was crazy. So, I took over for my group and started giving directions as if I were the sergeant. The funniest thing is that I just told men to line up and do the silly things we know we have to do in the service. They followed my orders as if I had been appointed in charge. I had not and just saw a void and filled it. But they listened.

Finally, a real sergeant came in and then a lieutenant. I was neither criticized nor thanked for what I had done to keep the troops in order. Instead, we were all given clothing to go to Korea and numbers to line up with our duffel bags. We then got to go on the ship.

## Shipping Off to Korea

Our ship was named after Quartermaster General Montgomery Meigs, one of the leading figures for the Union during the Civil War. We boarded and sailed out of the harbor. When we passed under the Golden Gate Bridge, the ship stopped and dropped anchor. We heard a voice over the loudspeaker.

"This is the captain," he said. "In the event we are attacked by submarines or planes and a compartment gets filled with water, we will automatically close it to save the rest of the ship." Hearing that, I made sure that I got the top bunk right next to the door of our compartment. I figured if we got attacked, I was going to hold the door open until I got out!

On the journey over to Korea, they fed us well. We had turkey, chicken, pork chops, and potatoes. After we ate, I had a chance to go up on deck and look at the water. I remember while I was up there, the ship's crew came out with all the leftover cooked potatoes, turkey, and other food and just threw them overboard. Yet when we had gone through to the food line, they only gave us a certain amount, like a wing or breast, on our plates. I was shocked that good food was being thrown overboard along with other things like boxes and anything they had no use for. It was such a waste and way of polluting the water.

We finally arrived in South Korea at the southern end of Pusan. Our compound was surrounded by a tall wire fence. We soon encountered a group of little Korean kids, aged five or younger, begging for food. Several older, departing troops started throwing rocks at them. Some of our new recruits got upset, and we nearly had a riot. One of the older departing soldiers explained the problem.

"Those kids look innocent," he said. "We used to want to give them food too. But then they threw a hand grenade at us when they got closer. So that's why we were trying to chase them away."

Our group was to be stationed in Seoul, the capital of Korea. The Korean president at that time was Syngman Rhee, an older gentleman who ruled his nation with a firm hand. Bombed roads prevented the ride north to Seoul by truck convoy, so we traveled by train through the mountains and tunnels. Once seated in the train, the lights would go out and we wouldn't see any daylight until we reached the next station, sometimes about 40 or 50 miles away. It was pitch black. Of course, I was always prepared for anything and had a little flashlight with me.

I again got up on the top bunk, which was not really a bunk but the luggage rack. I stayed there because I knew that I was relatively safe. I prayed that we wouldn't get bombed in the tunnel. Fortunately, we arrived without incident. It was a great relief to see the sun and smell fresh air.

## SERVING IN THE EVACUATION HOSPITAL

While at Camp Pickett for basic training, I was assigned to a medical group and learned about the Army's relay system for the care and treatment of wounded soldiers in Korea. The first line of care was at the battlefield, with an aid station and a separate forward collecting station. The wounded were triaged, diagnosed, and given immediate care. They were then transported, usually by helicopter, to a Mobile Army Surgical Hospital (MASH). The MASH unit – later depicted as a comedy in a novel, movie, and television series – was a very serious, small, hospital about 20 miles from the front lines. After initial treatment, a patient would be transported to an evacuation hospital. Once medically stabilized, he could be air lifted to a hospital in Japan, the Army medical center at Fort Sam Houston in San Antonio, Texas, or the Walter Reed Army Medical Center in Washington DC.

I was assigned to the 121st Evacuation Hospital in Yong Dong Po, South Korea, northeast of Seoul. It had been a hospital that had been bombed. Quonset huts were on the compound grounds for male officers, female nurses, enlisted men, and the hospital director. Wounded soldiers were brought to the hospital with many serious conditions, often needing specialized surgeries. My first day, I was on duty at 7:00 in the morning and was assigned to the intake room in a large gym. All over the floor were stretchers, and a soldier was lying on the floor screaming along with other wounded men. A soldier was crying, with blood running out of his pants. I walked around. It was like a muddy floor, only it was blood. I stood there in amazement.

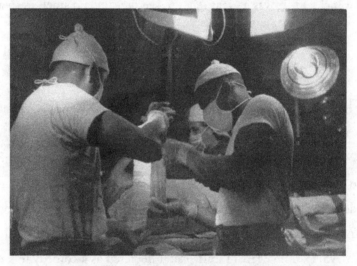

*Dan, right, operating room, Korea 1954.*

"Don't stand there!" a sergeant shouted at me. "Get to work and take care of our soldiers." So, I immediately got involved in caring for the injured. Then from what we called the emergency ward emerged a North Korean solider being carried by two of his comrades. We all stared.

"If they're in here and wounded, we care for them," the sergeant yelled.

I was soon assigned as a corpsman inside the ward. I stayed there for about a week before they realized I had some personal medical training, which I had gained from working with Dr. Church, the veterinarian. My papers indicated I had subspecialist skills, so I was quickly reassigned to the operating room. I became a scrub nurse, dealing with all kinds of wounds including belly wounds, burn cases, head wounds, and all forms of trauma. I assisted on every major and minor operation. I learned to be a cast technician, and I could do any cast that they gave me. Or they would give me the x-ray film to work with. Later, they assigned me to the instrument control group, and I had to reorder instruments once a week. In short, I was three things: operating room scrub nurse, cast man, and the instrument control.

It's important to understand that this wasn't the classic, modern hospital or operating room. It was a bombed-out shelter with water leaking through the roof and some type of lights connected which, if you moved a certain way, could burn you. We wore whites or greens in the operation room, and we had an autoclave to sterilize instruments, which was used often. We had two plastic surgeons always debating who got to use the Brown dermatome, a small machine for skin grafting. One surgeon rotated home first and took the dermatome with him.

I enjoyed working with the nurses and doctors, and I felt right at home. They had three other corpsmen in the operating room. Although I was usually the only Black, we were all treated as family. My first surgical experience was when a soldier came in with a serious sucking chest wound. After he was prepped, they kept him in the section called the operating room holding area.

During this first operation, I was asked to hold the retractors. These are L-shaped instruments that, when the body is opened, are placed on either side of the field inside to hold the chest open so the doctor can see what he is doing. Squeezed in between the doctors and nurses and with the burning lights on my back and no room to move, I got into position and saw all the blood. I got woozy and soon found myself falling right into what they call the "open field" of the wound. The doctor who was operating calmly used his shoulder to push me back. I fell and slammed my head on the floor. When I woke up, all the nurses were laughing because I had fainted. Meanwhile, they located and removed the three bullets lodged in the soldier's chest and afterwards he was flown to Tokyo.

I must say I've seen every type of case. I've scrubbed on chest surgery, arm and leg surgery, and finger surgery. I vividly recall one patient who needed brain surgery. They removed the top of his skull. He had a subdural hematoma. We could see the brain pulsing. As he was laying there strapped down, he started singing a song, famous at the time, by Doris Day.

"Once I had a secret love," he crooned, "who lived within the heart of me." Over and over he sang it, throughout the operation on his brain. The attendants all looked at each other in amazement. The operation continued. I don't remember now whether he lived through it.

## Saddest Story

The most tragic patient I worked on I will never forget. The Armistice had ended the war on July 27, 1953, but the fighting was still going on. Soldiers were coming in drunk or injured from some type of altercation or from getting caught by an enemy who didn't know that the war was over. During this time, there was a master sergeant who had just returned from stateside leave. He had one more month remaining before he would be discharged and go home to retire from the service. He had survived many battles over his 25 years of service in the military. I believe he was with the military police guarding the hospital compound.

Someone called and asked him to check out something on the front lines, about 40 miles north of the 38th parallel where the fighting was. A corpsman was with the soldiers on the ground to help immediately when they got wounded and take them to the field MASH unit. They took a jeep with three other guys to the front lines and started back on the way, all happy. Then they hit a mine that tore the jeep up. The sergeant came in on a stretcher with his face blown apart. His arms were dangling, and his two legs from the knees down were dangling. We put him in a smaller operating room. Two doctors worked on each limb. I personally pumped 22 pints of plasma into that poor soldier. Afterward he was taken to the recovery room.

The next day, as I always did, I went to check to see how he was doing. He was bandaged up all over his body, including his face and eyes.

"I can't wait to get out of here," he said. "I want to get home and run across the room and see my daughter and pick up her up in my arms."

What he did not know was that he had lost his eyes and his two arms and legs. I just left, totally in tears, because what he did not know is that, once stabilized, he would be shipped home to a Veterans Affairs hospital in his area. His family would probably visit him for a year. Then they would gradually fade away, and he would be by himself, a basket case.

I still support our military service, but some of the tragedies, like this one, are heartbreaking.

## The Morgue

Not all my experiences at the evacuation hospital were so sad. Several unusual and even humorous episodes occurred while I worked there. For example, one day in late July 1953, shortly after the war ended, the MPs brought in a soldier who was very drunk. They strapped him to a gurney.

Dr. Murphy, a very kind, cool, and gentle doctor, was on duty. It's important to the story to know what a beloved doctor he was, very professional, never got angry. He walked over to the patient for an examination.

"Ychh, ychh," the soldier moaned. Dr. Murphy leaned over him.

"Okay, soldier," he said. "I'm here to treat you."

"Aahhshit," he responded. "The hell you are!" And then he spit into Dr. Murphy's face.

Dr. Murphy picked up some gauze, wiped his face, and washed his hands. He then calmly picked up a large wad of gauze and shoved it - literally pummeled it - into the soldier's mouth. Everyone in the emergency room was shocked. It was so unlike Dr. Murphy.

We gave the patient some medication that put him to sleep, then we worked on him. Afterwards, we pushed the gurney out of the emergency room and started to pass the adjacent temporary morgue. It had a glass window on the door, and we could see about 10 dead men lying inside. As I recall, the sheets covered them only up to their necks. We looked at each other, opened the door, and rolled the patient in between the bodies. He was still tied to the gurney. As we left, his medicine started wearing off. We all stopped outside in the hall, looking through the glass window.

"He's waking up," someone said. The patient turned his head and looked around at the bodies lying near him.

"Hey, you guys, what happened to you?" No answer. He tried to sit up and exclaimed, "I said something to you!" Still nothing. Then he started swearing.

"Where am I? Hey, you guys are dead! Am I dead?"

We all cracked up laughing. Finally, one of our group said we should get him out of there, and we did. Afterward we felt bad about it, not for him but because this was really a desecration of those dead soldiers. After all, they were someone's father or son or brother.

## *Learning to Set Casts*

Corpsman Kearns taught me how to set plaster casts. A patient would come in with a broken arm or leg. He would be X-rayed and brought to me to put on the cast. I would first put on a soft cotton sleeve followed by protection for any protruding bone, followed by a roll of netting composed of plaster cast material, which hardens after it has been made wet.

Shortly after the end of the war, Corpsman Kearns was soon due to rotate back home. We had a party for him with lots of beer and booze. He got drunk, passed out and fell on the floor. An orthopedic surgeon looked at me and me at him. We took Kearns's clothes off, put a full body cast on him, and wheeled him into the recovery room. He was still out. In the morning, he woke up, and the doctor, nurses, and I were there.

"What happened?" He asked.

"You got drunk," the doctor responded. "You took a jeep and had an accident and broke your femur." Then the doctor touched his leg.

"Oh, Doc, don't do that!" Kearns exclaimed. "It hurts!" He yelled out in pain several times when touched, even though nothing had been injured or broken. Meanwhile, the nurses brought a urinal and bed pan and cared for him. He was very embarrassed.

I think we kept him there for three days. Then I took his cast off. He was petrified that I was going to cut him, but I was careful using a vibrating saw and cut just down to the netting. I was confident in myself, and I never cut anyone. Afterward, Kearns told us that he himself had played the same trick on a Colonel. I always wondered what happened to him.

## Sex in a Cast

We had a severely wounded patient who needed a full body cast. Because I was the cast technician, I did this one. It covered his complete torso, except for cut-out holes around his groin. Later, the soldier somehow came down with gonorrhea, a sexually transmitted disease. Back then, it could take 10 or more days for gonorrhea to incubate. But he was in his cast for much longer than that and had had no symptoms when he was first admitted to the hospital.

The doctors were all perplexed as to how he could have become infected. There were, however, many nurses there from Thailand. The rumor was that one of them had gotten on top of him while he was lying in bed. Of course, we couldn't prove it.

## Removing a Spear

One day, during the latter part of the war, a soldier walked in holding a bamboo spear on both sides of his body. It had gone through the exterior of his stomach, but fortunately missed his vital organs. We had never seen anything like it, although it was known that the North Koreans sometimes used bamboo spears.*

The doctors discussed how to remove it. They cut off one end of the spear, and carefully pulled it out. Then they stuffed the holes with, I believe, sulfur to prevent infection. They put some type of drain on both ends, wheeled him into the recovery room, and went on to the next patient. The last I knew I saw him walking and talking with others.

---

* In late December 1950, five American airmen in a truck convoy were ambushed by North Korean forces. Their bodies, discovered shortly after by a South Korean patrol, showed that the flesh had been punctured in as many as 20 different areas with heated, sharpened bamboo sticks.

*Light Bulb*

This is probably the weirdest story of all. Shortly after the war ended, I was in the emergency room, on call. Around midnight, a soldier walked in with two others on each side. He didn't seem to be walking differently, but they were very close to him.

"What's wrong?" I asked.

"I need to see a doctor," he said. "I have something in my stomach." A nurse went around to check him.

"Don't touch me!" he said. The nurse asked what the problem was. He hemmed and hawed, then finally responded.

"I have an electric light bulb in my rectum."

"How did it happen?" She asked. She was annoyed that he hadn't told her about it when he first arrived. At first, he said he did not know. Then he explained that he had been with one of our nurses, a "round eye" American, at her hut. Her husband, a helicopter pilot who had flown in with an injured soldier, arrived home and saw them through a window. The husband got a couple friends, and they fought with him, shoving a light bulb in his anus.

Everyone in the emergency room was shocked. A doctor arrived and asked what happened. The patient told his story again. The doctor seemed to enjoy the story. He gave the man medicine, something to relax his muscles. It didn't work. Then the doctor took long impaction forceps, the type sometimes used in delivering babies, and tried to retract the light bulb. But the bulb shattered. So, this became a full-fledged operation. The patient received anesthesia and the doctor went in and painstakingly removed all the shards piece by piece.

The patient survived, and I never saw him again. But I never forgot him and the moral of his story: stay away from married women!

# OTHER EXPERIENCES IN KOREA

## Swimming

I was lucky to be able to have a variety of other experiences during my tenure in South Korea. I had done a lot of swimming in my youth, and I was assigned to take a Red Cross Swimming Instructor training under Jim Garrett, who directed the program. I received the certificate, and during the summer months, I was chief lifeguard at the base's swimming pool.

*Dan, lifeguard at base's swimming pool.*

Our hospital had one of three concrete pools in Korea. The pool had been closed because the floor had a crack in the main section, so water seeped into the ground. At the time, groundwater in Korea was contaminated because human waste was used to fertilize gardens, plants, and shrubbery. Latrines were serviced by the common oxen-pulled "Honey Bucket," which collected the waste and distributed it to various locations throughout the area. Hence, the crack in the pool floor had to be adequately sealed.

Although the military had been integrated by Truman in his 1948 Executive Order, there were many military old-timers who detested Blacks being treated as equals. So, it was with me and the Company's Supply Sergeant Parino. When I went to him for lumber for the pool's fence, we had a major altercation, resulting in him slapping me across the face.

"You're too damn smart," he exclaimed.

The incident escalated up the chain of command with a supporting document that I retain to this day. I told the full story of what happened. The result was a subtle reminder from the Company Commander, who told me that records (meaning such as mine) can often be lost, putting a soldier's future and life in jeopardy, unless I dropped the case. I knew when to walk away, and I did!

I was able to scrounge enough lumber from the base, but I also needed to obtain 20 bags of cement to repair the pool. I knew I could not get the cement from Supply Sergeant Parino, so I would have to go to the main Supply Depot in Seoul. It was a Friday morning when I arrived at the main depot, a huge complex of all types of materials that had been delivered from the United States for the warehouse. It was almost a city within itself.

The compound was gated, but it opened for incoming and outgoing vehicles. There was a huge sign – and I do mean HUGE – painted in red and white: "Scroungers, stay out. This means you! All supplies and materials are for the program to rebuild Korea." I walked under the sign, up the stairs, and into the office complex. When I entered the office, I was met by a scornful Master Sergeant. I explained that I needed 20 bags of cement for our swimming pool.

"Can't you read?" he asked me, pointing to the sign. He turned around and left the area. Just then another office door opened, and out stepped a young, polished Captain who yelled at me for being on the compound trying to get cement. I told him about the need for the hospital pool, but he quickly ended the conversation. We saluted, and he went back in the office and closed the door.

It was well known that who really runs the Army were the Non-Commissioned Officers and Privates First Class. I went down the steps and around to the building that said "Cement." I entered and there were broken bags of cement in different piles, enough on the floor alone to fill our need. A Black sergeant come over, and I told him what I needed. My back was toward the entrance, and he was facing me as we talked. I was trying to work out some type of negotiation with him when he suddenly stopped talking and walked away. I turned around and there almost in my face stood the captain from the office. He yelled and threatened to get me court-martialed for disobeying his order to leave the depot.

"Can't we negotiate something for the troops?" I asked, defying his tirade.

"You don't have anything I want!" he screamed.

"We have 'round eyes," I quickly said. "Our hospital has many stateside nurses." His eyes lit up. I told him that if he would give us 20 bags of cement, I was sure that a couple of our registered nurses would enjoy meeting him. He readily agreed.

*Nurses Bochman, Paulie, and Frazier, picnic, 1954.*

I immediately hitched a ride back to the hospital and went directly to the operating room. I told two of my women nursing friends about the situation, and they agreed to help. Because the nurses were officers, they were able to obtain a jeep and driver. We tore back to Seoul to meet the captain. I stayed in the jeep as they went into his office. I don't know what arrangement they worked out for their Sunday night meeting at the Officer's Club, but it worked.

Monday morning, a truck arrived at the pool with 35 bags of cement. I got a Korean construction crew to repair the leak in exchange for the extra 15 bags of cement. Another lesson learned: "Life has no obstacles, only challenges."

### Olympian Dr. Sammy Lee

One of the highlights of my service was to become a friend of Major Sammy Lee. He was an ear, nose, and throat physician at the 121st Evacuation Hospital. I was honored and pleased that he usually requested me as scrub nurse for his many surgeries. Like me, Sammy was also a swimmer. He was the first Asian-American man to win an Olympic gold medal (at the 1948 Olympics) and the first diver to win consecutive Olympic gold medals in the platform event by winning again in 1952.

Sammy and I bonded as swimmers. At the hospital's pool, Sammy and I installed a makeshift diving board in preparation for his diving exhibition for the Korean public. I was petrified when he triple somersaulted into the pool, extremely close to the edge. It was magnificent but frightening.

Dr. Lee and I often discussed the burden of America's racial discrimination policies and practices – he as an Asian American, me as an African American. He was humble but gregarious, highly respected by his fellow physicians and Army colleagues. Indeed, there was great jubilation and celebration in the operating room in 1953 when it was announced that he was named Athlete of the Year.

Sammy died in 2016 at the age of 96. I was sickened to read in his obituary in *The Washington Post* about the discrimination he faced when he returned to the United States after serving in Korea. It took the intercession of then Vice President Nixon for him to even buy a house!

*Sammy Lee holds Olympic gold medal, 1952. Photo, Associated Press - File:Capilla, Lee, Haase Public Domain.*

## Gene Neff

My assistant who helped me get the swimming pool restored was Gene Neff. Gene was white, tall, and lanky. He played first base for the Detroit Tigers in his civilian life before and after he was in the military. He was a medic at our evacuation hospital and also oversaw the indoor recreation facility. We worked on special projects together, and he helped me in getting the pool ready for swimmers. Fortunately, he was not with me when I went to the cement depot in Seoul, as he would not have understood my private wheeling and dealing with the officials there. But he was a great guy, and we were real buddies. We went on hikes together and into town on occasion to Korean restaurants.

One day, driving back to the hospital compound from the swimming pool, the company was having an athletic field day. We decided that we would compete against each other. I thought I was a fast runner, but when the whistle blew, he left me in the dust - and I mean IN THE

DUST! That's how I learned what an athlete who has trained for his profession can do. After all, a large part of a baseball player's training is how to run. I called Gene a "White Jackie Robinson."

After Korea, Gene went back to baseball for a while and then to college at the University of Kentucky. He became a teacher and later a corporate executive. He died on January 11, 2021, while I was in the midst of writing my memoirs. A video interview of him was made in 2018.[15]

## Making Extra Money

Bi-monthly payment to members of the military is on a gradation basis, with, of course, the lowly private recruit receiving the smallest sum. All privates earned the same monthly amount, but all had their own, different, spending habits and needs.

In Korea at the time, women were viewed or typed as "mamasan" (older Korean women), "moosama" (younger Korean women), or "round eyes" (American women and other non-Korean women). It was not uncommon for soldiers to pay a moosama girlfriend for a half or a full month. The payment to the moosama was generally made on pay day. Three or four days before payday, however, she would often inform the soldier she had to see her aunt, mother, sister or some relative up north because they were ill. Or she made some other excuse. She, of course, often had another lover at a distant camp who also would pay her under the same terms. However, if lover number one came up with additional money, she would stay and not have to go up north.

We lived in Quonset huts that housed about 15 men. One Sunday, a private from another hut came into ours and said he needed money for his moosama. He asked each man if he could borrow $50. They said no. Then he came to me.

"I'll loan you the $50," I jokingly said, "but on payday you give me $100." Without blinking an eye, he agreed, and with a handshake we had a deal. On payday, 10 days later, he proudly walked in our hut and gave me $100. Soon I became a loan shark using the same formula. After the first month, I could not lose money because I used the profits for lending. I sent my extra money home to my bank account to save for college.

My term in Korea was almost up, and I had my papers to rotate back to the United States in two weeks. This meant my chance of seeing those buddies from Korean again might never happen. In walked the original borrower, who asked for $200 under the same terms. We discussed my rotating plans and his, and his ability to fulfill his obligation to me. I agreed, we shook hands, and I gave him $200.

I returned home and forgot about the deal. Some weeks later, I received a letter postmarked and stamped with all the stations I had been through to get home. There in the envelope was $400, the amount the soldier and I had agreed to. I didn't even remember his name. To this day, I remain amazed that he honored the agreement. It was another good lesson that I've never forgotten. Some people, even whites dealing with Blacks, can be honest!

*Last but not least in Korea, photo of Marilyn Monroe from a friend of Dan's. Marilyn visited Korea in Feb. 1954 – 10 shows in 4 days to more than 100,000 troops. Dan was unable to attend, but he saved and treasured the photo ever since and said, "I heard that she was so mobbed by troops that they moved her from a truck to a tank to protect her!"*

CHAPTER 7

# Interregnum: Working and Rescuing

## CONSTRUCTION

When I returned home to Connecticut from Korea, I knew that I wanted to go to college. I had the money I saved from my service in the war, and the GI Bill that provided, among other things, funds to veterans for college tuition and living expenses. So, I worked in construction for about a year to save more money for college. I found that working with white men on construction crews was not a problem as they learned that I could pull my load on the job.

Being a construction worker – a.k.a. day laborer – is not for the faint of heart. Back then, we would arrive at the pickup site or workplace while bringing our own lunch and protective gear, if any. My first construction job was in 1954 with C.H. Nickerson & Company, based in Torrington, Conn., 10 miles from Winsted. Their crews were renovating an elementary school. Early one Monday morning, I arrived at the open-air truck pickup site, dressed in working clothes, hoping for work, but I was not selected. I arrived at the same time for three days straight, still no work. One morning I dressed casually as if I were going to a ball game or a movie, thinking I would not be chosen. However, several of us were selected and driven to the work site. I had no glasses, hat, helmet, or work shoes.

At the elementary school, they had assembled a metal frame "stanchion," a type of scaffold. When I climbed on top of it with my ax to rip down the ceiling, I could only hunch down and slam my ax up into the ceiling to dislodge the plaster. Subsequently, all the debris including the asbestos insulation came down on my hair, face, and shirt. I continued all eight hours tearing down the ceiling. When we finished work and I got home, my mother hardly recognized me because I was so filthy. That was my introduction to day labor construction.

## Danger in the Trenches

Later, on a different construction job, I worked for a company that had the contract to replace the sewage pipe in the town. A trench was dug by a backhoe about six feet deep and four feet wide. One day I was down in the trench with another worker, catching and placing ceramic pipes. It had rained that Friday and Saturday but was dry on Monday morning when we reported for work. The contractor had not, as was required, braced the trench wall with prepared steel bracing or with heavy timber siding. To do so would cost him considerable time, money, travel, and equipment. This contractor eliminated that step. As I was holding one of the pipes, I noticed that the wall was weeping, slowly dripping water from the side.

"We need to get out!" I immediately yelled to my partner. "The wall is weeping."

I climbed out of the trench as fast as I could. My partner cursed at me, called me a coward, and continued working by himself. I was now on top of the side of the trench. There was sort of a rumble. Both sides crumbled, covering my partner almost up to his neck. I'm here today, but they had to dig him out of the trench! I was later told that he did not return from there alive. It taught me a good lesson: One must always be aware for his own safety.

## *Working for a Tree Surgeon*

Afterward, I searched and found another labor-intensive job working with veterinarian Dr. Church's brother, who, I believe, had a Bechtel subcontract throughout the state with a small tree surgeon business. My work continued outside, clearing trees for an electric "right-of-way" on Avon Mountain in West Hartford. Back then, men were into strength, lifting and carrying huge loads of material and proving themselves by their work ethic. I could measure up to almost anyone on the all-white crew with no trouble about race. Various crew members were always quick to team up with me as we took down trees.

Most of the crew had come from the Connecticut Hills, Canada, or Washington State and had experienced trouble with the law. They were all white. Our working foreman, Johnnie Godenzi, also white, was a local Italian, a bit older, and married with three children. He invited me several times to his home for dinner with his wife and children. I believe we were the only two crew members out of 10 who had never been in jail. Johnnie taught me how to eat and enjoy red hot peppers, which made my whole body warm in the freezing New England weather.

Generally, the crew at lunch time would gather at a location, make a fire, and eat our lunches. Their conversations generally were about sex and beautiful women. Always beautiful women. I thought I was educated in adult sex, but I learned a lot. One crew member, Ed, had a stint in the notorious New York's Riker's Island jail. He would repeat the same story during every lunch time about how the guards had sneaked a "woman of the night" into the jail for the guards and inmates to enjoy. She stayed with them for a whole week.

One day, at lunch in mid-August, we sat around the fire; the sun was high, and fall was around the corner. Crew members were discussing plans for their next job. The West Hartford tree removal project would be ending soon. As they discussed possible jobs, it became my turn to talk about my future. I spoke openly and without hesitation.

"I plan to go to college," I said. In an instant, I became an outcast with the crew, except for Johnnie Godenzi. They stood up and looked at me as if I had betrayed them.

"A college boy!" one of them sneered. They looked at me with such anger and contempt that I was almost hesitant to team up with my partner after lunch and go off into the woods with my ax and chain saw. It was not a nice time!

Johnnie, who undoubtedly could tell that I was distressed, insisted that I come to his home that evening for a delicious spaghetti dinner with his wife Naomi and their three children. I don't recall us talking about the day's events. I do remember the comradery I shared with him and his family. Over many different meals, we discussed my plans for college. He was happy for me, and said he hoped his children would go to college too. He had just built a dormer on his home, and he showed it to me.

Sometime later, while I was in college, Johnnie's wife Naomi wrote me a letter. She said that Johnnie had been out with his family on a local hunting trip. His young nephew mistook my good friend for a deer and fired his Winchester 30-O6 Rifle, hitting and killing him. I was stunned. It showed me again how precious life is.

## Painting a Water Tower

The tree-cutting job was terminated when we reached the end of the river. Then the guys were all looking around for work – these were all day laborers who made their living by doing odd jobs. Someone indicated that Nickerson needed workers to paint water towers, those big round, white circular towers that sit up in the air on spikes. They must be painted, by regulation I believe, every 10 or 15 years.

One of my buddies said he was going to do it, so I said I would try it too. It was good money. What one needs to know, however, is that those water tanks are not what people just look at from a distance. Up close, they are even more huge!

To paint, we had to get up to the top of the peak of the water tower and then somehow tie a rope around the pipe on them. There was often a hook designed for that purpose. We didn't have buckets on trucks in those days, we just had a climbing rope. We put our rope through the hook. Then we painted the towers. We could see on the top of it where they were painted before. Guys had missed some of the spots, and they were shiny.

So, I proceeded to paint. Some companies had mechanical sprayers, but this company did not. We used a paintbrush. I was okay painting the first round on my side until I happened to look down. I hadn't realized that I was that high up. The tank was so big, and it looked so far down to the ground before I would hit it if I fell. I really lost my stomach, and that was very unusual for me. I vomited all over.

The guys started laughing. I could hardly get my breath back because I kept looking down instead of looking up. But I painted my half of the water tank and then came down. I never went back up again. I entered college in September. My construction days were over.

## TEACHING SWIMMING

Because I had earned a Red Cross Water Safety Instructor Certificate while in the Army, when I returned home, I was asked by the Winsted local Red Cross director, Mrs. Skelton, to teach swimming to youngsters. There were two separate locations for swimming instructions. One was on the outskirts, south of Winsted, at Burr Pond. The other location was north in Norfolk, at Toby Pond. Both were inland ponds of water that would freeze in winter and thaw in summer. Parents from the local areas would sign up with the Red Cross office, which developed the list of students for us.

At both Burr Pond and Toby Pond, the students were all white. However, there was somewhat of a class distinction between students at Burr Pond and students at Toby Pond, the latter of which came from a more affluent community. Both settings were exceptionally breathtaking in the summer months when the foliage was in full bloom.

There was an Italian physician's family with three children, the youngest daughter of which, Paula, was about three years younger than me. She came to the pond one morning and said she would like to help with teaching swimming. Somehow, she had heard that I could stay underwater for 3 to 3-1/2 minutes and asked if I would teach her to develop that skill.

Paula became my assistant, and we developed a strong relationship. Since Paula did not have a car, I would often arrive at her home in the mornings, enjoy a cup of hot chocolate and something sweet that her mother made, then drive with Paula to the swimming area. I was not considered an extraordinarily strong swimmer, just a good swimmer. Paula on the other hand was both a strong and powerful swimmer. After classes were over, she and I would often stay and enjoy the water. Our love of the water and swimming together resulted in lengthy discussions and thinking about plans to swim the English Channel.

Oddly enough, there was an upsetting incident with her father. One afternoon following swimming class, Paula and I with her younger brother Johnny went hiking in the beautiful mountains. We discovered some bones right off the path, which appeared to have been there for some time. I used my t-shirt to gather them up and brought them back to their house for her father (a physician) to examine. He indicated that they resembled human bones, and he called the State Trooper's office asking for someone to retrieve them for further examination.

While he was on the phone, apparently the policeman asked where he got the bones.

"A colored boy found the bones and brought them to me," he replied.

Paula and I were standing on the other side of the desk. We were flabbergasted. To call me just a "colored boy"! Paula and her mother lashed out at her father for not indicating that he was familiar with me, and that the boy who found the bones was a swimming instructor and friend of the family. Nevertheless, Paula's father acted undeterred by their comments. I felt it was another example of a brain-washed American protecting the social understanding in our country.

In the fall of 1956, we left for college – Paula at Tufts University and me at Springfield College, both in Massachusetts. She later got married and moved with her husband to Waterbury, Conn. Occasionally, I would drop by their home when back from college and have dinner with them. One Sunday, about 10 years later, her husband Lennie called and told me that he had just returned from funeral services, having buried Paula. She was found floating in the local Waterbury Lyman Pond. I was shocked and devastated at the loss of my dear and good friend.

Afterward, there was talk in the Winsted area about Paula's death and others at the Lyman Pond. I later learned at one of our high-school class reunions that there was something mysterious about her death, given that she was such a good swimmer. Some suspected foul play. However, I never knew anything more about the incident.

## WINSTED FLOOD 1955

In August 1955, in a little more than a week two hurricanes passed by southern New England and produced major flooding over much of the region. Hurricane Connie came first, saturating the ground and bringing river and reservoir levels to above normal levels. A week later, Hurricane Diane assaulted New England, with rainfall totals ranging up to 20 inches in two days. The hardest hit state was Connecticut, and one of the hardest hit places was my hometown of Winsted, which was doubly damaged because of its old infrastructure, including earthen dams, and sewage and drainage issues.

The evening of Thursday, August 18, 1955, I attended the Burrville Dog Training Club located in the Burrville community of Torrington, Conn., about five miles south of Winsted. As was often the custom, halfway there I would meet my friend Mary Bowdoin with her dog, a Weimaraner named Miser. She drove from Pine Meadow, about a mile south of New Hartford and seven miles southeast of Winsted. I had taken the upper route (then the Torringford Road) to meet her. Mary had parked her car, and she and Miser rode with me and my Doberman dog Mark down to Route 8 to the Burrville club.

The weather was somewhat balmy, with a drizzling rain. Since we were training inside the building where the club met, we were unaware of Hurricane Diane causing havoc in Winsted. Indeed, news reports earlier in the evening had announced that there would be only moderate flooding in the lowlands throughout Connecticut. When the club meeting was over later about 9 p.m. that evening, the rain had decreased. We drove up the hill to where Mary's car was parked. She proceeded south toward her home in Pine Meadow. Along the way she encountered major flooding and roads destroyed. She parked her car in a dry, secure location near New Hartford and walked home with her dog, not retrieving her car until several days later.

As for me, I continued north on my drive home. Then on my car radio I heard the 11 p.m. news from WTIC, a station in Hartford about 30 miles southwest of Winsted. The reporter said the forecast for the next day would be some rain but little chance of flooding. At that very minute, however, Winsted had just lost its communications with the rest of the state. Around 10:45 p.m., the Civil Defense had been called out and immediately blew their siren. That was the last bit of power in our lines.

Driving into Winsted, I passed the Gilbert School on the way up to my mother's house on Gregory Street, which stood on a hill, untouched by the flooding. By that time, however, water from the Mad River, which paralleled Main Street, had begun to rush through the upper part of Winsted, destroying homes and stores.

Police and firefighters began going door to door in the dark, telling residents to leave for higher ground. Had I taken the lower Route 8 back to Winsted, I would have run directly into gushing water filled with debris. All highway lights were out, and I probably would not have survived the flood. When I arrived home, mother and I talked about the rain. Our electricity was out, so we had no other communication or knowledge about how bad Winsted proper was doing, especially Main Street, which bore the brunt of Hurricane Diane's wrath.

## Encountering the Flood

About 9 a.m. the next morning, I walked down to the St. Joseph's Roman Catholic Church, located on a hill facing Main Street. As I stood at the

*MainStreet Winsted, Conn. during flood, 1955.*

front driveway entrance of the church, Alfred (Al) Landi, a young Italian neighborhood boy about 11 or 12 years old, ran up and stood next to me. My family had recently moved from Chestnut Street, where the Landis lived up the street from us. Al's older sister Corrine was a year or two behind me at Gilbert School.

There are not enough verbs and adjectives to describe the horrific scene that appeared before us. The usually mild Mad River had become a torrent of violently rushing water, rising faster and faster along Main Street. Whole buildings were being demolished, trees uprooted, cars smashed. Pulitzer Prize-winning author John Hersey described it vividly in an article in the New Yorker magazine a month after the flood:

> "[T]he Mad River was brimming. Along Main Street, it was fifteen feet above its normal level, and the water was ten feet deep in the street itself. It was literally ripping up Main Street. The pavement and the sidewalks were being sliced away and gutted six feet deep. The water had broken the plate-glass windows of most of the stores

along the street and had ruined their stocks... All but
two of the town's twelve bridges had collapsed or were
about to. A four-story hotel at the foot of the street, the
Clifton, had floated off its foundation and into the river
and downstream three quarters of a mile, and had settled
on the town ballfield, more or less erect but with its two
lower floors worn away." [16]

The corner of Main and Chestnut Street was the center of attention,
along with Cornelio Avenue, a dead-end street north of Main and parallel to
Chestnut in the next block. People were trapped in their apartments by the
rising, rushing water. A huge 30- or 40-foot cylindrical tank had floated into
Cornelio Ave., bobbing back and forth, nearly causing major devastation including possible loss of life. Fortunately, the tank got stuck and settled in
place, eliminating a danger to residents and their rescuers.

People often come together to help victims whenever there is a catastrophe. So it was with the flood. The firefighters, whose names I cannot recall,
had worked throughout the night and early morning rescuing the families on
Cornelio Avenue by lashing together ladders and ropes to reach them. The
rushing water rose to the second-floor balconies of their apartments.

On the south side of Main Street, there had been screaming and
yelling for help throughout the night and morning by Joseph and Maria
Cornelio, who had arrived from Italy only two weeks earlier and spoke no
English. They were trapped in their tenement apartment building, the
foundation of which was in direct contact with the swift, overflowing Mad
River. Debris had built up on the north side of the dwelling. We could
hear the building moan. It was just a matter of time before it would be
demolished and washed away.

## The Rescues

I had left St. Joseph's Catholic Church and was now on the top roof of the Demartino grocery store, which was on the north side of Main Street. I worked with several other men to save the residents in the tenements on the near side of Cornelio Ave. Meanwhile, we could hear the screams and prayers from the Cornelios across from us on the south side of Main Street. How could we get a rope across to them, so a boat could be secure enough for men to reach them? Attempts were made by throwing a rock attached to a small rope for them to catch as the Cornelios hung and waved out the window. The wind was too strong, and all efforts fell short, or the rope got tangled in the electrical wires hanging between our "roof crew" and the Cornelios' tenement across the street.

Many men contributed to the rescue. One in particular was Dewey Plank, who was with me on the roof of the Demartino store. Dewey was an outstanding fly fisherman. He became the hero of the day. He ran home, obtained his favorite fly-casting rod, and returned. He flicked his line across the street to the Cornelios' building. It fell short. He tried again. No luck. He tried several more times, and then, through all the hanging, tangled wires, the line landed with precision not far from the window. The Cornelios reached for larger/stronger ropes to be attached. Everyone on our roof cheered.

Then a boat appeared, an eight-foot two-man skiff, and it was time for men on the roof to cross the turbulent river. Ropes were tied to both ends of the boat (bow and stern) along with a sort of check line rope, which was used to control the boat from debris coming down Main Street. While in the military in Korea, I had received my Red Cross Water Safety Instructor Certificate, which included boat and sailing craft safety. I was concerned that there would be too many people in the small skiff.

"Only two or three strong swimmers should get in it," I warned them. The boat crossed with three men. I remained on the Demartino roof, holding the check line with the other men and watching for debris that could impact the boat. The men in the skiff pulled themselves across on the main rope and managed to climb up and reach the window of the Cornelios' apartment. One of them placed a heavy winter Mackinaw coat on Miss Cornelio, tied a rope under her arms over the coat, and lowered her into the boat. They did the same for her brother.

Five people were now in the boat, headed back to the safety of the dry land. Looking up the river, Mrs. Cornelio and I saw at the same time a huge timber log, bigger than a telephone pole, coming directly toward the boat. She panicked, screamed, and stood up. The boat immediately capsized, spilling everyone in it into the violently rushing river, although all were lashed to the boat.

## "Negro Youth a Hero"

When Mrs. Carnelio stood up and screamed, my lifesaving training automatically kicked in. I knew someone would need help in that churning water. I immediately stripped to my skivvies and jumped down to the lower Demartino store roof and then to the ground. I raced down along the dry part of Chestnut on Main Street. I took off my wristwatch, a high-school graduation gift, and threw it up on the grass. Although I did not see her, my friend Corrine Landi saw my watch and retrieved it. She later returned it to me.

Then I dove into the river by the Demartino building. I recall hearing the screams from the hundreds of hysterical people on the banks of the Catholic Church. Everything was happening so fast. I noticed out the corner of my eye two policemen who were in trouble as they tried to lower themselves with telephone wire to save those who had been in the boat.

Once in the water, my muscle memory took over. I was in my swimming style or custom. I sucked in the filthy, sewage-polluted water and spat it out as I normally did in a swimming pool or lake. (Afterwards, I could never understand why I did not come down with typhoid or other illnesses.) I knowingly swam upstream against the current next to the buildings where the river flow would be less strong, anticipating that the center of the river stream would carry me back down to the capsized boat. It did!

The turbulent river, flowing about 20 miles an hour, swiftly swept me down past the boat into the area where a man was struggling in the water. I suddenly found myself with him swept into the swift-moving stream. He got caught going around and around in a whirlpool. His eyes were rolled back so I could only see the whites of his eyes. I was somehow able to grab his shirt collar and pulled him out of the whirlpool. The water swept us close to the washed-out rear of a building, which, now alert, he grabbed. Immediately. I was pulled back into the vortex of the whirlpool and was propelled back close to him. He grabbed my hand, and we both walked through from the rear to the front of the building.

I did not know the gentleman and never saw him again. By news accounts, it must have been Joe Horte, one of the men in the boat who had tried to save the Cornelios. When Mrs. Cornelio's rope slipped off her, he grabbed her, but his rope snapped. She broke away and drowned. John Hersey, in a syndicated article that was published in the Boston Advertiser newspaper, had a subhead that said, "Negro Youth a Hero."[17] I do think Joe Horte was a true hero also. Indeed, there were many heroes that day!

Emerging from the raging water, I was still only in my skivvies. As I walked up the street to go home, Mr. Royer, a local trashman, went into his house and got me a pair of pants to wear. I returned home late in the afternoon to find our house unaffected by the storms and flooding. Inside, my mother and sisters were sitting at the dining room table with a set of papers. They were startled to see me.

"The police came to the house," my mother said. "They told us that you had died in the Mad River rescue attempt." Apparently, the police and others had not seen me emerge when my swimming ordeal was over. Following a hug or two, I told my family what had happened.

"Put the insurance papers on Dan back in the chest," mother told my sisters. I still smile remembering her words.

## Aftermath

The next day, after the waters receded, downtown Winsted was in shambles. It looked like a war zone, with collapsed buildings and houses, most of the businesses destroyed, and huge blocks of concrete with tons of debris filling the streets. The Winsted Evening Citizen later reported that "95 percent of the city's businesses were destroyed or severely damaged; 170 of the city's 200 retailers were wiped out as Winsted lost 18 grocery stores, 9 barbershops, 16 restaurants and taverns, 8 package stores, 3 small hotels and several car dealerships." [18]

Seven people died in the flood. Residents who had lost their homes and all their possessions were distraught. Disease was a constant fear, as food and water supplies were contaminated. The Marines in helicopters brought supplies and the Red Cross. Local citizens pitched in and helped. Dr. Raymond B. Church, the veterinarian I worked for in high school, provided medical help and supplies, as not many regular physicians were available.

Writers from *Look* maga-
zine came to our house and asked if
they could take a photograph of me
perusing the damage in downtown
Winsted. It was later published in
the December 1955 issue of *Look*.
The caption read: "Danny Smith,
whose heroic actions saved the life of
at least one man, surveys the charred
ruins of a factory."[19]

Fifty years later, in August
2005, the citizens of Winsted held
events to commemorate the 1955
flood. I met up with many of my old
friends for whom memories were
still fresh and vivid. One of them –
Al Landi, the young boy who was

Danny Smith, whose heroic actions saved the life of at least one man, surveys the charred ruins of a factory.

*Dan viewing rubble from the Winsted Flood, Look Magazine, Dec. 1955.*

with me at the Catholic Church during the beginning of the flood – wrote
me a letter that I treasure most of all:

> I have to say that I don't remember too much about you
> as I was a pre-teen when you moved from Chestnut
> Street. However, one thing that is indelibly etched in my
> memory is when I was standing close to you on the church
> property the morning after the rains came when you dove
> into that absolute torrent trying to save Mrs. Cornelio. I
> have never, to this day, seen a braver or more selfless act
> and have retold that story hundreds of times over the last

50-plus years. The term "hero" is much overused. But
your attempt to save her without regard to your own safety
was nothing short of heroic.

*Dan on Main Street in downtown Winsted, 50th anniversary of
the flood, 2005. Photo by Loretta Neumann.*

As for Winsted, in August 2005 the *Hartford Courant* reported:
"After the flood, Main Street, which is also Route 44, was widened and
the buildings on the south side of the road were never rebuilt. The void,
which has left Main Street looking rather lopsided, is a lasting reminder."[20]

Similarly, at about the same time an article in the New York
Times said:

> The south side of Main Street, which backs onto the river,
> was virtually washed away. The damage was so bad that
> Winsted never fully rebuilt and just paved over the street
> where the businesses and tenements once stood.

Main Street today seems out of balance, with stores on one side of the four-lane street and nothing but road and the river on the other.[21]

I have a different view from the images left from both accounts. Despite the devastation that Winsted faced in the 1955 flood, today I find that most of it remains a charming New England town. Many of the older structures have been rebuilt along the north side of Main Street and 19th-century houses line the adjacent streets. The residents of Winsted – still predominately white – are as friendly as I recall from my youth. Best of all, I still consider it one of my homes.

## WORST RACIST INCIDENT

On August 22, 1955, the Monday following the Winsted flood, I returned to my summer job at Camp Jewell, a YMCA camp founded in 1901 in North Colebrook, Conn. After returning from the Army and doing construction work, I served as Camp Jewell's trips director for two summers. Located about eight miles north of Winsted, it was high and dry, and had been unaffected by the storms and floods that assaulted much of Connecticut.

Working at Camp Jewell was a great lesson for me in organizing and managing a program and overseeing teenage boys (all white, as I recall), mainly from good families in the Hartford/West Hartford area. Most stayed for two weeks or so; those who could afford it were there for the whole summer.

Nelson Yarbrough, the first-string quarterback from the University of Virginia, was my tent partner and became my assistant trips director. We organized many adventures, with a van for campers that pulled a wagon with our canoes. For example, we took campers to Canada, the Laurentian Mountains in southern Quebec. Big trees, beautiful waterways. We also went climbing in the White Mountains in New Hampshire and canoeing down the Saco River in Maine, shooting rapids and camping on the side.

Nelson Yarbrough, 2008

*Dan's partner at Camp Jewell, Nelson Yarbrough.*

One of my favorite places was the Adirondacks, a 5,000-square-mile mountainous wilderness in upstate New York. I especially loved Lake George, a beautiful recreation area with crystal clear water 40 feet deep. You could toss a quarter on the bottom of the lake and clearly see it. I remember one time when we were canoeing there; near the end we heard some boys and girls yelling at us from the beach.

"Get off the lake," they screamed. "A storm is coming!" They paddled over and invited us to their camp to spend the night. It was a delightful adventure.

The most memorable and difficult trip for me occurred when we were returning home with 10 campers after a visit to Lake George. We drove our van to Barkhamsted Reservoir, about 20 miles from Winsted, where I used to swim. I wanted to show it to them. The day was warm and sunny, families were picnicking, and kids were playing. When we arrived, there was a beach commotion which, as a former lifeguard, I knew indicated someone in the water was in trouble. I told our campers to go back to the van. I would have to dive in and didn't want them to get into trouble.

*Barkhamsted Beach, Conn.*

The edge of Barkhamsted sloped down and then abruptly dropped to a depth of at least 14 to 20 feet. A young girl, about sixteen years old, had walked into the water and suddenly fell into the deep end. Even a strong swimmer could have trouble dropping so quickly. I took my shirt off and dove in find the girl. I was not able to reach her, but another swimmer did, and he brought her up. He and I took her to shore and laid her on the sand. I felt her pulse on the side of her neck. It was reasonably strong, although I knew she still suffered from water inhaled into her lungs. I started to give her mouth-to-mouth resuscitation and other life-saving methods.

A uniformed police officer was standing on the bank with another gentleman, whom someone said was her uncle.

"Hey, you!" he hollered, as I bent over the girl. "You!" he yelled again. "She's dead, already dead!"

At first, I didn't understand. I knew she was still alive. Then I looked up and saw him glaring at me. He was large and burly, wearing a side arm and a broad hat. I believed he was a state trooper. Then it dawned on me what he meant. I was Black and she was white. He did not want my lips on hers. I saw his gun and knew what could happen. So, I got up and returned to the van with our campers. My usually rowdy group was totally silent. It was as if they had seen a funeral. All the way back to Camp Jewell, there was no discussion. They were as shocked as I was.

This remains the most racist incident I have ever experienced in my life. To this day, telling the story brings tears to my eyes. To think that someone would rather have anyone die rather than have her white lips touch my black mouth. Incomprehensible.

CHAPTER 8

# Springfield College, Learning More

I long had a goal of attending college, spurred by my bother Abe. After serving in the Army, Abe had returned to Connecticut, earned his GED, and was able to get admitted to the engineering program at the University of Chicago, which he attended using the GI Bill. He later became an aeronautical engineer, working on spaceships in Washington State and California. He was an inspiration to me, as was my sister Marion for all she accomplished both from nursing school and then college. They were excellent role models.

I was introduced to Springfield College in Massachusetts by Walt Malins, the director of Camp Jewell. A small, private New England educational institution, Springfield was established in 1885 as a young man's Christian college with emphasis on training for youth leadership and YMCA directors. Its mission from its founding is to educate students in "Spirit, Mind, and Body for leadership in service to others."* Sports were always a major focus. Best known for the invention of basketball and volleyball by Dr. James Naismith, the college housed the national Basketball Hall of Fame, established in 1959 and now relocated in the city of Springfield.

Walt Malins and William Cheney, dean of students at Springfield, had been roommates when they attended the college as students. Walt urged me to call Cheney and get an appointment to see him and visit the college, which I did. I was scared to call him and was very surprised

---

* In 1928, women were admitted to all summer courses including classes for coaching of track, baseball, and basketball. In 1951 women were first accepted as full-time students.

when the dean answered his own phone. We talked for about an hour. I was thrilled when he invited me to visit the college. He referred me to William (Bill) Lammers, the director of admissions, who later met with me, gave me a battery of tests, showed me around the campus, and gave me my application papers.

Subsequently, I was accepted!

When I entered as a freshman in the fall of 1956, I was 24 years old. The student body numbered about 2200 students, with only about one percent of African descent. Dr. Glenn Olds was soon to become president of Springfield College. He served from 1958 to 1965. I believe he was, at age 43, the youngest college president in the United States. He had a doctorate from Yale, where he had roomed with President Kennedy's brother-in-law, Sargent Shriver, a factor that became important in my life later, after I graduated. At Springfield, Dr. Olds was a great leader and teacher who worked well with students.

*Alumni Hall, Springfield College, Dan's freshman year residence.*
*Photo 2003 by Loretta Neumann.*

# FIRST COLLEGE EXPERIENCES

As for me, although I think my involvements in Korea and my work afterward better prepared me for college, Springfield was a great introduction to a new way of living and thinking. I learned to study better in college than when I was in high school. At Springfield, I first majored in pre-med then later changed my major to general studies with minors in sociology and psychology. Because these required fewer labs and less time, the change enabled me to get more involved in the school's activities. It also expanded my immediate employment opportunities when I graduated. And, despite the paucity of Blacks at Springfield, I never experienced overt racism from my professors (with one exception) nor from other students. My friends and roommates were mostly white.

Proficiency in swimming was a requirement for graduation at Springfield College during the 1950s when I was a student. As freshmen, we were required to take a swimming class, which included a lifesaving course under the direction of Springfield's Olympic coach Charles E. "Red" Silvia, a highly respected athlete in the international swimming community. Silvia pioneered the technique of two dolphin kicks for each arm action. He taught it to Springfield swimmer William (Bill) Yorzyk, who participated in the 1956 Olympics in Melbourne and was the first swimmer to win the Gold Medal in the new 200-meter "dolphin butterfly" event.[†]

---

[†] Yorzyk set 11 world records and won the U.S. national outdoor title four times from 1955-58 before retiring in 1960 at age 26. According to "The Complete Book of the Olympics," by David Wallechinsky, Yorzyk was even faster as he got older: "In 1984 Yorzyk, then a 57-year-old anesthesiologist, swam the 200-yard butterfly in 2:11.0 – faster than he did in his athletic heyday." Source: Karen Rosen "BILL YORZYK, FIRST BUTTERFLY OLYMPIC GOLD MEDALIST, DIES AT AGE 87," *Team USA*, Sept. 04, 2020. *https://www.teamusa.org/News/2020/September/04/Bill-Yorzyk-First-Butterfly-Olympic-Gold-Medalist-Dies-at-Age-87*

*Dan and Bill Babcock, Springfield Class Reunion, 2015.*
*Photo by Loretta Neumann.*

*Bill Babcock*

It was in one of those swimming classes that I met William Havens (Bill) Babcock. Bill was rugged, white, and an outstanding athlete in track and football. He was what I call a "land athlete" whereas I was a "water athlete." In addition to my Red Cross water safety instructor training in Korea, I had been swimming for many years. I had taught swimming to young campers and adults of all ages. For me, water was a second home. Without difficulty, I could stay underwater for three minutes. It was at Springfield that my classmate Richard Stevens of Longmeadow, Massachusetts, on a challenge, swam three laps underwater with me in the college pool.

During our swimming class, Bill Babcock and I were teamed together to practice lifesaving skills. Like other male students at that time, in the class we were both swimming in the nude. I portrayed the drowning victim, and Bill played the pool lifeguard to rescue me. Often in drowning cases the victim panics and grabs anything they touch, even the rescuer, to save themselves. That is the role I took, being towed to the side by Bill, when I broke away from him. I climbed up on Bill's backside, wrapping my arms around his neck.

For Bill to admit defeat or to give up was out of the question. I was pushing Babcock down deeper into the swimming pool. Then I felt him slap my thigh three times, indicating that he was out of breath and needed to come up for air. However, instead of just releasing him, I put my feet on his thighs and pushed off to swim out of the pool. That pushed Bill down further just when he was coming up for air. As I was about to reach the side of the pool, there was a tremendous chorus of shouting by our classmates.

"Dan, look out!" they yelled. Bill was coming after me for my swimming prank.

"I'll get you, Smith!" he exclaimed. "I'll get you!" I jumped out of the pool. Bill followed. He was relentless, chasing me from one side to the other. For protection, I dove back into and out of the pool, corner to corner. Bill followed. Finally, Coach Silvia blew his whistle.

"Stop running!" Coach Silvia yelled. He kept us on opposite sides of the pool until we calmed down. Then Bill and I started laughing, both realizing how we looked to our classmates, running around buck naked like two crazy people. Little did we know that was the beginning of a lifelong friendship.

After the first year, Bill and I decided to become roommates and live off campus for our sophomore year. We selected two other freshman classmates and rented a house within walking distance of the college. Our roommates were John Shirposki, a Korean veteran, and Gene Fox from Pennsylvania. In short, we had three white sophomores and one Black – me.

Springfield College fostered diversity as well as being concerned with helping people. Hence, we all worked together and had mutual respect. We also each had our own idiosyncrasies when it came to buying groceries and cleaning up after meals. Bill and I were always helping our younger relatives. Bill brought his young 13-year-old male relative to live with us because the youngster was having difficulties at home. In turn, I had my 13-year-old nephew stay with us. He was having similar problems growing into his teenage years.

I learned a great deal about being a father from Bill's father, Reggie. A yacht captain, Reggie would drive up from Florida to watch Bill play football. In addition, he would bring with him goodies from the yacht's refrigerator. One day Reggie arrived at our off-campus house with some huge steaks. While waiting for Bill to clean up from football practice, Reggie cooked the steaks for the meal.

"Dig in!" he said, as we roommates gathered around the table. I took my fork and pierced the biggest steak. Reggie placed his hand on top of my hand.

"No, that one's for my son Bill," he said. I thought it one of the finest examples of a parent's devotion to his child I had ever witnessed.

*Another Job – Phlebotomist*

Since we lived off campus, the cost for lodging resulted in an increase in my budget. Consequently, because of my medical experience in Korea, I responded to a Springfield Hospital advertisement looking for phlebotomists, and I was hired along with John Shirposki, one of my roommates. You could always know in which room John was taking blood by the screens and moans of the patient. This was long before the syringe and needle were replaced by the vacuum tubes and butterfly-type needle now used throughout the medical system.

I worked at the hospital as a phlebotomist for two years. Besides earning money, I gained good experience that was often useful as I applied for professional positions. Indeed, I have found that all my jobs, whether menial or skilled, aided me and in some way enriched my life.

# SPORTS

Unlike most other athletes at Springfield, I had never played sports in high school. I had grown up in a small rural farm/mill community for the most part, with only what we called a "Joe Louis" radio –a radio with static that sputtered and cut off at the most crucial part of a story or fight. We had no television to watch or from which to learn sports. Coming from a solid working-class community, I considered tennis, track, football, and basketball to be for the privileged rich.

Instead, from elementary to high school, we played "King of the Hill," where we threw boys off the top of the mound into a pile of other kids. It was sometimes called the "Nigger Heap." We also played tag, and I taught myself to swim. But I had zero knowledge about competitive swimming or the rules and regulations of other sports. In my social class we often looked with disdain on kids running up and down a field, when they could be working to make money for their family.

## *Football*

Consequently, I was "brain-dead" about organized sports when I entered Springfield. I could watch but knew nothing of the games except the scores. For example, I went out for freshman football and was proud to be given a uniform and helmet for use on the field. One day, Coach Ozzie Solomon told the "red shirts" to go up to the line of "scrimmage." I lined up next to my friend, seasoned player Bill Babcock, and knelt like the others.

"I don't see a scrimmage line," I told Bill. I did not know what the word even meant. Of course, the players all broke out into laughter. A couple weeks later I learned that the "red shirts" were to be pitted against seniors. I thought I had learned the game, but I still did not yet know the difference between the offense and the defense. I began running down the field when Coach Dunn blew his whistle.

"Danny, Danny Smith," he yelled. "You are running the wrong way!"

Talk about being embarrassed! Needless to say, I never got to play in a regular game. The last game of the season, I and others were sitting on the bench in the rain when Coach Ozzie came down selecting seniors and "red shirts" for the final period. He came to me, put his hand on my shoulder and smiled, but kept going down the bench line.

## Wrestling

I did somewhat better in wrestling. While I was in elementary school, I was very good at playing King of the Hill. I would flip kids over my back or wrestle them to the ground and then throw them in the pile below. It was all just roughhousing, no real competition or keeping score.

*Dan the wrestler.*

When I arrived on campus at Springfield for freshman week, following registration another classmate and I went to the wrestling coach office of Doug Parker, a Springfield graduate and all-American wrestling champion.[‡] Most important, Doug was an excellent teacher and coach. I walked up to him and said that I wanted to come out for wrestling.

"Good, we'll see you upstairs on the mat," he said.

"I want you to know that I will give you my all," I replied. He smiled.

"Good, because I'll get it!"

---

[‡] Parker served as head wrestling coach at Springfield College for 35 years starting in 1955 and concluding with his retirement in 1990. In that span, Parker's teams won 22 New England Championship titles, including 16 consecutive wins from 1955-1970. Overall, Parker finished his coaching career with 485 victories, 35 straight winning seasons, and 15 top-20 national rankings. On January 14, 2017, the Springfield College wrestling program became a member of the elite 1000-win club after defeating Theil College, joining Oklahoma State, Iowa State, and Oregon State Universities as the only programs in NCAA history to achieve 1000 dual meet victories.

He did get it, and I became a wrestler. Fast forward to when I was a junior at Springfield. I was wrestling at 177 pounds. I was not great, but I was holding my own with the team. I was especially thrilled when the coach selected me to be on the team going to West Point Military Academy in 15 days. He asked me to drop weight and wrestle at 167. Ten days later I made it down to that weight. When our team arrived at this famous, historical place, I and my teammates were mesmerized with the beautiful campus. The cadets were marching with sparkling, polished, pressed uniforms. And the West Point food training table was filled with all kinds of goodies.

As we walked into the wrestling hall, I noted the circular balcony above the wrestling floor. It was filled with uniformed cadets. Our team lost the two lower pound meets, so the coach asked me to wrestle up at the 177-pound weight. I felt very competitive when I saw my opponent. I went out to the floor and circled to defeat this West Pointer. The referee gave instructions and then stepped back and blew the start whistle.

Suddenly, there was a great roar from the balcony by the cadets who were standing up. I went to shake my opponent's hand, but I looked up, and he grabbed me, slammed me to the floor, and pinned me. What a shock to me and the team. Walking back to the Springfield bench was the longest walk I ever took. But the episode taught me a good lesson – not to be distracted or intimidated by grandeur but to stay focused on my goal. It has also, many years later, given me a good joke to tell my friends. I set the record at Springfield in wrestling. I got pinned in 13 seconds!

## Syracuse – Why I Refused to Wrestle

The former great Black football player James (Jim) Brown was a powerhouse at Syracuse University and, after graduation from Syracuse, was with the Cleveland Browns from 1957 through 1965. He ruled the field with his hard running. He then went to Hollywood and became an actor. He nurtured student Ernest R. (Ernie) Davis, a Syracuse student who was as powerful a running back as Jim Brown, and who became the first African American to win the Heisman trophy. Davis was also an outstanding wrestler in my same weight class.

My coach believed that I could beat Ernie Davis. I was in good shape and very competitive. The wrestling staff urged me to get ready and prepare for the meet. It was my perception at the time, and I convinced myself, that it was the coach's hidden agenda, whether he knew it or not, to see what we now term a "Mandingo" type wrestling exhibition. I assumed my coach hoped to see two Black titans "duke it out." In my travels and experience, I had seen many good-thinking white Americans act in many ways like in the old American South, without even recognizing what they were doing or why they did so.

I decided that I would not participate in that event. Hence, I made excuse after excuse for not going to the meet at Syracuse. Finally, the coach took me off the Syracuse travel list. Ernie Davis was later picked by the Washington Redskins and traded to the Cleveland Browns, but he died in 1963 of leukemia at age 23 without ever playing in a professional game.

## INTERRACIAL DATING

I met Diane Hazzard, a young white woman of Irish and German descent, at Springfield College in 1957. I was 25 years old, one of a few veterans from the Korean War who entered after our service using the GI Bill. It was my sophomore year. Diane and I passed each other on campus while she was an entering freshman. Those young 17- and 18-year-old female students seemed very immature to me and other veterans. However, by their late sophomore and junior years, those same freshman students seemed more grown-up!

Diane was on the cheerleading squad, and we noticed each other at various athletic games. One thing that caught my attention was her friendly smile and twinkle in her eyes. She had many girl-friends and was often mentioned by boys in my dorm as a girl that they would like to get to know. I was always a good listener at bull sessions and observed the talk about

*Diane Hazzard, Springfield College Yearbook.*

interesting, sought-after girls by the guys in our study group.

It is important to remember that this was the late 1950s when the civil rights movement was a growing issue. There were well-publicized demonstrations in the South against segregation and demonstrations at the Springfield Woolworth store. The Montgomery, Alabama, bus boycott had recently occurred. Churches were being bombed. Most important for Diane and me was the nation's social custom of race separation. A 14-year-old Black boy, Emmett Till from Chicago, had been murdered in Mississippi a couple years earlier, in 1955, for supposedly flirting with a white woman. Unwritten prohibitions against interracial dating were well entrenched in the brainwashed public's mind, in the North as well as the South.

I recall entering Professor Berger's sociology class and taking a seat in the rear of the room. Diane walked in at about the same time. She took the empty seat right next to mine. Dr. Berger would not likely have noticed us together. He was a bespectacled, older professor who could hardly see students, often calling them by the wrong names. When driving his Model

T Ford and especially when parking his car, he would often crash into the other car and leave his calling card on the windshield for the owner to contact him.

In Dr. Berger's class, the wooden seats were somewhat cramped together, resulting in close contact for students. Diane and I both soon noticed that our feet were touching, followed by our ankles and knees, in such a way as not to draw attention from others. We were playing "footsies." It would appear as just a casual body movement that seemed neither romantic nor purposeful. We also learned how to play elbow tag, which also always looked innocent.

## STUDENT BODY PRESIDENT

I later got involved in campus politics and elicited Diane's help with my campaign for student body president. She worked very hard, especially with the girls' dorms and particularly at Abbey Hall where she was in residence. She set up meetings and developed creative signs, including a huge cardboard hand which she hung in the student union. "Dan is reaching out his hand to help us," the poster said. It asked students to sign the hand in

support of my campaign. Another one had a mirror on it with the question in bold face, "Stop, Look at Me – Be true to yourself. Who is the best man for the job?" A third one said, "Vote for Dan, the Man with a Tan." We thought that was especially clever, but some people found it controversial.

I had a hard-working team, and we were all excited when I won. A couple of days following my victory, Diane and I decided to go off campus and spend some time together. I skipped classes and spent the afternoon driving around the area to look for a suitable location. I found an unpaved long dirt road off the beaten path up in the hills about 10 miles from the college.

*Police Encounter*

When I picked Diane up from her dorm at dusk, we were both excited and looking forward to celebrating. As we drove up the hill on the somewhat bumpy dirt road, shadows from the maple and birch trees looked like a welcoming gateway to a castle. We stopped at a flat location, and I turned off the engine.

In what seemed like only seconds, a police car with red lights flashing stopped behind us. We were both startled. Two imposing white police officers walked up to our car; one came on each side. Diane and I looked at each other, realizing that we were an interracial couple in unknown territory. I was asked to step outside my car and into the police cruiser to provide information. Diane was to remain in the car for questioning. She was nervous because both officers were tall and rugged looking. Her officer asked her if she was in the car "under her own free will."

"Yes!" She blurted out. "That's Daniel Smith, the student body president of Springfield College." Then she flashed that big smile. No reaction appeared on his face, however.

Meanwhile, I gave my driver's license to the police officer who was questioning me. I explained who I was, and he called the dean of the college to verify that we were, in fact, his students. Dean Cheney asked that they send us back to Springfield. The police officer then walked me slowly back to my car. Towering over me, he spoke in a very stern voice.

"Son," he said, "I want to tell you something. You were very lucky tonight. But in the future, if you ever want to park somewhere again, DON'T PARK BEHIND A FEDERAL PRISON!"

*Dan pledges service with President Olds, "Stepping Up Day."*

### Lesson from President Olds

After I was elected student body president, Dr. Glenn Olds had me meet with him at least once a month to discuss administration, leadership, management, and organizing. These were more learning experiences. At one point, there had been a student issue on campus, and because I was student body president, he expected me to handle the problem. We discussed the issue at one of our monthly meetings. His comments were most enlightening.

"Dan," he said, "I could have the whole student body line up to enter my office for money and a gift. Give each a dollar bill and a Hershey Bar. But before the tenth student reaches the exit door, someone will complain that he was not given a Baby Ruth candy bar!" He noted you can never please everyone. "If you try pleasing everyone, you end up pleasing no one." Another good lesson.

*Dan chairing Student Council meeting.*

## Springfield Alumnus

I graduated from Springfield in 1960, and I credit the college – faculty and students – for helping to make me the man I am. An active alumnus, I have served on the Board of Trustees and have attended many class reunions over the years. I have also appreciated the many opportunities to meet other presidents of Springfield, especially Richard B. Flynn (1999-2013) who did so much to expand the facilities at Springfield, and Mary-Beth A. Cooper (since 2013), the first woman president and one who has

*Dan's senior photo,
Springfield College, 1960.*

enhanced the programs. They both have greatly increased Springfield's leadership, academic influence, and prestige.

## CHAPTER 9
# Becoming Professional

## NORWICH – SOCIAL WORK AND RACISM

Following graduation from Springfield College, I accepted a position at Norwich State Hospital, a 3000-bed state mental institution about 45 miles southeast of Hartford. From 1961 to mid-1963, I lived and worked there five days a week as a professional social worker, covering the geriatric unit and maximum-security Salmon Building.

*Dan at Norwich State Hospital, Conn., August 2017.*
*Photo by Loretta Neumann.*

I was the only Black social worker at Norwich and may have been the first. I was told that few people of color held such professional positions at that time in Connecticut. But I had minored in sociology and psychology at Springfield College and passed the state examination for social workers. I also had previous medical experiences, from working at the veterinary hospital in high school to serving as an Army medic during the Korean War and a part-time phlebotomist while in college. So, I was hired, and I was excited to have my first professional job.

*Making Friends*

Once at Norwich, I settled in and made many friends among my colleagues. An upscale co-ed dormitory was provided for medical professionals and social workers such as me and interns and residents who came from throughout the nation and from other countries. (The international ones were referred to as FMGs – Foreign Medical Graduates.) Many were studying for their medical board exams or PhDs. A separate, on-site housing facility was also available for registered nurses. We often played volleyball after work, and sometimes the nurses participated. Our rooms did not have kitchens, so we generally had meals on the grounds at the professional dining room, with white tablecloths and servers who waited on us.

We were a very collegial and cohesive group. I recall several interesting people. One of my best friends was Barry Fritz, a PhD student in psychology from New York who was a social activist. Also, John Kehoe, a dentist preparing for his boards, and Bob Smith (no relation to me) who drove a Jaguar and was studying for his PhD in psychiatry. He had worked in a foundry in Pennsylvania and was still a bit rough around the edges. Bob Graham, MD, a short "munchkin" who always wore Irish suits with a shirt and tie, drove a Mercedes that everyone admired. When John F. Kennedy became president, Graham accused him of being intellectually dishonest. I disagreed, and we had some vigorous debates.

Dr. Olenick was an FMG from Poland. Every morning for breakfast he had a soft-boiled egg, cut off at the top, with butter and salt, plus a piece of toast. To our amusement, his diet never deviated. One day at our table when Olenick was absent, someone noted how bright he was and how bookish.

"Yeah, but he's still a peasant," commented Al Sashin, a "proper boy" from New York studying for his PhD in psychology.

In the evenings, we would find any excuse for a party, including an ample supply of beverages, lasting from 7 p.m. until quite late. With so many young unmarried men and women who were recent college graduates, there were several romantic interactions, all in the name of "summer love." I know I personally broke some hearts, and, in turn, one young lady broke mine, which was long lasting.

I recall an incident involving an FMG from Argentina, a young doctor who was seriously dating one of the young women at Norwich. At the same time, he was also seeing a married woman in Hartford. One day, the hospital superintendent phoned the Argentinian's older brother, also a doctoral resident at Norwich, and said that the woman's husband had called and said he was on his way down to do harm to the younger Argentinian. Quickly, our colleagues scurried around to find the brother and hide him before the husband arrived.

Fortunately, we succeeded. He was working with a patient in one of the 40 buildings on our grounds and was encouraged to leave. However, this incident caused a huge commotion with the young Argentinian doctor's Norwich girlfriend, who was very distraught when she learned of it. Always some form of drama going on! But as I recall, they were reconciled and later got married.

I especially remember one girl from New York who lived two doors down from me. I think her name was Sarah. She was attractive, what the guys called a "Jewish Princess." This was her first foray away from home and her first professional job. Early one Saturday morning I was preparing to leave the grounds to visit someone, and my pants needed pressing. I had an ironing board but no iron. I walked to Sarah's room and asked if she had an iron that I could borrow. She said her mother had given her one, and Sarah had just unpacked it. She was hesitant to loan it to me but relented, begging me not to damage it. I thanked her, took it down to my room, plugged it in, and set it on top of the ironing board. I had the iron for only about five minutes, and then as I went to get my pants, I tripped over the cord and knocked the iron on the floor. It broke. When I returned it to Sarah, she screamed and cried and called her mother. I felt bad and the next day bought her a new iron.

"I thought you were going to move and not replace it," she said when I gave it to her. I just smiled and got roasted by the guys at the party that night.

## Working with Patients

One of my patients in the maximum-security Salmon Building, where former prison inmates with mental problems were housed, was a man named Alexander. Newly admitted, he had been in prison, I was told, because he was the driver of a vehicle that the police had tagged as being involved in criminal activities. The story was that he had been picked up along with others, probably members of the Mafia.* While in prison, he became agitated and quite violent – so much that when he entered his cell he was handcuffed to the door. Even though handcuffed, when a guard entered the cell, Alexander had kicked and broken the guard's jaw. Hence, he was sent to Norwich State Hospital for mental treatment.

---

* Connecticut has a long history of Mafia involvement, dating from Prohibition in the 1920s to today. See Hoffman, Chris, June 2013, "The History of the Mafia in Connecticut," *Connecticut Magazine.*

As his caseworker, I had the responsibility of working with him at least twice a week. It should be noted that while he was in prison, guards carried big clubs and pistols for protection. However, when I went to see him, I was only allowed to take a pencil and pad of paper. Yet he never attempted to assault me. We had many discussions together. I tried to convince him that if he calmed down and accepted treatment, they might release him.

"No," he exclaimed, "they're going to keep me for life!"

He said he was fearful of being killed by the Mafia because he heard too much while driving their car. For example, they talked about one member of the Mafia who owned several silos for which he was paid by the federal government to be filled with grain for government surplus. However, the silos were empty and held no grain. While Alexander drove the car, they had numerous discussions about who else was involved in the payoff for the empty silos, and that Senator Estes Kefauver was part of the investigation. (Although Alexander told me this, I have never validated his story.)

In my discussions with him, I found that Alexander, like me, had a strong love of dogs. So, we often talked about how he could have a dog if he were released from the hospital. He was excited about this possibility. Over time, he became less agitated and less confrontational. He was subsequently discharged from the hospital and was able to get three German Shepherds.

I also remember a very serious, elderly patient who grabbed my arm one day as I was walking through the geriatric ward. I was stunned when he pulled the sheets off his legs and showed me his feet.

"They aren't taking care of me," he said. I looked at his feet. His toenails were extremely long and curved around his toes. They had never been cut. He also noted that he saw old people come into the geriatric ward with their adult children, who would sign some papers. Then two or three days later, the patients went someplace, and when they came back, they were very listless, obedient, no trouble to anyone. They would sit on a bed or a rocking chair and not communicate with others.

"They act as if they've had a lobotomy," he said. "This happens all the time. Children discard their parents for whatever reason."

I found it amazing that patients housed there for some length of time learned all the language and jargon used by medical professionals in the hospital. They know more than what people realize.

## Racist Incident

To earn extra money, I changed out of my shirt, tie, and jacket and worked as an orderly during the evenings at the Backus Hospital, an acute-care, not-for-profit community hospital about five miles away. I removed trash, emptied ash trays, and cleaned patients' rooms.

*Backus Hospital, Norwich Conn. 2017. Photo by Loretta Neumann.*

It was at Backus that I met Donna, a 16-year-old white patient, while I was doing my usual chores. She said that she had tried to commit suicide because her father had mistreated her. Among other things, he had made her listen to a tape recording of her parents having sex. I explained my role as a social worker at Norwich, said that I could help get her admitted if she had suicidal thoughts again, and gave her my office phone number.

Although I saw her at Backus on several occasions afterward while I did my usual duties as an orderly, we did not discuss her situation again. I did, however, inform my superiors at Norwich, both older men, probably in their mid-fifties or sixties. Then, a couple months later, she phoned me at my office. She sounded distressed, and said she felt she needed help. Her thoughts were again of suicide. I do not recall what issue prompted this, but she was clearly distraught. Although I was keenly aware of our racial differences – she white, me Black – and the then-national attitudes against male/female racial interactions, I felt obligated to help her.

I told her that she should take a cab to the Norwich emergency room and that I would meet her at the door. She did and came accompanied by her mother. I was able to get her admitted as a voluntary patient, and she was assigned a female social worker on the women's ward. I informed the director of social services and my immediate supervisor. They were concerned about my having a personal friendship with her, but I assured them that it was purely professional.

Several weeks later following medical treatments, Donna was scheduled to be discussed at the hospital's "grand rounds," a conference to evaluate her for possible discharge. Leading it was a psychiatric physician from Yale, Dr. Detrick, an eminent doctor with whom I had been in conferences on several occasions. Because I was familiar with the patient, I was seated in the room, although not at the conference table. As the meeting was about to get underway, I looked out the door into the hall, and saw the director of social services. With his finger he beckoned me to come out to him, which I did.

"You can't stay there," he said.

"Why?" I asked. He told me to come to his office, that he didn't want to discuss it in public. When I entered his office, he closed the door, and I sat down in the chair in front of his desk. He looked at me pointedly and said that the doctor from Yale was in charge of the conference. I said that I understood and that I had been in conferences with the doctor before.

"The doctor may ask you some questions that may be embarrassing to you and the hospital," he said. I took it that he was inferring that I had some type of personal relationship with the girl. I was perplexed and didn't quite know what to say. It was very warm in the room, however, so I stood up and took my jacket off. He immediately stood up too.

"What are you going to do? Fight?" he exclaimed.

I was shocked and disgusted. I knew what he had in his mind. No matter my professional credentials, experience, and proven capabilities, his stereotype was of a Black man interested in a young white woman, a Black man with uncontrolled anger. I believe that has always been one of the main racial problems of white Americans: they do not know Blacks. We knew whites because we had to live with them, but whites did not know us because they did not live with us.

I simply left his office and did not go back to the conference room. The next day, my supervisor wrote a lengthy memo about his perception of why I had been asked to leave the conference. He said he was upset with my lack of professionalism in working with patients. He clearly did not understand that these were racist attacks on me, both by him and by the director. Nevertheless, I retained my position at Norwich and continued working there until I was able to obtain a new position at what was then called the Seaside Regional Center for the Mentally Retarded in Waterford, Conn. Meanwhile, Donna was subsequently discharged from Norwich.

Several years later, I was passing through Norwich with my wife, and we stopped to purchase some groceries in a local store. An older woman in line at the register came up to me and introduced herself as Donna's mother.

"Were you the man who helped my daughter at Norwich Hospital?" she asked. I said yes. She smiled.

"Donna has done well, and I just want to thank you!"

## MLK- MARCH ON WASHINGTON 1963

One of the most profound events in my life occurred while I was working at Norwich. I often spent time after work with my friend Barry Fritz, the Jewish psychologist and civil rights advocate from New York, discussing the pros and cons of life in the United States and the potential impact of racial integration on American society. During the early summer of 1963, Rev. Martin Luther King, Jr.'s, planned march on Washington was a major topic. We focused on three key issues: (1) The purpose of the march and what it would accomplish; (2) safety and medical attention for participants who might be involved in riots during the march; and (3) whether civil rights was mainly a problem for the South to solve and not a Connecticut or northern or national problem.

As the march date drew closer to August, Barry and I debated going to Washington, D.C., to participate in it. I remember sitting at dinner and discussing it with our professional colleagues. They thought we were "nuts" to go and put ourselves in harm's way. They stressed the real possibility of civil disruption and riots that could occur. But finally, Barry convinced me that he and I, a Jew and a Black, should journey to the nation's capital to show our support for Dr. King and the civil rights movement.

We used Barry's car for the eight-hour trip south. We talked virtually non-stop all the way down about life in America, but were filled with anxiety the closer we got to D.C. Our car entered the city from the east, via New York Avenue. Much to our surprise, we were met by a white motorcycle police officer. We were alarmed, but he turned out to be extremely polite, professional, and helpful.

"Where are you going?" he asked. "Do you have a place to stay?" We explained that we had come from Connecticut to participate in the March on Washington. We confessed that we did not have any accommodations lined up for the night. The officer then proposed to escort us to a place where we might be able to stay. We followed him to a home owned by a white family where there were other march participants. They included members of the Student Non-Violent Coordinating Committee (SNCC) headed by John Lewis and the Southern Christian Leadership Conference (SCLC).

I distinctly remember asking our hosts if the local restaurants and hotels were segregated or open for all and was assured that they were open. They invited us to spend the night in their attic, which we did with about 20 other marchers from all over the country, using sleeping bags and floor mats on a nice oak floor. We were provided donuts, coffee, and orange juice the next morning.

I do not remember how far our housing was from the Lincoln Memorial, but I recall that the street quickly filled up with orderly, well-dressed Black and white marchers. Walking with the packed crowd past the Washington Monument, it took Barry and me about two hours to

*Dan interviewed in 2020 by German television at the Lincoln Memorial,*
*where he had watched Martin Luther King's "I Have a Dream" speech in*
*1963. Photo by Loretta Neumann.*

reach the Reflecting Pool at the base of the Lincoln Memorial. Along the
way, a newspaper reporter asked one of our marchers, "What do the Negros want?" The reply was "Equal rights under the law – no more, no less!"
That became one of our rallying cries.

As one who considered himself a group dynamics expert and or-
ganizer, I marveled at the size of the crowd and the unity of expressed
purpose. I had witnessed great crowds and crowd control while serving in
the military, but this was a huge mass of people of all races, genders, and
religions. They were singing "We Shall Overcome" and marching with
determined faces, yet in a festive mood. There were women pushing in-
fants in baby carriages and fathers with children on their shoulders. There
were nuns, priests, and rabbis; men in military uniforms; youths dressed in
Boy Scout uniforms; and union members passing out literature and pins.

*I Have a Dream*

In short, the Reflecting Pool was surrounded by a living sea of humanity, all trying to get closer to the Lincoln Memorial to see and hear Dr. King speak. Some people perched in trees, many waded into the pool, while others sat and dangled their feet to cool them from the hot pavement. Barry and I worked our way through the crowd, almost to within 100 feet of the podium at the end of the Reflecting Pool where Dr. King was to speak. Facing the Lincoln Memorial, we were on the left side.

There was a "buzz" in the crowd because of John Lewis, chairman of SNCC, who was considered a "firebrand." While young, he was well respected, and in 1961, was one of the original freedom riders and badly beaten. For his speech, Lewis had included stronger, more inflammatory language than the march leaders felt appropriate for the event. Because of this, there was even a question of whether he would be allowed to address the marchers. Lewis subsequently spoke, however, and his message was powerful. He stressed that Blacks could not be patient.

"We do not want our freedom gradually but want to be free now!" He appealed to people to get into the revolution that was sweeping the nation. He concluded: "We must say Wake up America! Wake up!" We were all very moved, and Lewis received strong applause

The other crowd "buzz" was whether President Kennedy would appear and address the marchers. He did not. (Indeed, Barry and I had predicted that he would not come because of security reasons.) Of course, there were many other speakers. But we all were thrilled when Mahalia Jackson, one of the most noted gospel singers of the time, sang at Dr. King's request one of her classic songs, "I Been 'Buked and I Been Scorned." In turn, she was apparently instrumental in urging Dr. King to deliver the best-known part of his speech, "I have a dream!"

We were all transfixed. Dr. King spoke with the thunder and cadence of a Black minister giving a sermon. "We will not be satisfied until justice rolls down like waters and righteousness like a mighty stream."

"Yes! Yes! Yes!" I kept repeating, as he talked.

There was an amusing moment, too, when Dr. King spoke of having a dream of little Black boys and girls walking hand in hand together with little white boys and white girls.

"Yes!" I exclaimed again.

"Do you think maybe Dr. King has gone too far?" Barry jokingly said. I just laughed. I already knew that day was here.

When Dr. King finished, we all joined in great applause. Many around us - Barry and I too, of course - had tears in our eyes. It ended with all of us once again singing "We Shall Overcome." Afterwards we drove back to Connecticut fulfilled. We understood that we had been involved in a truly historical American event, one that included all races and was not mired in riots. It was, in fact, peaceful in all respects.

## 50 Years Later

I have always felt that the March on Washington was such a pivotal point in the history of Black America that we should never let the memory die. So, I was pleased in August 2013 to be interviewed by Rick Lyman for a New York Times article, published a few days before the 50th anniversary. To my surprise, I was featured in the article with a large photo on the front page of the newspaper. It was quite a shock, as I had thought I would be just one of many old marchers included in the article. Two professors were quoted, along with Lonnie Bunch, then-director of the National Museum of African American History and Culture. They shared mixed views on the success of the march in thwarting racial discrimination.

The article summarized my life story as the son of a man born into slavery and, in response to the issues raised about Dr. King's effect on racism, concluded with a quote from me:

"It's like you run a race and you hit a wall and you have to work with yourself to get past the wall….That's what happened to America. We made great progress and then we hit a wall and the wall started to push back and America just has not pushed through that wall yet." [22]

The next year, in March 2014, Springfield College held a special program with a panel discussion in honor of the 50th anniversaries of both the 1963 March on Washington and Dr. King's 1964 commencement address at Springfield. Barry Brooks (class of 1964), Bob Parsonage (Springfield Chaplain 1963-1973) and I (class of 1961) described our experiences on the 1963 march.

*Springfield MLK program with Daniel Smith,*
*Bill Parsonage, Martin Dobrow and Barry Brook, 2014.*
*Photo by Loretta Neumann.*

I was not at the 1964 commencement, but Barry and Bob spoke of it as a lesson in courage. The president of Springfield College, Dr. Glen

Olds, turned down a million-dollar gift offer to the college because the donor did not want Rev. Martin Luther King, Jr., to deliver the commencement address. At the same time, Dr. Olds defied pressure from the FBI to retract the invitation for Dr. King's speech, which was given under armed guard on July 14, 1964.[23]

I understand that Dr. Olds was also instrumental in getting Dr. King released from a southern jail, where he was incarcerated for being on the beach and swimming at an Atlantic Ocean hotel. Dr. Olds and Springfield College later conferred on the civil rights leader an honorary doctorate, the first school to do so.

## SEASIDE REGIONAL CENTER

After Norwich Hospital, I was offered a position as a social worker at the Seaside Regional Center, beautifully located on Long Island Sound in Waterford, Conn. It was the first of its kind in the nation, a state-operated facility for the care and training of mentally retarded but educable residents.

My supervisor was Marilyn Gravink. In those days it was unusual for women to supervise men, but I highly respected her. She was bright, tall, and attractive, from the Midwest, professional, and enjoyed her job.

*Seaside Regional Center, Waterford Conn, 2017. Photo by Loretta Neumann.*

Many years later, she served as a consultant for a federal program I directed, called the Area Health Education Centers (AHEC). She also wrote a strong, supportive letter on behalf of the program and its director.

## *Teaching Life Outside*

At the Seaside Regional Center, one of my duties was to train and prepare some of the residents for life outside the facility. I developed several classes, usually of 10 residents, both male and female, ages 18 to 35. One was a course that I developed on etiquette, especially how to eat properly at the table, how to hold their utensils, and to use napkins instead of their fingers. For that I used Amy Vanderbilt's book of etiquette along with the Vogue book and the one by Elinor Ames.

Other classes were on how to enjoy the world of work and how to perform a job once hired. For example, I taught them how to dress appropriately for certain types of jobs, to arrive on time for work, to listen and appreciate their supervisor, and always to return things to where they got them. Also, how to live by themselves, to care for their accommodations, and to handle basic money management.

In addition, I instructed them on hygiene – to wash and dry their hands and to use their own handkerchief. As a demonstration, I took pieces of copper sulfate crystals, placed them on the ground, then put a huge block of ice on top. I had the students watch how long it took for the copper sulfate to rise to the top of the ice, which showed them how bacteria travels and how we must be careful about the things we touch before our finger goes into our mouth.

They needed to know these things because the positions they were preparing for were at a very basic level. These included cleaning restaurant tables, washing dishes with or without machines, cleaning floors, washing clothes and folding them properly, cleaning bathrooms, etc.

Following the completion of instructions, unfortunately I did not think to provide them with a certificate, which they would have appreciated, but we always had a special evening meal for the graduates. Most important, I would work to locate for them a position in an acceptable establishment in the local community, which included hospitals and restaurants. I would visit the establishment, meet with the manager, and explain what the residents had been trained to do.

## Walter Meets Howard Johnson's

I vividly remember some of the residents that I worked with. One was a man named Walter. He was about 30 years old, wore glasses, about medium height, had a good gift of gab, and was very friendly. I had negotiated a job for Walter at an orange-roofed Howard Johnson's Restaurant. The restaurant manager had been there only two weeks. I also found Walter a room in an acceptable apartment house within walking distance of the restaurant. I drove him there, and he met his landlady. She showed him his room and explained the financial arrangements.

Afterwards, I walked with Walter to the Howard Johnson's and pointed out to him the orange roof. I introduced him to the manager, and the manager and I broke bread together over lunch. One of the perks of my job! When I left, I told Walter that I would be back in 10 days to see him. Ten days later I returned to the Howard Johnson's to talk to the manager and check on Walter's progress. The manager said he hadn't seen him lately.

"He came on time for two days, but I haven't seen him since." I was concerned and drove to Walter's apartment house to talk to the landlady.

"He's been leaving before 8 a.m. in the morning and returning after 5 every night," she said. I was perplexed. Then, as we were talking, Walter walked in.

"Walter, the manager at the Howard Johnson's hasn't seen you," I said. Walter looked surprised.

"I've been working there every day," he replied.

"But the manager said he hasn't seen you," I said again.

"That's funny – I walk to the Howard Johnson's. I thought it was a long way." It hit me that he may have passed by the original restaurant and kept walking till he found another orange-roofed Howard Johnson's. We got in my car, and as I drove Walter showed me where he had been working. There it was, another one with an orange roof, some distance past the original Howard Johnson's. I talked to the manager there.

"It was the funniest thing," the manager said. "I came in late one morning, and here was this guy I'd never seen before, washing dishes and cleaning the floors. I walked up to him and asked why he was there. He lit into me. 'Can't you see I've been getting here on time and working all day? Aren't I doing a good job?'"

The manager asked his name and wrote it down. "I have to give you some money," he said.

"Yes, you do!" Walter exclaimed. After that, he kept his job there, despite the long walk. He liked the people he was working with and wanted to stay. And they were pleased to have him.

## A Sad Ending

A not-so-happy story involved a teenage resident at Seaside, Peter, who was about 13 or 14 years old, good looking, and friendly. I met his parents, who were obviously wealthy. They lived in Maine where his father had a high-profile position. I felt that Peter was an embarrassment to them because he had epilepsy.

I always thought Peter was more than educable and never felt that he was retarded (the term used back then). There were other medical facilities in Maine where they could have placed him for assistance with his mental challenges. My speculation was that his parents moved him far away so they would not need to have him in their family community.

Peter and I, however, bonded very well. He was always turning up in my office, wanting to talk. He considered me a friend, and I tried to be one for him. But I was on my own professional path, making my plans to go to veterinary school at the Tuskegee Institute in Alabama. When the day came for me to leave Seaside, he was crying, and very emotional. I saw him in my rear-view mirror, as he ran, following my car to the highway. I never reconnected with Peter.

# CHAPTER 10

# Moving South to Alabama

Although I enjoyed my time as a social worker, because of my love of animals, my dream had long been to become a veterinarian. As I have noted before, during my high school years I worked for Dr. Raymond B. Church, a local white veterinarian in Winsted, who took me under his wing. It was with his encouragement that I applied to the Tuskegee Institute School of Veterinary Medicine in Alabama. I had been told by my New England family, friends, and associates that Tuskegee Institute (now Tuskegee University) was one of the premiere Black colleges in the United States, attended by the sons and daughters of prominent Black doctors, lawyers, and judges. At that time, its veterinary medicine school was one of only 19 in the country, and it had a fine reputation. In preparation, I took additional prerequisite courses, applied to Tuskegee, and was accepted for the 1964 term.

Before I left for Tuskegee, my mother hosted friends to her house for some treats and to wish me well. I recall their serious discussion about wanting me to be "mechanized" before I left. This was during the early 1960s when lynchings of Black men were still occurring in southern states. One of the women produced a skinny, holstered .45 pistol revolver for me to take for protection during my journey and while I was in the South.

Although I was very familiar with rifles and pistols from my experiences in my days of hunting and in the military during basic training and while in the Korean War, I chose not to take or carry a weapon. I felt, rightly or wrongly, that I could protect and defend myself alone with my big Black hands instead of a gun.

So, I packed my little two-tone green Hillman Husky wagon with my personal belongings, including my recently purchased set of a Britannica encyclopedia. With my mother's and sisters' boxes of food (not knowing where in the segregated South I would be able to eat), I headed out for Alabama at 3 a.m. in the morning. I had charted my route through the American Automobile Association (AAA) map system, as I did not have a copy of the "Green Book" used by Blacks for travel. I checked the course several times in the weeks prior to leaving.

I especially wanted to be sure that I could maneuver through Washington, D.C., without getting tangled in traffic. But of course, given my unfamiliarity with the signs and directions in and around D.C., I arrived at the height of its morning commuter traffic. My car seats were packed with books and clothing, so I could not see clearly out of the right-side window. As a result, I got caught in the middle of the city at Dupont Circle, driving around and around the circle. I couldn't tell which exit to take that would lead me out of D.C.

Suddenly, a white policeman stood in the center of the road, blew his whistle and, stopping traffic in all directions, walked stiff-legged over to my car.

"Sir, where do you want to go?" he calmly said. I nervously explained that I was trying to get through D.C. to go to school in Alabama. To my relief, he just smiled.

"Follow me," he said. Meanwhile, other drivers got out of their cars and started clapping and waving as I followed the policeman. He walked me around the circle to the exit I needed. I was more embarrassed than afraid but felt relieved after he got me off the circle and I was able to head out of the city.

## A Scary Stop in Georgia

Afterward, the drive was uneventful. I refueled along the way and had no problems except for a major thunderstorm in Georgia. The AAA directions were accurate, and I followed the map's yellow markers quite well. As the day went on, I got tired. I was not yet drowsy, but not necessarily as alert as I should have been. My map showed a "Y" in the road, and I turned right instead of taking the main road to the left. As I drove, I noticed I was on an incline, going up a steep hill into the woods of Georgia.

At the bottom of the hill, I had noticed a one-pump gas station/garage with five or six white men sitting around talking and drinking beer. I had thought nothing of it, but when I reached the crest of the hill, the half striped, yellow road signs disappeared. I immediately realized that I had taken the wrong turn. I swung the car around to head back down the hill when the Hillman sputtered and cut off.

Well, that was just the predicament I was warned about and feared could happen – a Black man off the beaten path in the Deep South, with no idea where I was, no way to communicate, and my car broken down. At least it was daylight and warm outside. So, I got out and turned the Hillman to point down the hill. I got back in, put it in neutral, held on to the hand brake and inched my way down to the gas station. As I came close to the men who were there, they began to stand up and look at each other and at me. One of them appeared to be the owner. I guided the Hillman into the midst of the group, jumped out, and looked at them cheerfully.

"Can you help me?" I asked. I explained my dilemma with the car and that I was heading for veterinary school. To my delight, they all gathered around the Hillman and tinkered with it, added a wire of some sort, and got the car running smoothly again. I offered payment, but they wouldn't accept it.

"If you're going to take care of my horse," one man yelled, "I'll take care of your car!"

As I left, I smiled and waved, and they smiled and waved back. When I arrived at Tuskegee Institute and told my story, the guys in my dorm said, "You did WHAT?"

## INTRODUCTION TO TUSKEGEE

*Tuskegee Institute (now Tuskegee University), National Historic Site.*

Entering the Deep South was, to put it mildly, quite a surprise. I had grown up in the 1930s and 1940s as one of a handful of Blacks in Winsted, and our educational institutions were not facing state-sponsored segregation. The schools I attended were integrated and my friends were all white. I served in the integrated Army during the Korean War. In college most of my classmates and my major girlfriend were white. After college, my social work was with mostly white professionals with whom I had cordial relationships.

The Tuskegee Institute was my first all-Black educational experience. It was an eye-opener. They initially placed many Army veterans in the dorm with young freshman students who were having their first experience away from home. I remember vividly a conversation with my first roommate when we met. He spoke with a very southern accent, and I spoke with what I presume to him was an equally unfamiliar New England voice.

"Hi," I said.

"H'Rummm," he replied. He repeated it a couple times. It took me awhile to understand that he meant "Hi, roommate."

Another student, desiring to learn more about this Yankee, asked me, "Were you in the woh?"

"Was I what?" I replied.

"In the woh!" he exclaimed. "W. A. R. You know, the Korean Woh!"

Other male students I met (and most of the "Vet Med" students were men) had questions too. They were very curious about my northern experiences. Had I ever dated a white woman? I had, they had not. Also, I was older than they were. I had a car – most of them did not – and many had never even had a driver's license. While I had been very poor as a youth, I had saved money from my post-college positions and had the GI bill to help pay my school expenses. In short, I stood out a bit from the other students. It was my first foray into the Deep South and my first introduction to the Thursday smell of chitlins being cooked.

In any event, the veterinary school was not a walk in the park. Its classes were quite demanding. We studied animal anatomy, histology, bacteriology, etc. The classes were like the ones that first-year medical students take. I remember one occasion when I was cramming for a test in the early morning. I was eating Twinkies and drinking Cokes, all forms of junk food. Then I felt as if I were going to vomit or have diarrhea. I went to the rest room, passed out, and woke up in the campus's John Andrew Memorial Hospital. It was diagnosed as a hyperglycemic attack (too much insulin in my blood system). It's a condition that I've monitored all my life.

## CIVIL RIGHTS –
## SELMA TO MONTGOMERY MARCHES

While I was in Tuskegee, I got involved in a cause that was very important to me – the struggle for civil rights. This was during the early 1960s, and civil rights activities were at their height. The Freedom Rides on buses and sit-ins in places such as Greensboro, N.C., had begun. There were lynchings across the South and many riots. Malcolm X, the famous minister, orator, and human rights activist, appeared on the scene. Rosa Parks awakened the conscience of Black Americans. Reverend Martin Luther King, Jr., was deeply involved in the bus boycotts. John Lewis was hyper-active with the Student Non-Violent Coordinating Committee. Stokely Carmichael and Julian Bond were working directly in the movement as well. Alabama sheriff and segregationist Bull Connor in Birmingham was beating up peacefully protesting Black citizens with his dogs and water hose. Alabama's racist Governor George Wallace, who had blocked seven Black students from entering the University of Alabama in 1963 until stopped by President Kennedy, was still shouting, "Segregation now, Segregation tomorrow, and Segregation forever!"

In early March 1965, hostilities erupted as civil rights activists attempted to march from Selma to Montgomery, the capital of Alabama, in support of Negro voting rights. The first attempt, on March 7, was led by 25-year-old civil rights activist John Lewis. It was brutally thwarted at the

Pettus Bridge in Selma when 600 marchers were tear gassed, whipped, charged by horses, and beaten with chains and nightsticks by state and local police and vigilantes. Lewis himself was severely beaten. The event was so violent and brutal, it was later named "Bloody Sunday."

On March 10, Rev. King led the second march, again starting in Selma. As he was standing down Governor George Wallace's troopers, however, he knelt in prayer and obeyed a court injunction that stopped the march. Meanwhile, over in Montgomery, a convoy of cars and chartered buses arrived carrying 700 student members of the Tuskegee Institute Advancement League and their chaperones. They had come to peacefully present a petition for Negro voting rights to the governor. Wallace refused to see them.

Undaunted, the students held an outdoor rally and gave speeches. Most of them returned to Tuskegee later that day, but 200 of the students staged a sit-down strike at the behest of James Forman and members of the SNCC. They took shelter in a nearby church. Several students were later beaten by Montgomery police officers as they left.

The third march from Selma to Montgomery, led by Rev. King over several days and 54 miles, was completed on March 25. This time, I decided to participate, having been inspired by my attendance at Dr. King's speech in Washington in 1963. I traveled to Selma with great trepidation, as I am not one by nature to be non-violent if assaulted. Also, given what had happened on the previous marches, no one was sure if violence would occur again and whether the march would be completed.

This time, however, marchers were protected by federal troops. The march was successful, and, for me, it was thrilling to be able to support the movement and march next to Rev. King and his wife Coretta; United Nations Under-Secretary-General Ralph Bunche (the first African American Nobel Peace Prize winner); civil rights activist and Rev. King's chief partner in the civil rights movement, Ralph D. Abernathy; and singers Joan Baez; Tony Bennett; Peter, Paul, and Mary; and Harry Belafonte and his wife.

As I was walking with the marchers, I looked on my left and to my surprise saw my white English professor from Springfield College, Edward Sims. We chatted as we walked up to the Alabama State Capitol, then he got lost in the crowd.

Despite the relative peacefulness of the march, one of the marchers, Viola Liuzzo, a white mother of five from Detroit, was shot and killed in her car in Lowndes Country by the Ku Klux Klan (KKK) while returning marchers back to Selma. In retrospect, all these recollections remind me of the turmoil when President Kennedy and Dr. King were assassinated, and, many years later, when students were involved in the Arab Spring uprising that erupted in 2010. The more things change, the more they remain the same, as the January 6, 2021, insurrection at the U.S. Capitol demonstrated.

# TUSKEGEE INSTITUTE SUMMER EDUCATION PROGRAM

I am an Episcopalian, and in Tuskegee I attended the local, primarily Black, St. Andrew's Episcopal Church, as did the president of Tuskegee University, Luther Foster. One Sunday Dr. Foster spoke to me following church service. He said that he and Dean P. B. (Bert) Phillips, Dean of Students, had a program that he planned to initiate and wanted to discuss it with me.

*Dr. Luther Foster, President, Tuskegee Institute, 1953 – 1981.*

At a subsequent meeting at his office, Dr. Foster described a new summer program that would be funded by the Federal government as part of President Lyndon Johnson's "War on Poverty." Sponsored by the Economic Opportunity Act of 1964, the program was to provide tutoring to disadvantaged school children and adults throughout Alabama during the summer. Tutoring would be done by college students, primarily from Tuskegee Institute but also from other institutions of higher learning.

President Foster indicated that he had recently met my former Springfield College President Glenn Olds at a conference. Dr. Olds told him about the effective leadership positions I had held at Springfield. President Foster suggested that perhaps I could find a way to postpone or delay my veterinary pursuit.

"Perhaps you can use your administrative experience now to help our people in Alabama," he said. A short time later, Dean Phillips asked me to serve as Associate Program Director of the new program, the Tuskegee Institute Summer Education Program (TISEP).

So began my adventure with TISEP. Dean Phillips was the Program Coordinator and a true visionary. He foresaw college students not only providing tutoring services to the disadvantaged but also serving as role models for what a good education can accomplish and, as a result, being transformed themselves into better citizens. He brought in students from Tuskegee and reached out to other colleges and universities to participate. Paul Ware, a high-school principal from Birmingham, Ala., was hired as Program Director. He helped organize programs in 10 counties of Alabama,[*] working with other principals and teachers to find facilities

---

[*] Participating counties were Barbour, Bullock, Elmore, Jefferson, Lee, Lowndes, Macon, Montgomery, Pike, and Russell.

and placements for student tutors and the people they would tutor, known as "tutees."

My role as Associate Program Director was to maintain a healthy rapport among the staff, members of the Tuskegee "family," the community, and the program coordinator. In addition, I handled personnel matters – not an inconsiderable task given that there were about 100 group directors and general staff members. In addition, I was to act in the capacity of the Program Director in his absence. Later I was given responsibility to oversee transportation, which was critically important to both the tutors and the tutees.

## TISEP Orientation and Training

I remember vividly the first time that Tuskegee students came to learn about TISEP. It had been announced around the campus, and the first meeting was scheduled in the evening in the gymnasium. I arrived 15 minutes early to find the gymnasium packed with interested students eager to hear about this new program. Of course, a major inducement was the fact that, if selected, they would receive a salary for their work as tutors during the summer. Most of these college students had never worked in a semi-professional job; if they had employment, it was often at manual labor. This would be a great opportunity for them as well as for the tutees.

Dean Phillips addressed the students. He explained the importance of this program and its philosophy. He challenged them to use their education to serve others, noting that by doing so they would not only be helping others but also themselves. They could be role models as well as tutors. He was loudly applauded when he finished speaking. It was a stirring address. We all felt proud to be part of this new initiative.

The preliminary phase of the training program was held for a month in late spring, ending in early June. For the most part, it was under my direction. We held periodic meetings with Dean Phillips to plan the training program. Four to five hundred active students, freshmen through graduate, participated as tutors.

It is hard to describe now, more than five decades later, the sheer poverty and ex-

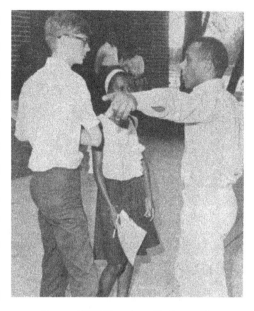

*Dan and TISEP students, Tuskegee, Ala.*
*The TISEP Reporter, September 2, 1965.*

tremely poor living conditions faced then by most Black residents of rural Alabama. Their homes were often decrepit, unpainted shanties without electricity or indoor plumbing. Their segregated schools lacked the educational amenities and higher quality teaching of the white schools. Many Negro children had not learned basic skills in math, English, and science.

It was a daunting task to orient Tuskegee students to these conditions. Although Black themselves, most of them came from somewhat advantaged homes and backgrounds. We were fortunate, however, to have Dean Phillips explain the problems of rural Alabama and the culturally deprived people who lived there, as well as the historical background of the southern Negro. Dean Phillips and I also demonstrated the concept of "role playing" to them by showing what might be done.

*Summer Program*

The first TISEP, funded by the federal government under the Economic Opportunity Act, operated 32 educational centers in low-income rural and urban areas in 10 counties in Alabama. TISEP had an enrollment of about 6000 tutees in grades 7-12, with 780 of them adults who attended night classes. The program staff consisted of about 100 people from a variety of backgrounds: principals, teachers, coaches, priests, supervisors, and graduate students. The tutors, about 600 of them, worked for 13 weeks.

The Tuskegee students were augmented by students from other colleges and universities: Auburn, Bennett, Central State, Clark, Fisk, St. Olaf, Hampton Institute, Howard, and state universities of Alabama, New York, Michigan, and Minnesota.[24] Over the course of the summer, they taught classes in regular subjects such as English, mathematics, science, and social studies. In addition, an Art Group provided 13 tutors for six of the counties who taught arts and crafts related to the academic studies and to nature. Because there were not enough art tutors for every center, they took a mobile exhibit around to the others. A Music Group held classes in music appreciation, culminating in performances at 23 centers. A Drama Group was smaller, but they brought at least two one-act plays to each center. A Beauty Culture Group visited 21 centers and presented lectures and demonstrations on personal grooming. A Community Development Department provided services such as clothing distribution, home improvements, library books, and repairs of used clothing and household goods.[25]

A newspaper, *The TISEP Reporter*, printed 11 editions chronicling the program with stories and photographs. It was informational and educational, not only for student participants but also for the communities, so that tutees and their families "would begin to think of themselves in relation to education as part of a new arm in the civil rights movement, to feel that they were important enough to be written about as individuals rather than poverty statistics."[26]

While tutees were learning, the hundreds of Black and white college students who worked with them also gained tremendously from their experiences. They learned new skills and made friends with people from other races and cultures. Indeed, for many if not most, this was their first opportunity for interracial encounters. I recall especially the students from St Olaf College, Minn., about 50 of them, all white and likely not aware of the dangers they would face in coming to the deep South. But they persevered and even seemed grateful for the opportunity to be there. Dean Philips was later awarded an honorary PhD by St. Olaf College for his outstanding work with TISEP.

". . . I have found myself pulled into another way of life . . . new attitudes, new values, and new habits . . ."

*Black and white college student tutors, TISEP, summer 1965.*

## Challenges

TISEP was the first program of its kind in Alabama if not in the country, and not surprisingly, it experienced problems as well as successes. To dwell too much on either would be unfair. This was a completely new program that had great goals and objectives, but it suffered from disorganization and a lack of clear direction. It was by necessity put together quickly, which meant that it did not have the advantage of long-term planning. There were also problems with funding. (Federal funds did not arrive as quickly as anticipated).

For me, it was a difficult situation, as I was accustomed to the "chain of command" that is used in the military and the bureaucratic hierarchy of large institutions. Because of my administrative experiences and skills, I was often able to see issues that were developing in the program before others were aware of them. Frequently the problems were caused by a lack of communication. Transportation issues were especially daunting, given the 10-county span of the program.

A major problem was housing college students who tutored in counties far from Tuskegee and were unable to use on-campus accommodations. Some tutors found places to rent where they could live together. They faced fewer problems than those living with families. Instances were reported where tutors were a burden on the disadvantaged families they lived with. In one example, a tutor lived in a house with 14 children, two parents, and another tutor.

"This was a four-room house which had no running water or bathroom," the tutor wrote. "Four people slept in one room, and you can imagine where the other 13 people slept."

## Program Evaluation and Recommendations

Fortunately, I was able to get the help of Dr. Barry Fritz, my colleague and friend who had worked with me at the Norwich State Hospital in Connecticut. A psychologist, he had become a professor in New York. He served as the TISEP Evaluations Director.[†] For three months, Dr. Fritz and his staff followed the work of TISEP and provided guidance. At the

---

[†] Barry Fritz, PhD, later became a professor of psychology at Quinnipiac University, Hamden, Conn. He died in 2004.

*House in Macon County, Ala , being repaired by TISEP college students.*
*The TISEP Reporter, September 2, 1965.*

end, he thoroughly reviewed written reports and recommendations made by tutees, tutors, and teaching supervisors.

"For the most part, the writings are full of praise for the program," he stated in his final report. "The tutees love the program, the tutors feel it has been a memorable and valuable experience, and the teaching supervisors see it as a boom to their locality."

Indeed, many student tutors had been led to believe that they would be treated in a hostile manner by the tutees in the communities. This did not happen. For the most part, they were met with enthusiasm, few disciplinary problems, and a willingness to learn. This was rather overwhelming to many of the tutors, and it took them some time to adjust to the attitudes that tutees exhibited toward them. Clearly the transformative aspect of TISEP envisioned by President Foster and Dean Phillips, whereby the lives of the tutors themselves would be altered and enhanced, was realized.

*Aftermath and Reflections*

It is also important to remember that this was a time of tremendous social upheaval in the nation, especially in the South, over racial issues – especially school integration and voting rights. Just a year earlier, the Civil Rights Act of 1964 outlawed major forms of discrimination against Blacks. It outlawed unequal application of voter registration requirements and racial segregation in schools, at the workplace and by facilities that served the public. On August 6, 1965, President Johnson signed into law the Voting Rights Act. It outlawed discriminatory voting practices, such as literacy tests, which had been responsible for the widespread disenfranchisement of Blacks. White segregationists in Alabama fought implementation of these new laws, and they terrorized people who tried to integrate restaurants and register Negros to vote.

While TISEP was not directly involved in the civil rights movement, those who participated were not immune from the ramifications of what was occurring. Local police often stopped and harassed our drivers, issuing tickets for cars with out-of-town tags. It was a perilous time for young people of different races to be seen together. Adjacent to Lowndes County, Alabama, where TISEP sponsored several tutoring centers, was the home of the militant Black Panther Party and an area where the Ku Klux Klan was especially active and violent.

I do wish there were a way to find out what happened afterward to the other TISEP participants – staff, tutors, and tutees. I am confident that we would find a great many success stories that can be attributed to TISEP. But for now, it's important simply to note that with all the problems people faced at that very difficult time in the nation's history, Tuskegee Institute, with the support of the federal government, did its part in making life better for everyone, Black and white, in Alabama. I am proud to say that I was a part of that effort.

## MARRIAGE

Back when I was working at the Seaside Regional Center in Connecticut, my oldest sister Marion was employed as a nursing instructor at the prestigious Institute of Living, a psychiatric hospital in West Hartford. On occasion, I would journey to her home in West Hartford and enjoy dinner with her husband Lew and her handsome young son Phillip. One day, Marion phoned me and told me about a concert being held in West Hartford. She

*Sandy Hawkins.*

encouraged me to attend and said that a young Black nursing student, Sandra (Sandy) Hawkins, who was on rotation at the Institute, would be there. Marion wanted me to meet her.

When I arrived at the concert hall, I was seated next to Sandy, an extremely attractive, light-skinned, intelligent woman. An only child, she had graduated first in her class at a private high school, in Lenox, Mass., went to Reed College in Oregon, and returned to attend Saint Luke's School of Nursing in Pittsfield, Mass. We found we had mutual interests and arranged for an "official" date. After that, we dated off and on for some time.

Subsequently, Sandy's rotation was terminating, and I volunteered to give her a ride to her family's home in Lenox. I recall that it was the same day, November 22, 1963, that President John F. Kennedy was assassinated in Dallas. Hence, there was almost total chaos in the city. I remember she gave me directions on how to leave the city but sent me up a one-way street.

When we finally arrived at her home, her mother and father – Mauzell (Hawk) and Amy Hawkins – invited me to spend the night, since my plans were to drive to Rutland, Vermont, to see an earlier girlfriend and her family. I asked Sandy if she would like to go with me. She replied that her mother stated that she would have to get permission from her father. I was somewhat amazed because this was the mid-1960s, and I thought Sandy was old enough to make that decision on her own. I had made all my own decisions since I was 14 years old. In any event, we discussed with her mother whether Sandy could go and how to approach her father, who was in the adjoining bedroom.

I left them talking and went to the room where her father was sitting on the bed laughing. He could hear the discussion through the walls. He did not object to Sandy going and, in the morning, we drove to Rutland, which was about 95 miles away. We stayed there two days with Marion and Bill Murray and their three children. Marion and Bill were both teachers and graduates of the University of Connecticut. They had lived in New Haven, Conn., before moving to Rutland.

Sandy and I continued to date, and on Christmas 1964 at the Hawkins home, I presented her with an engagement ring. Afterward, I left my position at Seaside to go Tuskegee to fulfill my dream of becoming a veterinarian. Then, on August 28, 1965, at Saint Helen's Episcopal Church in Lenox, Mass., Sandy and I were married. I flew up from Alabama, and we had a beautiful wedding and reception with about 75 guests. I remember that a friend of her father donated Cornish game hens for the reception as a gift to the wedding party.

My college roommate and friend Bill Babcock was my best man. (I was best man at his first wedding.) Peter Aldrich, a high school friend, Al Sashin from Norwich, and Bill Murray served as my three groomsmen. It was interesting that several of my groomsmen developed long-term connections with my wife's bridesmaids. Sandy and I spent time in New York City on our honeymoon then flew to Alabama. We rented a house in Tuskegee, where our daughter April was later born.

*Dan and Sandy's wedding, with her parents Mauzell and Amy Hawkins and Dan's mother, Clara Wheeler Smith.*

# CHAPTER 11
# Fighting for Civil Rights

After my experiences at Tuskegee with TISEP, I felt compelled to leave the study of veterinary medicine to work directly in the civil rights movement. I was appointed by the Lowndes County Christian Movement for Human Rights as executive director of a new seasonal farm workers' education program. It was an anti-poverty program established by Sargent Shriver, director of the federal Office of Economic Opportunity (OEO), funded under a nine-month $241,604 federal grant. The purpose was to provide education classes and pre-vocational training for adults in Lowndes County and to prepare them to be able to vote. The previous July, racist Governor George Wallace had vigorously opposed the grant and held it up for several months, claiming that the sponsoring organization was closely allied with the Black Panther political movement, the Lowndes County Freedom Party.

Lowndes County was one of the poorest, most segregated areas of Alabama. Although 80 percent of citizens in Lowndes County were Black,

*Article on Dan starting anti-poverty program in Hayneville, Ala. Southern Courier, Feb. 11-12, 1967. He called himself "D. Robert Smith," so people would not call him by his first name.*

only two Blacks were registered to vote there. This area of Alabama had a history of violence. In August 1965 civil rights activist Jonathan Daniels, a white Episcopal seminary student from New Hampshire and valedictorian of his class at the Virginia Military Institute, was gunned down in broad daylight in Hayneville. He had been arrested for participating in a voter rights demonstration and had just been released from jail. He saw a shooter and rushed in front of a shotgun blast intended for a fellow activist, Ruby Sales. The shooter, volunteer deputy sheriff Tom Coleman, was later acquitted of killing Daniels by an all-white jury.

A few months later in Tuskegee, on January 3, 1966, Sammy Younge, Jr., a 21-year-old Tuskegee Institute student whom I knew from school, was murdered by a shot in the back of his head after a skirmish over his wanting to use a restroom reserved for whites at a gas station. Earlier, he had escorted Negro applicants in Tuskegee to register to vote. The man who shot him was arrested but was found not guilty by an all-white jury. I often drove by that same gas station but refused to stop and use the "Colored Only" restroom. I don't recall ever using one anywhere in Alabama. In effect, I adhered to the rules of the southern whites only by ignoring them and then only for self-protection.

Indeed, while we had anticipated it, my wife Sandy and I were both appalled by the acute segregation in Alabama, which we had never encountered in Connecticut or Massachusetts. We simply led our lives each day, without the amenities we had grown up with and expected. Sandy obtained a part-time position as a nurse at the John Andrew Memorial Hospital on the Tuskegee campus, which was a center for Black physicians in the Deep South to receive postgraduate training, and for Black patients to receive care. I recall that she was also taking courses to complete her bachelor's degree which, given her keen intelligence, was a breeze for her.

Although we had some colleagues from Tuskegee and acquaintances from the Episcopal church while we were there, we had few real close friends and little time to socialize. To care for our baby daughter April, we hired a local farmer's wife, who lived some distance away. She acted like a surrogate mother to April in our home, and she even planted a huge vegetable garden for us. We could not have gotten along without her. Neither Tuskegee nor Hayneville had opportunities for recreation and no suitable restaurants. In short, we did not have "fun," but we had our own home, and we were happy.

## MY ANTI-POVERTY PROGRAM

When we began the OEO-funded anti-poverty program, we were accused of operating a segregated program just for Blacks. I consistently stated, however, that it was offered to provide basic education to both white and Black low-income groups. To qualify for the training and $20-a-week stipend, participants were required to be between 18 and 55 years old, with net incomes less than $1000 a year and functioning at the sixth-grade level or below. We initially started with morning and afternoon sessions for groups of 25 people at two centers in

PEOPLE LEARN SKILLS FOR LIFE AND WORK

*Training photos from program brochure.*

the Ash Creek and Calhoun communities, near Hayneville, Ala. They were taught an hour each of communication skills, arithmetic and reading, spelling, and writing. During the last hour, men learned skills in farming, plumbing, masonry, carpentry, and electricity; women learned personal hygiene and how to care for their homes.[27]

My headquarters office was constructed in an old, abandoned church in Hayneville, the county seat of Lowndes County, a town of less than 1000 people. Under the direction of John Hulett, founder of the Lowndes County Christian Movement for Human Rights, local contractors and laborers were hired, and members volunteered many hours of work to prepare the office. We initially opened it in February 1967 without telephones or electrical service, which we were able to obtain only with the help of a white probate judge, Harrell Hammond.

One afternoon, an elderly Black man came up the stairs and into my office. He looked a bit sheepish but also proud.

"Excuse me, Mr. Smith," he said. "I want to show you something." He then reached into his pocket and pulled out the check he had been given for his $20 stipend. He showed me that he could sign it with his full name and not just an X. He cried. I cried. Tears of joy. We both knew the significance of this, that it validated him as a man. I cannot imagine a white person ever having that same experience.

*Headquarters in abandoned church.*
*Photo from program brochure.*

Then on Sunday morning, March 12, I woke to a telephone call from one of our teachers.

"The church is burning down," she sobbed. It had been torched, presumably by the KKK. According to reports, the blaze began at 5 a.m., and, as described by the local newspaper: "Ten hours later, flames still flickered in the heap of rubble that had once been the anti-poverty office. All the carpentry work done by John Hulett, Sidney Logan, Jr., and other Christian Movement volunteers was destroyed, and the new desks and chairs were reduced to twisted masses of melted steel."[28]

I was devastated but not deterred when I saw it. We knew the FBI could not prove that the fire had been deliberately set, most likely as a warning to white people who had cooperated with our program. Indeed, also burned was the barn of white Probate Judge Hammond, and 21 of his black angus cows were poisoned. This was undoubtedly done because he was helping our program get electric lights and a telephone. That same night and the next day, three Black churches in nearby counties were firebombed.

FBI AND STATE POLICE SURVEY THE DAMAGE

Fortunately, the contents of our building had been insured and I had kept duplicate copies of all our paper records at my home in Tuskegee. Hence, I was able to continue the program the very next week after the fire. Several white people from Alabama contributed and raised funds to re-establish our

THE PROGRAM BEGINS TO DIG OUT

*Headquarters church after the fire.
Photo from program brochure.*

headquarters in a trailer until a new office could be built.[29]

Unbeknownst to me, a much nicer activity had taken place as the result of the burning of my headquarters. I was being investigated at the request of a Mrs. Collings. A white woman about 55 or 60 years old, Mrs. Collings was close to the Episcopal Church and was appalled by what was happening to Black Alabamians. She wanted to help. She elicited the assistance of several local religious men of the cloth who had met me at Tuskegee or in a church setting. Mrs. Collins was pleased with their positive views of my moral and ethical standards and sent me a $6000 check to rebuild our office and "do good things" for the colored people in Lowndes County.

## Guns at the Gate

After the burning of our church headquarters, everyone was on edge with high tension in the area. The following Sunday, as director of the program, I was scheduled to speak to the community and make plans either to rebuild our headquarters at the same place or to move to a different site deeper away from the white establishment. What people in the community most wanted to hear, however, was whether I was going to stay or to leave and go back to a safe haven in Connecticut.

In the meantime, Jess Portugal, the director of the federal antipoverty program Volunteers in Service to America (VISTA) in Washington, D.C., reached me by phone. He said he wanted to come to discuss the establishment of a VISTA program in the Lowndes area. Jess's father, a local bank president, was later helpful in securing a large office-type trailer that would be situated on the site of the bombed headquarters.

*Trailer office after the fire. Photo from program brochure.*

At the time, I lived 60 miles away in Tuskegee with my wife Sandy and our baby daughter, April. On Sunday, Jess arrived at our home in a red Hertz rental car. He broke bread with us and after we talked, he drove us to the community meeting where my future with the OEO anti-poverty program was to be discussed. It was being held at a church in the back-country of the Hayneville area. As we drove through town in Jess's red rental car, people who recognized my wife and me waved and asked us to stop. They thanked us for the education program. It was getting dusk as we entered a long dirt road in a very rural area. We could see a wooden gate that swung open and closed to control cows. There was no movement at the gate when suddenly two local Black men on each side of it appeared with shotguns. They looked us over.

"Mr. Smith, we're just checking," they said and smiled.

My wife Sandy, an only child, was raised by her father and mother to be non-confrontational. She was petrified at the site of seeing so many Black Americans with guns. As we drove further into the church yard, we could see two men on the roof with rifles, and two men at each corner pillar and at the center of the church. As we entered the church, there were two men with rifles at each entrance. The community was prepared to do battle!

The church was packed. There was not even standing room, with spillover hanging on the outside of the door. Jess Portugal, Sandy, and I were escorted through the crowd and seated on the east side of the sanctuary in the front of the church, across from the altar. Following the normal intro-prayer by the robed minister and music from a choir, Jess made his comments about the VISTA program.

I was then introduced with loud applause, cheers, and amens. I told the gathering about plans to continue the program without delay, because I had anticipated such a situation and had photocopied and retained copies of all business and student records at my Tuskegee home. But most important to the community, I stated that I was going to stay in Lowndes and move the program forward. In addition, we would rebuild on the same site to show that we do not run. I also shared that a white Alabama woman, Mrs. Collins, had given $6000 to support our work. There was great jubilation, clapping, and more amens by the people.

"It's great to have the community on your side," I whispered to Sandy and Jess.

The minister then called up one more speaker. From the rear of the church, a young man with a huge afro hairdo headed up to the front. His name was H. Rap Brown. He looked at me and the gathering and said that he and Stokely Carmichael, who had a meeting that night in another state, wanted the new headquarters building to be in a Black-owned community. He then received a thunderous cheer and even more amens. Of course, I was bewildered to have opposing views in the community on the site location, with solid support for both proposals within just a few minutes.

## My Interaction with Stokely Carmichael

I found that the prospect of money turned members of the community into different people. When I had received the $6000 from Mrs. Collins, I immediately sought counsel from attorney Fred Gray, who I later learned had been the attorney for Rosa Parks, Martin Luther King, Jr., and the Montgomery Bus Boycott, which began the modern civil rights movement. [30] He and his partner, Solomon Seay, helped me set up the Lowndes County Community Fund, where I deposited the donated money. However, some members of the Board believed I was using the money to buy the new red car from Jesse Portugal's Hertz Rental. This idea was fueled by Stokely Carmichael and H. Rap Brown, who wanted the money to go to the Lowndes County Freedom Party (Black Panther Party.)

I was opposed to this because they were not supporting Rev. Martin Luther King's nonviolent approach to civil rights. Stokely had broken from SNCC and focused his efforts with the radical Black Panthers, of which he was one of the founders. In Lowndes County, while he worked to expand voting rights, he went throughout the county visiting churches and giving speeches. He became like a "god" in Lowndes. Yet following Stokely's ranting and raving in the church about Black Power, he would exit walking down the aisle and next to the last seat would be an attractive blond woman who would walk arm and arm with him to his car.

Stokely, who later changed this name to Kwame Ture, was a unique individual. It was Stokely who introduced the terms "Black Is Beautiful" and "Black Power," raising the consciousness and pride of Blacks in the United States. A true leader, he always had something positive to say to the group to which he was speaking. He was highly revered in Lowndes County and, regardless of what my Board agreed to at board meetings (e.g., location of the office), the Board would always follow Stokely's advice and recommendations. Most frustrating!

Later in the week after the meeting in the church, Stokely came into my office and tried to convince me to transfer Mrs. Collins's money to the Black Panther Party. I informed him that the money would not be transferred. I had placed the funds in a local bank requiring at least two of three signatures for withdrawal (me, the Board Chairman, and the Financial Officer). Stokely was wide-eyed. He rose from his chair and got directly in my face, nose to nose, almost touching.

"Dan, you don't understand," he said, "we are at war between the Blacks and whites of this country, AND IN A WAR, A LOT OF INNOCENT PEOPLE GET KILLED."

He got my attention! Undaunted, however, I subsequently contacted Mrs. Collins and returned the $6000 to her.

## TERROR ON THE HIGHWAY – KKK NIGHT RIDERS

That night, I was working alone in my Hayneville office on a report to the government. It had been delayed because of my lengthy discussion with Stokely. A typically hot summer night in rural Alabama, there was no breeze, and it was quiet enough to hear the bark of a dog or music in the distance. The office was in an open field, encircled by a black macadam road. The front and rear entrances were lit; otherwise, the area was dark.

I was oblivious to the time, but at about 9 p.m. the chairman of my program board arrived. He told me to look out the window.

"I received a call at home stating that a car was circulating the building and that you were alone," he said. I looked out and saw the vehicle, which slowly drove away.

"You need to leave for home immediately," he insisted. So, I did.

It was about an hour's drive from Hayneville to my home in Tuskegee. To get there, I would pass through the city of Montgomery, the capital of Alabama. The area was quite dangerous for Blacks, especially at night.

My car, the two-tone green Hillman Husky, had no air conditioning, and the weather was very hot. I rolled the windows down to catch the faint breezes as the Hillman proceeded through Hayneville. The drive was uneventful at first, but when I arrived at the entrance to the dark, rural highway, things changed. Although mentally still focused on my report, I noticed some headlights on a car some distance from me in the rear. Then suddenly the headlights came closer and closer. The car behind me sped up, and the headlights beamed even more closely. I realized that I was being followed.

Even with excess speed (my little car would only get to about 65 miles per hour), I knew I had 25 to 30 minutes on the highway before reaching safety at a gas station just on the outskirts of Montgomery. It was at that point their car slammed into my rear bumper and then pulled alongside of my Hillman. The driver and three other young men were in the car. They were screaming at me and waving what appeared to be white tee shirts.

"PULL OVER, NIGGER!" someone shouted. "YOU BLACK COON!" I held tight to the steering wheel as their car repeatedly rammed my rear bumper. They drove alongside again, yelling obscenities and shouting for me to pull over. This time, I yelled back.

"Not this coon! Not this Black coon!" You're not getting me, I thought.

Although I was keenly aware of the many Blacks who were chased and caught by the KKK night riders and never seen again, I was initially more angry than scared. I tightened my grip on the wheel and floored the gas pedal. The race to survive was on. I thought about my friends and family, whom I might never see again, and the report that I had not finished, and my no longer being able to take long swims. I remembered my high school buddy Alfred Youmatz and my college friend Bill Babcock.

"WHERE ARE YOU NOW WHEN I NEED HELP!" I yelled out to them.

The bumper chase seemed never to end. Suddenly they rear ended my Hillman again, in such a way that it was nearly sent off the road to the right into a ditch. My little car righted itself and continued. Then at one point my engine sputtered. It seemed as if I would never get to that gas station. Not until I saw the station's lights did I recognize my extreme terror. I was almost safe, but not yet safe. They were still close behind me.

I sped the Hillman into the driveway of the station. My pursuers were right on my tail. I nearly clipped another car that was exiting. Then I slammed on my brakes and stopped just about two inches in front of the glass garage doors. The vehicle behind followed me into the station, but then turned around and headed back. I composed myself, got a Coke, and proceeded on the 15-minute drive home to my family in Tuskegee.

I seemed calm, but when I got home, I began shaking, with chills and goose bumps all over my body as I thought of that episode. Indeed, the memory of that night has never left me, and when I remember it, the chills return. But I have no regrets for the time I spent in Alabama, and the work I did to help the impoverished people of Lowndes County learn to read and write so they could vote.

## LEAVING ALABAMA

While directing the migrant program in Alabama, I also worked with officials from the Office of Economic Opportunity in Washington, D.C., to bring a health program to Lowndes County. The program was stalled because Dr. Griffin, a white local physician, urged Governor George Wallace to prevent northerners from coming to Alabama and "spoiling" the Black citizens of Lowndes County. He called me an "outside agitator" from Connecticut. He was clearly a racist. Local Black citizens often repeated the Lowndes' lore that Dr. Griffin supposedly did a "complete" physical examination on a fully dressed elderly African American woman during the winter without her removing any clothing, including her heavy winter coat.

I was increasingly frustrated by Stokely Carmichael and H. Rap Brown. At the same time, my OEO contacts in Washington urged me to relocate to the nation's capital and work in their headquarters office developing neighborhood health centers. So, I agreed. I was tired of the tribulations and ready to leave Alabama. The new position would give me an opportunity to do good things at the national level. Stokely Carmichael's warning that "in time of war many innocent people get killed" did not go unheeded, and I wanted to have a home and family. I was being squashed between multiple interests, including the Black Panther Party and the KKK plus Governor George Wallace.

Leaving Alabama, my friends there, and my position was a challenge. I met and told the Board that I had accepted a position in Washington, D.C. I left the program in the hands of my business manager, L.H. Anderson. I understand that he later bought land elsewhere and moved the program to his property, deeper in Lowndes, away from the center of town in Hayneville.

In addition to resigning from my position, I had to sell our home in Tuskegee. When my wife and I were first married, we had rented it, but one day I was called by the owner who lived in Muskogee, Oklahoma. She said she wanted to sell the house because she was not going to return to Alabama, and she was behind on her mortgage payments.

"Can I buy it?" I asked.

"Yes, but you'll have to make up the foreclosure payment," she responded. I agreed. My wife and I were thrilled to own our first home. It was a 10-year-old frame house on a cul-de-sac located about a mile from the Tuskegee Institute campus. One story, with two bedrooms, a large living-dining room, and kitchen. Not huge but nice, and best of all, it was ours!

When we put it up for sale, we advertised in the newspaper and then waited. No takers. Then three days before we were to leave, someone arrived who was interested in buying it. A large, Black man in full police regalia drove up in his police car, got out, and knocked on the door. It was Sheriff Lucius Amerson, who had been elected in 1966 as the first African American sheriff in the Deep South since Reconstruction.[31] I recognized him immediately.

"I hear your house is for sale," he said. "I'd like to buy it."

"That would be fine," I said, "but we have to act quickly, as my family and I need to leave in three days, to be at our home in Bethesda, Maryland, when our moving truck is schedule to arrive." That was okay with him.

Fortunately, I was referred to a Black lawyer in Tuskegee who agreed to help us close on the house. We could not have been in better hands. He was Fred Gray, the same lawyer handling prominent civil rights cases who had helped me earlier in setting up the Lowndes County Community Fund. We were able to close quickly.

My "going-away party," a true southern Black barbeque, was arranged by John Hulett, a resident of Hayneville and one of my strongest supporters in Lowndes County. A prominent civil rights activist committed to voting rights, John was the founder of the Lowndes County Freedom Party[32] and became one of the first two Black men in Lowndes County to vote.[33] Around 100 people attended the barbeque. It was held outdoors at a church and featured fried fish, chicken, ribs, collard greens, and other soul food. Even Stokely Carmichael came, and we grilled ribs together. It was a great send-off!

## CHAPTER 12

# Move to Washington:
# Becoming a "Fed"

My wife Sandy was very apprehensive about moving to Washington, D.C., because of what I think she perceived as its glamour and intrigue. She said she didn't feel "ready" to move there. But I was excited about the opportunities it offered us and convinced her that it was a good idea. I flew to Washington, rented a house, then returned to Alabama. Sandy and I drove up from Tuskegee with our six-month-old daughter April and our Great Dane, Thor. This drive was much less eventful than when I first moved to Alabama.

The house we rented was on Edward Avenue in Bethesda, Md., a suburb of Washington. It was about five houses up the street from the home of attorney Clarence Thomas, later a Supreme Court Justice, and his first wife, Kathy Ambush. My wife interacted with Kathy and the children, but as a family we had no serious social gatherings.

## HOUSING DISCRIMINATION

Fortunately for us, in 1968 the federal Fair Housing Act had been enacted prohibiting discrimination in the sale, rental, and financing of housing. Prior to this, most Blacks found it difficult, usually impossible, to purchase or rent homes in white communities. They were systematically refused loans guaranteed by the Federal Housing Administration, which also discouraged banks from loaning money in areas with any African Americans.

And throughout the United States were "sundown towns," described by sociologist James Loewen as any jurisdiction that kept African Americans or other groups from living in it and was thus "all white" on purpose. Many towns passed ordinances barring African Americans after dark (hence the word "sundown") and/or prohibiting them from owning or renting property.[34]

*Dan's sister Jenny and her husband Charles Brown, 2007. Photo by Loretta Neumann.*

There were, however, some exceptions. In 1967, a year before the Fair Housing Act passed, my sister Jennie and her husband Charles (Charlie) Brown moved into a new home in Glastonbury, Conn., an upper middle-class suburb of Hartford. I was told that they were one of only eleven Black families to own a home there, at a time that the population numbered 17,000 people. It is cited as a "probable" sundown town on the Internet list begun by James Loewen.

Jennie and Charlie lived comfortably in Glastonbury for over 50 years and raised their two children – a son Charles (Chipper) and a daughter Jeannette. I have met some of their neighbors, all of whom spoke fondly of them.

But the town is still predominately white. According to the 2020 census: Whites alone are 85.2 percent; Black or African Americans alone, 1.6 percent.

## *Our Encounter with Discrimination*

As for Sandy and me, in 1968 we were looking at homes to purchase in Bethesda. It was (and still is) mainly a white, upper-class community. Despite the recently enacted Fair Housing Act, however, we were turned down for the first house we tried to buy. Along with our realtor, who was white, we searched for homes in the area and found one off Wisconsin Avenue on Chillum Street. A nice six-room house, it was listed for $27,000. Most importantly, it was in a good school district. After my wife and I viewed the house, we signed the contract using the GI Bill. Because we were a Black family, I upped the sale price a thousand dollars to $28,000 to make certain that the seller knew we were serious about purchasing. We then left that weekend for New England to visit our families in Connecticut and Massachusetts.

When we returned from our travels, our realtor called and said he wanted to come over and talk with us. My wife was instantly upset and blamed me because she thought I had bad credit and that is why we would not get the house. When the realtor arrived, however, he indicated that our credit was fine. The issue was one of race, he said, and he relayed the issue to us. He said that when he arrived at the house to meet with the multi-listing agent, the seller was not yet there. But the agent, a woman, was more than alarmed.

"I'm glad you have a buyer," she said, "because I understand that realtors have been showing this house to colored people."

"What's wrong with that?" our realtor replied. "In fact, this contract is with a colored family." The listing agent then grabbed the contract from him, ran out of the house, and met the owner who was just coming up the sidewalk.

"They are selling your house to colored people!" she screamed. She kept repeating this to the owner. "You don't want to sell your house to colored people, do you?"

"Of course not," the owner, an attorney with the State Department, said. My realtor met him and asked, why not sell to colored people?

"I can't stand the thought of colored people using the same bathtub and toilet that my mother and sister used!" We did not get that house.

Shortly thereafter, our realtor found us another very acceptable house on Roosevelt Street in the Glenwood section of Bethesda, located off Old Georgetown Road. To the west side was Suburban Hospital and on the east was the National Institutes of Health. About 8 to 10 blocks north was St. Luke's Episcopal Church, where I later became the church's Senior Warden (the lay leadership of the church). Also, our new home was in the same good Bethesda school district of Montgomery County.

There was, however, a 1942 restrictive covenant as an addendum to the original deed, which prohibited Negros or others listed in it from using or occupying the land. It said:

> Subject to the covenants no part of the land above described shall ever be used or occupied by, or sold, demised, transferred, conveyed unto, or in trust for, leased or rented, or given to Negros, or any person or persons of blood or origin, which racial description shall be deemed to include Armenians, Jews, Hebrews, Persians, Syrians and Turks; except that this covenant shall not be held to exclude partial occupancy of the premises by domestic servants of the owners of the land above described, the survivor of them, or his or their heirs or assigns.
>
> —Glenwood, recorded December 3, 1942, Liber 897 Folio 169.

Fortunately, such covenants had been ruled unconstitutional in 1948 by the Supreme Court[35] and, just a few months before our housing search, made illegal by Congress in the Fair Housing Act of 1968. Nevertheless, as we were unpacking our car and beginning our move into our new house on Roosevelt Street, a neighbor came and informed us that our soon-to-be next-door neighbor had developed a petition for nearby residents to sign to prevent us, Blacks, from moving into the neighborhood. To their credit, however, no neighbors would sign the petition!

## Moving In

It was on a Sunday when our U-Haul truck arrived at our new home with our belongings. The driver backed the truck from the road, halfway on the lawn so that it could easily be unloaded. The truck, however, was partly blocking the road. I had gone to get some "yummy" Montgomery Donuts for the driver and several neighbors who came over to help us. When I returned, there were

*Dan at Roosevelt House with daughter April and son Rob, ca. 1973.*

two police cars and four policemen. My wife and others were upset and somewhat frightened.

I asked the officers if they were there as the Bethesda Welcoming Committee.

207

"Move that truck, or we'll have it towed," one of them snarled. I just smiled.

"Do you want to help us move in?" I smiled. The police did not appreciate my humor. They gave us a lecture on road safety, etc. Several additional neighbors emerged and had a warm dialogue in our favor with them. The police subsequently left with our group clapping.

Despite all of this, we and our children found that our white Glenwood neighborhood was a unique, friendly community, which we thoroughly enjoyed.

## OFFICE OF ECONOMIC OPPORTUNITY

My new position in Washington, D.C., was with the Office of Economic Opportunity (OEO), which had funded the education program I directed in Lowndes County. The OEO administered most of the War on Poverty programs established pursuant to the Economic Opportunity Act of 1964, as part of President Lyndon B. Johnson's Great Society agenda.[36] OEO was created by Sargent Shriver (husband of Eunice Kennedy Shriver and President Kennedy's brother-in-law) who also served as its first director. It included VISTA, Job Corps, the Community Action Program, and Head Start.

While my government papers were being finalized for OEO, I was first hired on a temporary basis by a private consulting firm, Policy Management System, Inc. My position would be working for VISTA, founded in 1965 (now part of AmeriCorps). I had no understanding of the government classification of employees and the numerical "grades" that they were given. Fortunately, a woman government staffer was assigned to help me.

"Based on your education and work experience, you should easily qualify for a grade GS-12," she told me.

"Why can't I get a grade 13?" I asked, not knowing the difference. She looked at me with surprise.

"You don't realize," she exclaimed, "there are federal employees who have spent many years as only a grade nine!" She explained that I was just a bit short on management experience. However, she and her team reviewed my management and administrative experiences while in Alabama, which had been funded by OEO although I was then not a federal employee. They determined that I was more than qualified for a GS-13 rating, which is what I received on entering the government.

I was then assigned to the OEO Office of Health Affairs in the Executive Office of the President. It was directed by Dr. Joseph English, a psychiatrist who headed the "mental side" of the Peace Corps from 1962 to 1966.[37] In 1966, he moved to OEO and became Director for Health Affairs, developing the Neighborhood Health Centers program, as well as the health programs of Head Start, the Job Corps, and VISTA. Dr. English was a friend of Sargent Shriver. I soon noted that most of the leadership in OEO was associated in some capacity with the Peace Corps. So, it was for the most part like a family affair.*

Several staff members at the Office of Health Affairs worked as project analyst officers. Many moved on to higher positions. Among these was Dorothy Manne, a Black secretary who, through the new government program Upward Mobility, became a program analyst and with further

---

* I recall many of the cast of characters in charge of the OEO Office of Health Affairs at 19th and M Street, which included young medical doctors and activists. In addition to Dr. English, there was Dr. John Frankel, a highly respected senior physician who was director of the Health Services Office, Community Action Program, and who was followed in that position by Dr. Gary London; Dr. Robert Kalinowski, deputy director of the Office of Health Affairs; my friend Dr. Franklin (Frank) Stroud, a pediatrician and OEO medical director; and Donald Pugliesi, a former priest who arrived at about the same time I did and who became chief of operations for the OEO Neighborhood Health Centers.

education became the California Region 10 Health Administrator. The Upward Mobility program was excellent, because it allowed clerical staff who did not have a bachelor's degree, mostly women stuck in lower-level jobs, to move up to a higher position in the government.

## *Neighborhood Health Centers*

Another product of OEO was William (Bill) White, who worked tirelessly and incorporated the OEO Neighborhood Health Centers into the current Community Health Centers. To my surprise and pleasure, Dan Zwick, executive officer of the Health Affairs Program, informed me that I was being appointed assistant chief of Health Affairs for Program Development. It was through that position that I later received my GS-14. Among other things, my job was to help develop Neighborhood Health Centers (NHCs) that were being established pursuant to the Economic Opportunity Act of 1964, which authorized the formation of local Community Action Agencies. The centers were envisioned to be high-quality comprehensive ambulatory health care centers using a medical team approach in underserved areas.

The first OEO-funded Neighborhood Health Centers were created in 1965 by two medical doctors – Dr. H. Jack Geiger, MD, from the faculty of Harvard University and later Tufts University, and Dr. Count Gibson, MD, also from Tufts University. The first Neighborhood Health Center was urban, the Columbia Point Health Center (now renamed the Geiger Gibson Community Health Center) in Dorchester, a neighborhood of Boston. The second was rural, the Tufts-Delta Health Center (now the Delta Health Center) in Mound Bayou, Mississippi. Dr. Geiger believed a health center would not only provide much needed medical relief and social services, but also a path toward community empowerment and direct citizen action.[38]

Among the staff I hired was Marcy Gross, a young white woman who graduated from the University of Maryland in 1967. She began at OEO as a research assistant and became a very capable, loyal, and efficient professional employee. We worked with several communities to develop Neighborhood Health Centers, including in St. Louis, San Francisco, and New York City. Marcy Gross later joined me in the Area Health Education tion Centers (AHEC) Program at the National institutes of Health. Afterward, she became a senior adviser with the Department of Health and Human Services and helped build the foundation for federal policies regarding sexual assault and other women's health issues.

- *Saint Louis:* In St. Louis, for example, a center was in one of the most poverty-stricken and crime-infested neighborhoods in the city - the infamous 23-acre racially segregated Pruitt-Igoe complex. In keeping with OEO's emphasis on community participation, a local board was formed for the Neighborhood Health Center in 1968, and it was officially chartered in 1969. The board chose Morris Henderson, a prominent Black civil rights leader in St. Louis, as its first chief executive director and Myrtle Hilliard Davis, a Black nurse, as deputy director. As with our other centers, they were in charge. I met with them, and we worked well together. Indeed, they gave me an award in 1974 after I had left OEO. My job was to help them follow the regulations and keep within the budget. They were successful, and the center remains in operation today, renamed as the Myrtle Hilliard Davis Comprehensive Health Center.[39]

- *Chinatown:* I also developed a Neighborhood Health Center within the San Francisco Chinatown community. Because there was limited space to use in Chinatown, we had to negotiate an air rights location for the center, building over one of the streets. I remember they treated our team to a fabulous Chinese dinner. It hooked me on Chinese food. Afterward, our consultant, Dr. Albert Parker, took me back into the kitchen. The cooks were all Black! Sometime later, my wife and I invited the Chinese team to our Bethesda home for dinner while they were in Washington, D.C. We splurged. She made and served Beef Wellington. They did enjoy the dinner!

### Consumer Affairs Office

I soon saw the need for better communications with the residents served by the Neighborhood Health Centers. After much discussion, I convinced the leadership of the Office of Health Affairs to allow me to establish a Consumer Affairs Office, and I became its chief. I hired Mary (Broadhead) King, the daughter of a Methodist minister as an assistant. At one point in her life, she had worked as a consultant for the Student Nonviolent Coordinating Committee, headed by civil rights activist John Lewis. It later ended badly for her, however, under Stockley Carmichael's reign with his sudden dismissal of whites (without pay) from SNCC.

The goal of the Consumer Affairs Office was to train consumers – residents and their families who were receiving service from the NHCs in their community – on how to serve as advisors. Every center had a community board or advisory council. A member of our staff and I would visit the centers and meet with them and provide training on how best to express to doctors and staff the needs of the community. From them we also learned a lot, such as what food they enjoyed and the language to use or avoid with different ethnicities. In turn, they learned communication skills that could be used to help them become members of corporate boards – what to wear, how to think and speak to be accepted. In 1970, I co-authored an article about consumer participation with OEO-assisted Neighborhood Health Centers for the Public Health Journal with Gerald Sparer, director of the Program Planning and Evaluation Division and George Dines, a Black program-coordination officer.[40]

I also took on the task of developing, through a contractor, a booklet in Spanish that spelled out the rules and regulations written in English. To augment my responsibility, I hired a young Spanish-speaking man from Mexico, David Martinez, who had worked with his family on the migrant workers route picking vegetables. David and I became good friends, and he became the godfather of my son. He later left OEO and earned a master's degree in public health from the University of Michigan. He became top assistant to Cesar Chavez, whose position David was expected to assume when Chavez retired as head of the Immigrant Union. However, David got outmaneuvered by a competitor.

## My Ego

I do want to take this opportunity to apologize to a Yakima, Washington, family, whose name I now cannot recall. In 1969, the story had gotten around of how I had escaped being killed by night riders, presumably from the Ku Klux Klan, while in Alabama. At OEO headquarters in DC, I was being contacted by people throughout the country asking me to share my experiences. There had been riots and burning the previous summer in

1968 following the death of Reverend Martin Luther King, Jr. Another "long hot summer" was anticipated and covered extensively by the media.

After one of my speeches, a gentleman approached me and begged me to come to Yakima and share the same stories with his community.

"They should know what life is like outside of Yakima," he said. I understood that I had something to offer, and I accepted, even though I was not really in the league with the likes of Dr. King or John Lewis, Julian Bond, Stokely Carmichael, and others. True, I had some major experiences that most people did not have, but I was not like some civil rights activists who fought to develop their own organizations and public recognition. Some were trying to get the biggest headlines or television coverage so minorities would finally be recognized in the white media, and they would gain support from white "do-gooders."

However, once I hit Washington, D.C., in 1968 and was in demand as a speaker from different sectors of the country, I internally let it go to my head. My ego allowed me to make pronouncements I had no knowledge about, except that I was Black. Hence, there I was, my last evening in Yakima. I had delivered my speech and, having been treated extra well by the community at the potluck church gathering, I journeyed with my host back to his home for some special tea. During our discussion with his family, he asked me a question.

"This will be the last time my whole family will be free and able to take a cross-country trip together," he said. "Should we plan to go, with the newspapers predicting a long hot summer?"

I hemmed and hawed a bit.

"I would not take my family on such a cross-country summer trip this year," I pronounced.

Afterward, I recognized that I had no factual basis for my statement. It just made me feel good to say so. My ego was satisfied, because I thought that I was important. I never learned if the host and his family did in fact take the trip. I still feel sorry for what I said.

## Bedford-Stuyvesant

On one occasion I was given the responsibility to develop a Neighborhood Health Center in Brooklyn, New York's Bedford-Stuyvesant community. My colleague and I arrived from D.C. at La Guardia Airport around 11 a.m., but we didn't arrive at the clinic's destination until around 5 p.m. The taxi cabs we hailed (there were four different ones) would not go to "Bed-Stuy." The drivers all made excuses why they could not go there – mother was ill, cab did not have enough gas, or it was just too dangerous because of the crime.

When we finally reached the building, we walked upstairs into a large room with empty chairs placed around a long table. The room was packed with neighborhood people, but no one sat down. So, I sat in a chair at the end of the table. Finally, a huge dark man entered and sat at the opposite end from me. All the other chairs quickly became occupied.

We both introduced ourselves. Then, as soon as he shared the community's history, he reached in his jacket pocket and slammed his 45- or 38-caliber pistol on the table.

"Okay, feds, let's talk!" He got our attention.

I was stunned, but simply explained what OEO was and how it developed Neighborhood Health Centers, with the community being an integral part of the decision-making process via having a community advisory board. The meeting went well, and we left the leader with papers and forms to be completed and returned to our office in D.C. for the next stage of the process. (That episode so startled me that afterward I half-joked that I should take some toilet paper with me if/when I went there again.)

I had previously been in communication with Shirley Downes, a staffer for Congresswoman Shirley Chisholm who represented the Bed-Stuy Community. Rep. Chisholm was extremely helpful in "smoothing the waters" with her constituency so we "feds" would be trusted as we worked with her community. She and I shared several lunches together, and I remember her later discussions about the pros and cons of being the first Black woman to run for president of the United States.†

## WATTS AND MLK ASSASSINATION

It was April 4, 1968, and the Watts Community in Los Angeles had gone through a horrific semi-race riot just three years before. Our office arranged for a site visit team to meet with the Watts center over issues related to their OEO award program and, of course, the budget. I believe there were about six team members, all having their own responsibilities with the program as related to their expertise. I was the lone Black on the team, and my expertise was community participation. I had just set up the Office of Consumer Affairs, which dealt with problems that the local community had with the Office of Health Affairs developing a Neighborhood Health Center. There were many discussions, especially with the interaction of Blacks with Latinos and Hispanics.

At Watts, our team was seated in a large conference room at the health center with windows that faced the sidewalk and the road. About

† Shirley Anita St. Hill Chisholm was the first African American woman in Congress (1968) and the first woman and African American to seek the nomination for president of the United States from one of the two major political parties (1972). "Shirley Chisholm," Debra Michals, PhD, National Women's History Museum, 2015, *https://www.womenshistory.org/education-resources/biographies/shirley-chisholm*

25-30 center personnel were attending the meeting. We were in mid-discussion when someone from the center opened the door and announced that Martin Luther King, Jr., had been assassinated. We were shocked. I assumed the meeting would be terminated out of deference to Dr. King. However, the OEO team leader said that because of so much planning, plus the cost of flying seven employees to California, the meeting should continue. I disagreed.

"To continue would be disrespectful and show a lack of sensitivity to the community," I said. "Plus, it could endanger the safety of everyone."

Suddenly, the street dynamics changed, reminding me of the energy change when there is a pool drowning or a sudden crime scene. Loud noises erupted. People outside started throwing large trash barrels in the street. Some were on fire. One barrel bounced off the building next to the room we were in. Crowds began to gather outside, and I saw small groups run after cars with white drivers. I knew we should not be in Watts at that time.

But how to get a ride to the airport? No cabs would take a white group through town. After much discussion, the Watts Center director and I arranged for one of their ambulances to remove stretchers and other material and equipment so the team could all fit inside. It was a very quiet ride to the airport. We all peeked through the ambulance's windows, watching people taking over the streets.

As I recall, our team flew back to National Airport in Washington, D.C., on the same plane. We were all surprised to see smoke coming from various sections of the city. Few taxicabs were available, if any. The city had somehow arranged for buses to take us through the District. As we rode the bus, we were stunned to see people looting and rioting and the National Guard on duty holding loaded rifles.

*Washington DC after riots following assassination of Martin Luther King, April 1968.*
*Photo from Library of Congress.*

"Do you have real bullets?" I asked a solider. He looked at me sternly, but nodded in the affirmative.

Heading north, the commercial streets outside of downtown looked like a war zone, with buildings burning and firemen with trucks trying to distinguish the flames. Smoke penetrated the bus and our clothing. Fortunately, I arrived home in Bethesda at 11 p.m. safe and sound. My wife and I watched on television the D.C. situation with the chaos in the streets and reporters repeating the history of Dr. King and his death. We saw presidential candidate Robert Kennedy announce that Martin Luther King, Jr., had been assassinated. It was an incredibly sad night.

*OEO Epilogue*

After President Richard Nixon took office in January 1971, the days of President Johnson's War on Poverty were numbered. President Nixon attempted to impound the funds appropriated by Congress for OEO, but in 1973 this was ruled unconstitutional. During President Ford's administration, OEO's name was changed with its reauthorization in 1975, to the Community Services Administration (CSA). Then it was transferred to the

Office of Community Services within the Department of Health and Human Services (HHS) by President Reagan in 1981. Most of the agency's programs continued to operate, either by HHS or by other federal agencies.

Today, Community Health Centers are the outgrowth of OEO's Neighborhood Health Centers. They are community-based and patient-directed organizations that serve populations with limited access to health care, and they are supported by the Health Resources and Services Administration (HRSA), an agency of HHS. The centers must be in or serve a high-need community (designated Medically Underserved Area or Population). Nearly 1,400 health centers now operate approximately 13,500 service-delivery sites in every U.S. state, D.C., Puerto Rico, the Virgin Islands, and the Pacific Basin. More than 255,000 fulltime staff provide care for more than 29 million people. One in 11 people in the U.S. relies on a HRSA-funded health center for medical care.[‡]

In short, this part of President Johnson's War on Poverty continues, in modified form, and I feel immensely proud to have been part of the agency, OEO, that initially started it.

## Tobytown

While I was working for OEO, I also became involved as a volunteer with a project to help Tobytown, an impoverished Black enclave founded by freed slaves in 1875. Located within Montgomery County, Md., one of the wealthiest counties in the United States, Tobytown lies in Potomac, an affluent, census-designated suburb of Washington, D.C., named after the nearby Potomac River. For nearly a century, residents of Tobytown owned the land with their homes, worked the neighboring farms, and

---

[†] Health Resources and Services Administration, Bureau of Primary Health Care, last reviewed: October 2022 *https://www.hrsa.gov/about/organization/bureaus/bphc/index.html*

raised their own meat and vegetables. Until the 1960s, they lived in shacks with wood-burning stoves, miles from public transportation, and accessed only by a single dirt road. The community had one outhouse and one outdoor well for water.

As the county grew, the farms gave way to enormous mansions on vast tracts of land that eventually surrounded the shanties of Tobytown. Dozens of the new homes are larger than 10,000 square feet and now sell for millions of dollars. As the rich, car-centric suburbs expanded, farm jobs evaporated, and Tobytown grew increasingly isolated. With few resources for improvement, the dilapidated community became an embarrassment to its neighbors.

In 1968, a group of white Potomac citizens, including Luttie Simms and Carl Mathison, formed a committee called Tobytown Associates to help the residents and improve the area. They sought a Black resident to head the association, and first identified Preston Martin, a laborer who was one of the few Tobytown residents with a full-time job. Most others were unemployed, and few of the children had completed high school.

A colleague of mine, a respected white physician, Dr. John Frankel, was a resident of Potomac. We became social friends, and my wife Sandy and I hosted them for a brunch at our home. Sandy, an excellent cook, prepared eggs Benedict, and John's wife complimented her on her Hollandaise sauce. In turn, Dr. Frankel wined and dined us at his home. He then told me about the Tobytown project and asked if I would assist them.

"We need a Black person to direct it," he said candidly. "And you have demonstrated at OEO the leadership skills they need."

I subsequently went with Dr. Frankel to a meeting of the recently established Tobytown Associates. At the meeting, they elected me as the volunteer president of the group and Preston Martin became vice president. The leaders gave us a partial outline of what they wanted to accomplish. The list included organizing the Black citizens of Tobytown, developing an educational plan for children of all ages, and collaborating to develop a turn-key housing project using their own "sweat equity." The organizers of the Tobytown group worked with me, and we obtained funds through their networks and grants from the Montgomery County government to support this cause.

Consequently, during the week, after my regular full-time government job developing Neighborhood Health Centers, I would work for three nights and often on weekends with the citizens of Tobytown and the Associates. My first effort was to develop a community center for social and other activities. This project started in 1969, and we finished the center two years later with plans drawn by a local architect, the hard work of the citizenry, and the help of government funding.

Another issue I stressed to the Board was the need to build the self-esteem of the Tobytown citizens.

"They should not be intimidated by the wealthy Potomac residents who surround them," I said. So, we brought in local Montgomery County teachers, several of whom were Black, to provide special tutoring to the children of Tobytown. That was extraordinarily successful.

In 1972, however, the county housing authority bought most of the land and, with loans from the federal government, demolished the shacks. Twenty-six brick and wood shed-style townhouses and single-family homes, ranging in size from one bedroom to six bedrooms, were built. None of the original homes were left.

The Tobytown Cemetery, located near the Pennyfield Lock along the C&O Canal next to the Potomac River, is the only remaining relic associated with the original Tobytown. The cemetery contains the remains of former slaves and their descendants. It has not, unfortunately, been well maintained by Montgomery County.[41]

When the community center and housing projects were completed, a big celebration and ribbon-cutting was held with the first elected Montgomery County Executive, James Gleason. Episcopal Bishop John Walker opened the ceremony with a blessing. My family, including my two young children, attended the event, and I was presented a plaque honoring my service. After this, however, I stepped down to attend to my personal obligations with work and family, which were increasingly demanding more of my attention.

As I look back, I recall that the goal had been for the low-income residents to eventually purchase the inexpensive dwellings. However, I later learned that the Tobytown residents were paid very little for their property. Over the years, seventeen families purchased their own homes for about $16,000. But nine units remained in the control of the housing authority, which also maintained the community center and grounds. Montgomery County still owns over five acres of original Tobytown land. The land around the Tobytown townhomes is owned by the Housing Opportunities Commission.[42] I do not know how many former residents were forced to leave because they could not afford the new homes. My understanding was that the residents had options for temporary housing elsewhere.

The isolation of Tobytown led to increased transportation problems for residents to get to jobs and schools outside the area. Most of the people who lived there could not afford cars. They had no way to get to jobs, schools, or grocery stores until bus service started in 2016, which the community fought for many years to get.[43]

Despite the continuing problems that have faced Tobytown, I am proud that I was able to be part of the efforts in the late 1960s to improve the lives of the people who lived there.

## CHAPTER 13

# Growing Our Family

While I worked for OEO, my wife Sandy had become employed at the National Institutes of Health as a Registered Nurse in the Clinical Unit. Our daughter April was still a toddler when our son, Daniel R. (Rob) Smith, Jr., was born in 1970 at Sibley Hospital in Washington, D.C. Sandy and I were fortunate to have good babysitters while we both were away at work. Later with the help of Sandy's efforts, we were able to find appropriate schooling that met our standards for the needs of our children.

During that time, there was great movement in the neighborhood for first-time starter home buyers. Most of our neighbors were moving up to their second home. Hence, we sold our house on Roosevelt Street and purchased a much larger one on Fairfax Road. We later sold the Fairfax house and relocated to Earlham Drive. All our homes were in Bethesda.

Although we were the only Blacks in our Bethesda neighborhoods, we had many close white friends and enjoyed community social events and dinner parties with neighbors. Our children played together too. Among our closest friends were Chris

*Dan and family: April, Sandy and Rob*

and Andrew (Andy) Haire. Chris was an amazing interior decorator, whose home was always beautiful. She was the type of good friend that I could count on in an emergency. Andy was a brilliant civil engineer.

The Haires had three children, two about the same age as my two children, April and Rob. They played together, had sleepovers, and toured the neighborhood on Halloween. We always had great fun at a crab feast at one or the other's house, along with some other invited neighbors. The feast consisted of corn, salad, and, of course, Maryland crabs, for which Chris and I often secured the best price.

## SAINT LUKE'S

We were members of Saint Luke's Episcopal Church in Bethesda, which was near where we lived. I was honored to become Senior Warden, the highest elected lay official in the church. I recall being told that I was the first Black to hold that office. I was dismayed, however, to find that the church was without a Rector, $20,000 in debt, and generally in disarray. Many church members worked with me to correct the serious physical problems. We got paint and brushes and painted various rooms, along with the Rector's office. We also developed a special budget fund and selected a good contractor to replace a deteriorated roof.

Several years later the Rector, Rev. David S. Pollock, wrote a very complimentary letter about my stewardship and what I had accomplished: "Through his leadership, two years later when he [Daniel Smith] finished his term, the parish had a new Rector, the budget was running a surplus and most of the debt had been paid. He has continued to be of great help to the church."

My wife Sandy was also deeply involved with St. Luke's. Among her activities, she chaired the Bishop's Visit breakfast meeting, a major event, which tore into our family budget (unnecessarily, in my view). As in many marriages, there are often different views on the use of finances, and we were not the exception. Indeed, she was a "do-gooder." When asked to participate on a committee or assist on a project, she had an exceedingly difficult time saying no. She later worked diligently as a volunteer for California Governor Jerry Brown's campaign for president.

Nevertheless, Sandy always did an excellent job on the tasks she undertook. For example, I remember an occasion around Easter. She had worked as a nurse all day, came home and worked with me on the house, and then at 5 a.m. the next morning, got up and prepared an amazing Easter breakfast. Afterward we went with April and Rob to church, returned home, and she prepared an equally amazing Easter dinner for the family, all with about four hours of sleep.

## DAUGHTER APRIL

*Young April.*

My daughter April, as I indicated earlier, was born in Tuskegee, Alabama, while I was a civil rights worker in Lowndes County. When my wife Sandy and I moved to Bethesda, April grew up with many friends. She was a bright, imaginative, and energetic child. I recall several incidents that involved her.

- *April vs. National Cathedral School.* We had hoped that she would be admitted to the National Cathedral School, a then-predominately white Episcopal private school in Washington, D.C., for girls in grades four to 12. We had prepared her accordingly. She was around nine years of age. Unfortunately, she did not

226

want to attend that school, so when she took the admission test, she purposely wrote the wrong answers on it. She even deliberately misspelled her name. As a result, they would not admit her based on the scores on the test. We did not learn about her disqualifying herself until sometime later.

- *April the Athlete.* While she attended Bethesda Elementary School, they had various athletic events. At a social one evening, one of the sets of parents was distraught, because they thought their child was the fastest runner. However, April came in first in all the races, and subsequently, became the outstanding soccer player.

- *April the Cook.* April always insisted that I taste her cooking. She used to mimic her mother who was a very good cook. One day, I had watched her make a concoction that included water, plenty of salt, food coloring, paprika, pepper, and anything she could put into it. After mixing her concoction, she ran after me to persuade me to taste it. I knew it would be awful, but she screamed, hollered, laughed, and chased me around until I finally tried it. It was the most disgusting mixture that I ever tasted. She got a great kick out of it.

- *April the Party Giver.* For her ninth or tenth birthday, April wanted to have a party, and she invited her neighborhood friends. She insisted on putting up a sheet and cutting a hole in it for me to put my head through so they could throw whipped cream pies at me. It really got out of hand. Someone tore down the sheet, and all the kids started running after me with pies to throw at me. It was all great fun for the kids, but I was so glad when my wife interceded with cake and ice cream.

## Ithaca College and the KKK

As an undergraduate in college, April attended Ithaca College, a private college in Ithaca New York. When she was an incoming junior, she had planned to continue with her roommate from sophomore year (we will call her Marcy)* and reside in the off-campus Hudson Heights apartments owned by the college and reserved for upperclassmen. But Marcy was offered an on-campus resident assistant position, which she accepted, leaving April alone without a roommate.

*April's high school graduation portrait.*

Although disappointed initially, April looked forward to having her own apartment, a situation coveted by most college students.

April was a member of the soccer team and had to go to college early every year for pre-season training. She arrived there in August, two weeks prior to the opening of school, moved into her apartment, and was fully settled in for at least a month. During this time, there was a "room freeze," when no room changes or transfers were permitted. A freshman

---

* Names of people involved in this incident have been changed to protect their identity.

student (we will call her Karen) needed housing because all the dorms on campus were full. She was offered the opportunity to be in an off-campus apartment – April's apartment – and was given a tour of it while April was there. Karen eagerly accepted the offer and moved in the next day.

Karen, a white student from New Hampshire, seemed nice enough. The only problem April had was that she was messy, a kind of a female version of the *Odd Couple*'s character Oscar Madison. This could have been somewhat tolerable if the apartment were a traditional apartment in which each person had her own room; however, this was a studio apartment where both beds were in the common area adjacent to the kitchen and the bathroom. Therefore, April not only had to endure and navigate Karen's dirty clothes, unmade bed, and belongings that were haphazardly strewn throughout the common area, but also to contend with Karen leaving dirty dishes around the apartment. Although the situation created some tension, another, much more alarming problem ensued.

Karen had a boyfriend who lived in New Hampshire, and they frequently talked on the phone. One day Karen was talking with her boyfriend, and the conversation turned untypically and noticeably quiet. There was sudden whispering, and the conversation had a different, almost mysterious tone to it. April was doing schoolwork across the room when, in the midst of a cryptic conversation, Karen announced, "April, don't listen to this."

A "red flag" went up in April's head, because during the many phone calls with the boyfriend, Karen never had requested this before. April nonchalantly agreed, believing that the conversation between them must have been something of a "lovey-dovey" personal nature that April had no interest in listening to anyway.

Curiously enough, however, the conversation began to get more puzzling. Karen was whispering phrases such as, "I will," and "I'm not sure if I can," and "I don't know," and "I'll try, but I don't think I can." These comments were disturbing, so, after Karen hung up the phone, April confronted her.

"I couldn't help overhearing. What was that all about?" April asked.

"I don't want to upset you," Karen responded. April continued to question her, and finally Karen responded very matter-of-factly.

"You know my boyfriend lives in New Hampshire," she said. "Well, he's the son of the Grand Imperial Wizard of the KKK, and he's upset that his girlfriend is living with a nigger." She also stated that what he said were his beliefs, but that she did not feel that way. April was understandably shocked and angered at this response. Before she could even react, however, Karen unloaded even more disturbing information that left April with more fear than she had ever felt in her life.

"He said that I should try to get out of this apartment," Karen said, "and if I can't, then I shouldn't eat your food, especially any that you prepare. Don't borrow any of your clothes, stay as far away from you as I can, and make sure that I clean the toilet before I use it so that I don't get a disease from you." April was dumbfounded. Then Karen delivered the most terrifying information about her boyfriend.

"He said that he wanted to make sure I was safe and protected from you. So, he has had his KKK members in Ithaca watching us."

Karen said at first she did not believe him, but then he told her some things that he could not have known unless he had been there. April was speechless. A multitude of emotions — anger, confusion, and terror — were building up inside her as she attempted to gather the appropriate words to react to the tremendous racist bomb that had just been dropped on her. But before April could respond, Karen announced that she was going to be late for class and flounced out of the apartment as if it were business as usual.

Following this, I received a phone call from April in which she calmly, but noticeably disturbed, informed me of what had just happened. I told her to pack a bag, stay with a friend, tell a trusted adult, and I would handle it. I immediately called the Office of Residence Life to inform them of the situation and to get a new location/roommate for April. The director informed me of their "room freeze" policy and that April would not be able to change her room. There was little consideration for the fact that my daughter's life could be in danger.

"Surely an exception could be made for this particular situation," I said. I was not taking no for an answer. "If this isn't addressed and rectified immediately, I will make sure that the story is on the front page of the Washington Post." In addition to communicating with the college, I also touched base with several federal legislators who had contacts with upper New York State representatives to make sure that they would support me if we had to expose the situation in the media.

As expected, that got the attention of the director, and he agreed to address the issue and meet with both April and her roommate, which they did next day. April and Karen confirmed the information that I had provided. Karen was asked specifically why she agreed to live in this situation if she knew that her boyfriend would have such a problem with it. Her response was unbelievably cavalier and matter-of-fact, according to April.

"Well, I thought it would be cool to live in an off-campus apartment as a freshman," Karen answered. "Besides, I don't feel that way."

The resolution to this situation was that because Karen herself was not a direct threat to April, the college could not force her to vacate the apartment. They would, however, offer April placement in another one off-campus. Fortunately, a player on April's soccer team was also in an apartment without a roommate, so April moved in with her. The rest of her junior year continued without incident.

## Epilogue to April and the KKK

As frightening and unbelievable as this true story sounds, it greatly demonstrates the reach of the KKK and white supremacists, especially when they feel one of their own is threatened. I thought that by having April attend a school in the North, she would be shielded from the evils of racism. Unfortunately, however, it still reared its ugly head. Racism was alive and well then, and it still is today.

I believe that the Black community generally can take a significant amount of abuse themselves, but they will defend their children to the death if confronted with a dangerous situation. This is probably because, for the most part, the only real thing that many Blacks have are their children. If we cannot take pride and defend our children, we feel somewhat of a failure in life. Therefore, that is why it became so alarming to me, because I was not immediately available on the campus to defend my daughter.

White Americans often try to rationalize or do what they think through their lenses is best for the Black community. My view is that whites too often talk at but never listen to what Black Americans say. Blacks who have lived around whites understand them. However, most white Americans have never lived with Blacks and hence they do not understand us.

## ROB, MY SON

My son Rob was born while we were living on Roosevelt Street in Bethesda. He was always a very bright and active child, well-liked by his peers at any age. However, I experienced a strange phenomenon when Rob was five years old. I remembered that I was age six when my father died by a hit-and-run driver. So, when my son neared that age, I was overly concerned that I might pass away. For several years, I was

*Young Rob.*

extremely anxious and triply careful not to put myself in any harm's way. My anxiety over that did not dissipate until Rob was about nine years old.

We enrolled Rob in St. Columba's Nursery School, a ministry of St. Columba's Episcopal Church. He was there at the same time as Bishop John Walker's son Carlie. They became close friends. Later, in 1984, when the Walker family went back to Jamaica to visit with Mrs. Walker's relatives, they invited Rob to go with them. It was a very enjoyable experience for him to visit another country.

After nursery school, we enrolled Rob in a private elementary school, where he loved his teachers, especially Mr. Richardson, a great English teacher and soccer athlete. During Rob's elementary school years, I served as the volunteer soccer coach for the Montgomery Soccer Incorporated Team. Rob was always a formidable competitor, and desired to learn more to become a better athlete.

As he grew older, he and I would stay after soccer practice and do drills, especially goal kicking. In addition, we would drive to the Medical Center Metro Station. Rob, much to my and the public's amazement, wearing ankle weights and a backpack filled with weights, started from the bottom, and ran up the escalator stairs to build his body. Plus, we would go to the Walt Whitman High School, which had a steep incline behind it. He would push a loaded wheelbarrow up and down from the bottom to the top of the bank 10 times, which was not an easy task. Rob was an outstanding athlete and received some competitive awards.

Later, Rob entered the public school system at the Walter Johnson High School, in Montgomery County, Maryland. We had begun living on Earlham Drive in Bethesda, and I was employed at the National Institutes of Health. One day, I arrived home early in the afternoon and found that the girls had discovered Rob. They had baked him a "welcome to the neighborhood cake" and brought it to the house. Rob was clearly very well-liked by his peers.

## Like Father Like Son

Soon after Rob entered high school, his mother left the family, and Rob and I were home alone. His older sister April, who had also been living with me, left to attend Ithaca College in New York. I was determined my children would continue to enjoy the same status they were accustomed to. I did a lot of cooking, and in the mornings before he left for school, I would serve bacon, eggs, and pancakes. I prepared so many eggs every morning that, unbeknownst to me, they raised his cholesterol level to a dangerous point. Fortunately, the doctor doing his

*Rob Smith, high school graduation portrait.*

required athletic physical caught it and called me. I quickly reduced the number of eggs I cooked.

One Saturday morning, I came downstairs and smelled something cooking. Rob was fixing scrambled eggs. As I watched, he would reach on the shelf where the spices were located and take one down and sprinkle it on the eggs. He did this several times. I did not think much of it, until I noticed that he put cinnamon in the eggs. I asked why he was using those spices.

"I saw you reach on the shelf and put different things in there, so I did too," he replied. I laughed and explained that there are certain ingredients used for different foods. For example, you do not put cinnamon on eggs.

I recall also, when he was home living with me, I was going on a trip to South Africa and asked him to water the plants while I was gone. When I returned, however, the plants were all withered and dying. I asked him what happened.

"I did like you asked," he replied. "I watered the plants every day." The upshot was that he discovered that plants could die from overwatering.

Indeed, in both cases, like me with cooking too many cholesterol-laden eggs, Rob learned from those experiences.

## College and Independence

Following my son's graduation, he enrolled at the University of Maryland's Eastern Shore campus, which serves as a feeder school for the main campus in College Park. Rob worked hard, and I served as his mentor from my home, especially as it related to term papers. It was a lot of fun because it kept us in close contact. Rob made the Honor Roll in the second semester and Dean's List in another semester. Rob then applied and was accepted at New York's Syracuse University where he received a partial track scholarship. He was on a track relay team and appeared once in the *Syracuse Herald Journal* and *The Washington Post*.

Unfortunately, he had to withdraw from Syracuse for financial reasons because I ran out of college funds. Rob transferred to the University of Maryland's Main Campus and was encouraged by a drama teacher to enter the entertainment world. It was of interest to him, as we had dragged him to dinner theatres when he was young in support of his sister April, when she was acting. He took a series of elective acting courses.

Then one day, Rob called me and said he had an opportunity to audition in New York City to enter American Conservatory Theatre (ACT) in California. I was not pleased since he had not yet received his bachelor's degree. However, he made a commitment that if I supported him and he were accepted at ACT, following graduation he would return to classes at Syracuse to receive his Bachelor of Science degree. Three years later, following his ACT graduation, he reenrolled at Syracuse and received his degree from Syracuse. Following graduation, Rob participated in marketing a phenomenally successful Wendy's commercial while he was living in New York. He has also had several roles in television programs.

I am very proud of my son. It is gratifying now to know that Rob is working at his craft, totally self-sufficient, and living in New York City, which allows us to be in easy communication. In fact, we have been in telephone conversations every Wednesday and Sunday since he moved to New York.

## CHAPTER 14

# AHEC Part I – Starting the Program

By the time this part of my story began, I had participated in the national battle to end the unequal treatment of Blacks, while also occasionally experiencing such treatment in my own life. Now, however, that unequal treatment would be ramped up against me, directly and egregiously. It culminated in a full-fledged legal fight for my rights, my reputation, my government position, and, indeed, my livelihood.

During the next two years, this battle raged, keeping me awake at night and struggling to stay above water during the day. I have carefully kept detailed documentation of the entire episode, in the hope that someday I would get the chance to share my story with the world. My goal is to offer publicly a first-hand, well-documented example of racism inside one of the nation's highest public institutions, to demonstrate the depth of the problem and add my voice to the plea for change.

*New Federal Health Program*

In early 1972, I was still working at the OEO, developing Neighborhood Health Centers throughout the United States. Meanwhile, President Nixon appointed as director of OEO a former Republican Congressman from Illinois, Donald Rumsfeld, who had voted against the creation of the agency. Rumsfeld was supposedly appointed to reorganize it. However, the staff knew that he and his assistant, Franklin Carlucci, were really trying to shut it down.

Hence, senior staff and others, myself included, were scurrying around the government looking for new positions with another agency. I learned of one from John Myers, a budget director at one of the National Institutes of Health. He was a member of Bethesda's predominately white St. Luke's Episcopal Church, which we both attended. I was the Senior Warden, the head lay leadership position of the church.

John and I were social friends. One day he and I were both heading downtown for different meetings, so we shared the dual seat on the bus. As we discussed several issues, including employment, John told me that he was aware of a pending appropriations announcement regarding a new position at the National Institutes of Health (NIH). The position would be to develop a $60-million program, recently enacted by Congress, to establish Area Health Education Centers (AHECs).

"It's designed to train primary care and family practice physicians along with related health workers in under-served areas," John told me. "With your background, you would be a good person to direct it. And it's the type of program that would give its director a great legacy."

Since the position was competitive and needed to be filled in three weeks, John urged me to update my Form 171, a government background resume, with my qualifications. John thought that many others would also apply. In addition, all program funds had to be allocated by September 30, 1972, just a few months away.

I submitted my application and was contacted by the NIH personnel office to come to NIH's Building 31, one of the main NIH administration buildings, for an interview with the deciding official, Douglas Fenderson, PhD, Director, Office of Special Programs in NIH's Bureau of Health Manpower Education.[*] My colleagues at OEO volunteered all kinds of suggestions as to how to impress him.

"Arrive an hour early," they advised. "You don't want to get lost on the sprawling NIH campus." They also suggested that I purchase a new suit or wear my one dark "power suit" and red striped tie. My former wife used to say that federal civil service bureaucrats are the worst dressed men in D.C., and I was president of the club. However, I elected to wear my favorite brown suit, which had served me well on previous occasions.

I arrived at Dr. Fenderson's office on time. In talking with him, it was obvious to me that he had reviewed my credentials, and I felt that he really knew me. I concluded that he respected my direct responses to his questions. He was now trying to decide between me and the top two other candidates, whom I had learned from the "grapevine" were both white. I felt that he was probably struggling internally with how the NIH system would react to him for hiring a Black man in this high-profile medical education position and whether, if selected, I would be able to navigate successfully within the NIH community. He asked when I could start, if selected.

"I'm ready to now," I replied. He then rose from behind his desk, indicating our conversation and interview had been completed. He began walking toward the door.

"I'll be back in contact with you within three weeks," he said. I instinctively asked if I could ask him a question. He agreed.

---

[*] Dr. Fenderson was highly respected, and in the 1980s was appointed by President Reagan as Director of the National Institute of Disability and Rehabilitation Research. He returned to his home state of Minnesota and became Director of Continuing Medical Education at the University of Minnesota Medical School, where he retired as Professor Emeritus in the Department of Family Practice and Community Health. He died on February 10, 2019 (age 90).

"What has four legs in the morning, two legs in the afternoon, and three legs in the evening?" I asked. He looked startled at me and, with a smirk on his face, opened his office door. Thus, I assumed he knew the answer to the Sphinx's question – a man.[†]

"Can you start work here in ten days?" he asked. I had the position!

When I have told this story, people have often asked me why I raised the question of the Sphinx. I have said it was to credential myself, to show that I was not only an educated person who would fit into the NIH world, but also that I was different and stood out from my competitors. Many years later, I saw the film *The Butler*, in which a Black man being interviewed for the butler's position in the White House suddenly showed off his knowledge of fine liqueurs – he too got the job.

## MY INTRODUCTION TO NIH

NIH has its roots to 1887, when a one-room laboratory was created within the Marine Hospital Service (MHS), established in 1798 to provide medical care for merchant seamen. Over the years its mission was expanded and, in 1930, the Ransdell Act included federal support for scientific medical research and established the National Institute (singular) of Health under the Public Health Service (PHS). In 1948, its name was changed to plural, the National Institutes of Health (NIH). In the 1950s, its budget was increased extensively, and its parent agency became the cabinet-level Department of Health, Education, and Welfare (HEW).

---

[†] In Sophocles' play *Oedipus the King*, the Sphinx, a creature with the body of a winged lion and face of a woman, destroyed travelers on the road to Thebes who failed to solve the riddle. When Oedipus answered correctly, the Sphinx destroyed herself. The answer is man, who crawls on all fours as a baby, walks upright in the middle of life, and uses a cane when elderly.

By the time I was employed there, NIH had 15 institutes, and by 1998 it had 27 institutes and centers including several that concentrated on various diseases–including typhoid, sickle cell, cancer, and heart disease. Today, NIH has become one of the largest, best, and most renowned health agencies in the world. I was (and still am) proud to have been appointed to work there.

Following my meeting with Dr. Fenderson, I arrived for work 10 days later back at Building 31. I noted that nearly all the doctors, professionals, secretaries, and support staff were white, while the security policemen and janitorial staff were all Black.

One day, soon after I started work, I was walking down the hall and met Dr. George Blue Spruce, DDS, the first American Indian dentist in the United States. His office was about four doors from mine. He beckoned me to come in and get acquainted. Dr. Blue Spruce was very astute and friendly. We had a good conversation. He understood what it was like to be the only one of a kind in such a huge research institution. He said he had been at NIH for about a year and had learned a few things about it. He indicated that they had a large, figurative peg board and would decide what peg hole you belong in.

"They will then proceed to pound you in that hole," he said. We both laughed. I was to find out later that he was correct.

## *AHEC Funding and Operations*

AHEC was established under legislation enacted in 1971 entitled "Health Manpower Initiative Awards."[44] It was an outgrowth of a report by the Carnegie Commission on Higher Education issued in the fall of 1970, *Higher Education and the Nation's Health*.[45] The Commission identified the need for federal support to improve the accessibility of needed health services in the United States, both by specialty and geography, through training of primary care physicians and other health-care providers.[‡] In June 1972, the Department of Health, Education, and Welfare placed the AHEC Program in the NIH Bureau of Health Manpower Education, headed by Dr. Kenneth Endicott. [§]

For the most part, funding was awarded to NIH through Congressional legislation. Such awards were designated for the various institutes when NIH submitted their annual budget needs to the Congress. As with some other government agencies in the pre-1972 era, except for agency administration and specific targeted projects, NIH awards were made to the individual institutes with grants. The grants allowed flexibility to explore various methods in finding solutions to health issues. Grant awards were often open-ended.

By contrast, NIH awards to medical schools for AHECs were made by contracts. Unlike grants, they are much more specific, directive, and less flexible, often with a set termination date from time of the award. They also often require milestones that are expected to be met. That was the case with the AHEC contract awards.

In the case of the AHEC contracts, following a pre-bidder' conference with medical schools, a Request for Proposal (RFP) went out, the submitted proposals underwent peer review, and the selected medical schools

[†] For a detailed explanation of AHEC and an extensive evaluation of its early implementation, see: Charles E. Odegaard, Area Health Education Centers, The Pioneering Years, 1972-1978 (Carnegie Council on Policy Studies in Higher Education, 1979).
[§] Dr. Endicott began at NIH in 1941 in the division of pathology. In the early 1950s, he was scientific director of the division of research grants, was an associate director of NIH during the late 1950s and served as director of the National Cancer Institute for nine years. Dr. Endicott then became director of NIH's Bureau of Health Manpower, where he helped establish new federal programs to provide financial support for institutions that train health professionals. He retired in 1977, with the U.S. Public Health Service rank of assistant surgeon general. Joseph D. Whitaker, "KENNETH MILO ENDICOTT, 71, EX-HEW ADMINISTRATOR, DIES," *The Washington Post,* July 19, 1987.

were awarded contracts.** Putting all this together was an enormous undertaking not only for my office but also for the recipients.

When fully operational, an AHEC would become a health "Center of Excellence" and would develop a subcontract with a community college, medical society, hospital, or advocate organization. The medical school would send interns or residents to the center where they would learn to treat general ailments such as appendicitis, minor wounds, and gynecological issues, rather than concentrate on more esoteric medical professions such as neurosurgery, ophthalmology, or other specialties.

In turn, students would provide health services to the local community within the geographic area where the center operated. It was found that students on rotation to the AHEC from the medical center were more likely to stay and practice in the AHEC area. In addition, the AHEC would develop a purchase agreement back to the medical school for certain areas of expertise that the medical school could directly provide.

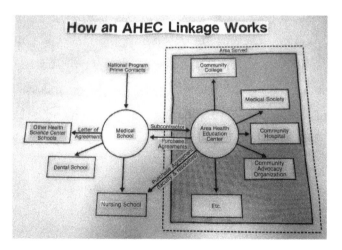

** The medical school in turn subcontracted with an outlier medical institution (hospital, nursing complex or other health institution some distance from the medical school). This outlier institution was the actual Area Health Education Center, which then attracted and promoted both local physicians and high-profile, national health professionals as speakers or special consultants.

*Congressional "Support" (Interference?)*

Each of the AHECs had a director and staff. The directors often called my office with questions about issues they could not understand, bypassing the medical school (the prime contractor) where they should have gone with such questions. They also frequently tried to go around us to contact their politicians to get additional funding.

This was the case one year with the University of Maryland's Medical School AHEC, which elicited Congressional support for additional funds through Senator Paul Sarbanes of Maryland. One day, a year or so after the program started, two staff members from the University of Maryland came to my office. One of them stayed at the office with me. The other, a senior project AHEC director, left and went to the senator's office and had him call me to ask for additional funds.

"I hear that AHEC is a very good program," Senator Sarbanes said, "but ours is short of funds. I wonder if we could work something out."

"Well, I think you have been misinformed," I replied. "These are not grants but contracts. They had the opportunity to submit a proposal to NIH and spell out how much they needed. If they received an award, they received the amount that they signed the contract for. I'm sure you understand that."

Senator Sarbanes thanked me for my time and said he knew I was very busy. He did not pressure me further, and the funding was not increased. Sometime later I met up with him at a reception in Baltimore and introduced myself. He smiled and was very cordial.

"You are doing a good job," he said.

## AHEC BEGINS - 1972

When I first started at NIH, I was immediately interviewed by the NIH Public Relations staff regarding the AHEC Program and my background.

I was shown my first office, modest in size (we used to call it "the closet") and absent any clerical support.

I quickly tried to recruit staff, starting with a full-time secretary, but I was rebuffed by an upper-level administrative staffer responsible for securing support staff. He always presented me with a rationale for delaying his providing me a list of clerical candidates. Instead, he gave me 60-day to 120-day part-time help, such as high-school trainees. These were "work study" employees, most of whom had never worked before. As supervisor I was expected to teach them the world of work.

The first receptionist/secretary assigned to me was a very inexperienced young woman. She could barely type, and her grammar was poor. This was her first job, and she demonstrated that she was not prepared for a front-office position. I recall her answering the phone one day as I was leaving the office. Someone had asked for me.

"He be gone," she answered. I was mortified.

In the meantime, the days were slipping by. On June 12, 1972, I sent a letter on behalf of the AHEC office announcing the program to those institutions that had requested information. They were given only 13 days – until June 25 – to respond. Those that intended to apply for developmental or operational support for an AHEC were required to provide a two- or three-page letter describing the major features of the proposed AHEC, the extent to which collaborative relationships could be assured, their proposed work schedule spread over a five-year period, and the ways in which the proposal responded to the underlying theme of manpower shortage in medically underserved geographic areas.

Remarkably, in such a short time, 85 institutions – medical schools and health science centers – attended a pre-bidder' conference and indicated an intention to apply. Of these, 27 were selected to be sent a Request for

Proposal (RFP), which I produced. They were given 30 days to send their written contract proposal back to my office. These would then receive peer review by a team of 12 professional reviewers, whom I selected.[††]

In the end, 11 institutions were chosen to receive contracts.[‡‡] This created an even more enormous headache for my office once they were all funded. The medical schools were spread all over the nation, and each had different concepts about operating their institutions and developing the AHECs.

Fortunately, I was then allowed to select and bring on staff: Project officers Jim Becraft, Doug Pendoton, Karen Hanson, and Attila Kadar, MD, and budget officer John Reed. Yet that still meant we had only a handful of professionals to supervise relations with the 11 widely scattered projects. Over three months, from November 1972 through January 1973, we visited each of them on-site to get to know their personnel and their projects.

Meanwhile, a buzz went around NIH about there being no clerical staff for Smith's AHEC Program. Then, out of the blue, one afternoon a secretary arrived who worked for an upper-level administrator in another institute. She came into my office and said that she and others wanted to volunteer to help me. I was overwhelmed. It was a truly unexpected and very welcomed gesture by that secretarial community to lend support to my effort.

One must remember that this occurred in the early 1970s, when no one had personal computers or internet access. Secretaries and clerks

---

[††] The reviewers represented a range of health-related professions, ranging from academic researchers to educators to heads of major national programs.
[‡‡] University of California at San Francisco; University of Illinois; University of Minnesota; University of Missouri (Kansas City); University of New Mexico (serving the Navajo Reservation in the four-corner area of New Mexico, Arizona, Utah, and Colorado); University of North Carolina; Medical University of South Carolina; University of North Dakota; University of Texas Medical Branch, Galveston; Turfs University (serving Maine); and West Virginia University.

were still using electric typewriters and carbon paper. Even the IBM Selectric typewriter, with its little self-correcting balls, was not on the scene. However, my newfound secretarial friend and I worked out a system: I would give her my hand-written material; she would type it; then she would farm it out to the other helpful secretaries for corrections and to make duplicates; and finally, they would make a copy and include it in a folder for each medical school/health science center in the AHEC office.

Getting typing done, however, was not my only problem. We did not, for example, have access to the photocopy machines, because my office did not have a key to the photocopy room. In those days, keys were restricted to each office. For some reason, my office was not given any keys.

So, I worked out another system. I arrived in the morning at 8:30 and would leave work around 7 p.m., then return to the office at 3 a.m. the next morning. The Black janitors had keys to all the rooms and offices, and they would open the doors of the photocopy room so I could get my material copied. They would also help me collate and staple the documents. I think they were proud of me and wanted to help me become successful. One may think this was insignificant, but it was a great help to the AHEC program and the nation. I only wish I could remember their names and be able to thank them.

Meanwhile, it was extremely difficult for me to obtain minimal essentials such as telephone service, typewriters, supply cabinets, desks and even, at one point, pads, pencils, pens, and manila folders. I wrote notes and memos to Dr. Fenderson's assistant director, Dorothy Reese, pleading for assistance. We finally obtained photocopy services. But it was not until August 1973, through my own personal scrounging, that I found a clipboard for maintaining copies of my correspondence. I could not even get manila folders for the

AHEC files. When we asked the procurement office for manila folders once, we were told that it would take six months to get them!

*Dan with James Walsh, 2018*
*Photo by Loretta Neumann.*

## Help Arrives

Fortunately, I had developed a positive relationship with James (Jim) Walsh, the agency's executive officer. With his help and that of Dr. Fenderson, who also repeatedly complained up the chain of command, I was able to obtain some part-time help. This included Mrs. Gray, a very competent, older Black woman who was extremely happy to be employed at NIH and especially to work for a Black supervisor. Indeed, she was very protective of me. Also, Jean Riley, a white secretary who was also highly effective, a hard worker and a self-starter.

In addition, I was able to bring onto my professional staff Marcy Gross, a smart and well-organized white woman who had worked with me at OEO developing Neighborhood Health Centers. Marcy was intelligent, loyal, hardworking, and creative. In addition to "having my back," she was committed to helping me implement the Congressional AHEC mandate. She and I worked tirelessly, often around the clock and on weekends.

Marcy quickly understood the reason for my difficult situation. A major problem for AHEC was that the program was totally new to the NIH leadership. Our perception was that the leaders were also not accustomed to having such a major program with so much money directed by a Black man. Marcy and I were determined not to let the system – the NIH bureaucracy - defeat our team from moving the AHEC Program forward.

Marcy stayed with me several years then left the AHEC Program to work in women's health. The public often hears politicians and others complain about lazy civil servants, but that only demonstrates their ignorance of the strong work ethic that I have seen in many hardworking civil servants like Marcy, who toil in the public's interest.

During all the turmoil I experienced at this time, I did not see or hear about other managers at my level (all white) having problems like mine with obtaining clerical staff and support.

## CONFRONTING THE BUREAUCRACY

Anyone who has had the pleasure of working in a large medical, religious, corporate, or governmental institution has probably encountered conflicts over turf within it. I have observed this and found it to be extremely challenging, especially as leaders vie for upward-mobility positions within their respective systems. In my case, in addition to my AHEC responsibilities, I had to deal with other agencies that had been vying for the same government funds from the Health Initiative Legislation. They included Regional Medical Programs, the Veterans Administration, and the National Library of

Medicine. All of them, I believe, had received an initial award before HEW decided to have NIH serve as the lead on the AHEC Program.

*Dan talking with Edward Knisley, director of Medical Science,
University of Baltimore at an AHEC conference, mid 1970s.*

So, besides serving as Chief of the AHEC Program, I was named the National AHEC Coordinator. This meant I had to attend the other AHEC meetings, provide them with advice, and encourage them to modify their directions in accordance with the Carnegie Model Consortium, which was the model that NIH had chosen for the AHEC program.

In 1973-1974, I worked on a Management Information System (MIS) that outlined the timelines and milestones for the AHEC projects. At the same time, we took the necessary steps to begin an evaluation of the AHEC program. A contract was let to Abt Associates of Massachusetts, chosen under the regular competitive procurement process. To say that the evaluation, which included looking at each of the 11 AHEC projects, was a nightmare would not do it justice. The AHEC project staff held meetings upon meetings to work out a system of evaluation that would fit all projects.

## *HEW Reorganizes*

In July 1973, in just the second year of the program, the Department of Health, Education, and Welfare decided to decentralize and move many health programs, including AHEC, to regional offices. None of the eight regional offices to which AHEC was assigned had staff prepared to handle the program. So, it was up to my office to educate and train the regional staff about the 11 AHEC programs and how they worked, both the programs and the contracting. Responsibility for allocation of AHEC funds, however, remained with my office. Because of the decentralization, the staff of my office was reduced to me as the national coordinator and a part-time clerk-typist until mid-1975.

Thus, I was the only one left to oversee all the AHEC projects plus the regional offices. As noted in a 1979 report published by the Carnegie Council on the AHEC program, prepared by Dr. Charles Odegaard:

"Conditions were chaotic because the central office was crippled, and the regional offices were slow in building staff. New program officers had to learn about the unusual and complex programs of multi-institutional character; and new contracting officers had to learn about the procurement problems peculiar to the AHEC type of operation."[46]

Amid this chaos, Dr. Fenderson was in the process of leaving the government. Before departing, he twice recommended me for promotion from the GS-14 grade level to a GS-15 level. In a memo to the Personnel Office, he noted the increased responsibility I was assuming as the program decentralized.

"Mr. Smith will need to provide policy leadership and direction in relating this 12-million-dollar per year, five-year effort to the expected changes and extensions," he wrote. "Mr. Smith has worked very hard, put in long hours, has set aside his own plans at times to assure the effective performance of his responsibility. He has taken the initiative in 'staying on top of' the workload. He has been supportive of and responsive to this office."[47]

Despite his strong recommendations, I did not receive the promotion. Dr. Fenderson's assistant, Dorothy Reese, a woman with the Public Health Service Commissioned Corps, was moved into his position and would oversee my office. A quiet "company woman," she demonstrated little knowledge of the program and minimal administrative skills. I repeatedly asked her for more staff support and she continually denied it. Without notifying me, she took away the one part-time clerk-typist that I had. As a result, I did not learn until 4 p.m. one afternoon that my son needed immediate medical attention that morning because of a high pollen count. My wife had not been able to inform me of the problem since I had no telephone coverage.

Ms. Reese repeatedly rebuffed my attempts to obtain staff support and denied my workload.

"You are spoiled," she said. "You should grin and bear it."

In August 1973, Dr. Fenderson announced that he would be leaving by the end of the year, and that Ms. Reese would become acting director of the Office of Special Programs. My lack of staff continued, and I repeatedly pleaded with her for help.

*More Problems*

That was not, however, my only problem. Indeed, one episode with Ms. Reese stood out. I wanted to let a contract to a non-AHEC firm to produce a list of the AHEC-type programs nationwide, including data about each state, medical school, personnel, amount of award and related information, which could be useful at a quick glance for us, Congress and others. Three different companies submitted proposals, and I selected one, C.E. Pagan Associates from Baltimore, which had the highest review rating and lowest bid for price. It happened to be Black owned; of the other two, one was Black and the other white. Ms. Reese wanted to select the white company, which was considerably higher in price and had received a lower review rating. I, of course, objected.

This resulted in a major meeting with heads of different Bureau of Health Manpower Education departments who were not even associated with the AHEC program. Most of those in attendance were in the Public Health Service Commissioned Corps. I was not deterred, even though Ms. Reese bought in higher level officials to help her with her problem.

About 10 people attended the meeting, one of whom was Dr. Harry Bruce, a friend of Ms. Reese. He was a real bulldog, but well thought of within the Commissioned Corps and the Bureau. In addition, I remember two other people at the meeting. One was a Dr. Green, who took a neutral position, and Cliff Allen, a highly respected Black Korean war veteran. He and I were the only Blacks at the meeting. In the end, I held my own about the low bidder receiving the contract – C. E. Pagan Associates, which later produced two very useful publications.[48] This upset Ms. Reese and other Public Health Service officials.

Another episode with Ms. Reese involved an elderly Italian secretary who had worked for Dr. Fenderson. I recall her name was Rose. He had hired her because he had trouble spelling, and she was good at it. When he left, Rose was absorbed into Ms. Reese's office. In those days, like most secretaries, Rose had only finished high school as a typist. One day she came to me with tears in her eyes.

"Will you help me with a paper that Ms. Reese gave me?" she cried. "She wants me to determine by this evening the 'gestalt' of the subject. I don't know what she means."

I was shocked. I thought it was inappropriate for Ms. Reese to expect this of a woman educated only as a typist. When I calmed down, I started working with Rose on it. Fortunately, while I was fuming, a good friend with a master's degree in philosophy walked into the office and took over helping the secretary.

Afterward, I went to Ms. Reese to complain about the inappropriateness of asking a secretary with so limited an education to take on such an intellectually sophisticated task.

"Dorothy," I asked, "what is Myristyl-gamma-picolinium chloride?" She looked at me, puzzled. I explained that it was a medical term for a treatment used for osteoarthritis in dogs. (I had learned this while studying at the veterinary school at Tuskegee.)

"If you don't know that, then why would you expect someone who has only been trained in high school to be a typist to know what 'gestalt' means?"

Shortly thereafter, I was given a white staff person who had worked for the Washington, D.C., government. She was not racially friendly, and she expected to have special privileges on the job. For example, without informing me, she met with Ms. Reese and received a one-week leave of absence, which was granted without contacting me. So, Ms. Reese and I had another warm discussion over administrative matters.

*Recentralization*

A major shift in the program came again, resulting from legislation enacted in October 1976, which directed that the administration of health manpower programs be recentralized, including bringing AHEC back to the central office, effective October 1, 1977. This caused another upheaval in my office and with the AHEC projects. To handle this, I initially had only one other professional staff member, Marcy Gross, to help. We assumed responsibility for preparing and negotiating the sixth-year contracts awarded in September 1977. Regional offices were still responsible for monitoring the remainder of the initial five-year contracts and the official project files.

Fortunately, I was helped by Paul Daily from the Bureau of Health Management Education's contracts office. Paul was willing to take on this task even though he was grieving the death of his son, who had been killed by a drunk driver. Paul later played a major role in developing the Mothers Against Drunk Driving (MADD) program. He and I negotiated the sixth-year contracts on a back-to-back basis, which took us five days with much sweat and frustration.

For me, recentralization also meant rehiring staff and reorganizing the central AHEC office. As the 1979 Odegaard report on AHEC noted: "The assembly of staff for ultimate recentralization was as slow as assembly of staff for decentralization four years previously, imposing a hectic and uncertain burden on both federal and institutional officials linked with responsibilities for AHEC contracts. In addition...there was a substantial shift of personnel associated with the presidential change of administration early in 1977."[§§]

Finally, I received a full-fledged secretary with all the skills needed for the task, Joanne Van Vechten. Joanne was a highly effective and efficient worker. She, Marcy Gross, and I made a good team. We were, however, extremely busy and constantly had to make many decisions. As a result, when it came time for me, as Joanne's immediate supervisor, to do

---

[§§] Odegaard, Area Health Education Centers, 23.

her performance review, I told her that she was an excellent secretary, but I just did not have the time to develop the necessary paperwork for her in-grade promotion. The following day, Joanne came back to me and closed the door in my office.

"If you think I'm doing an excellent job, you ought to take the time to complete my excellent rating," she said. "It also means more money." Of course, I made the time that evening to provide her with an excellent rating from her supervisor.

*Despite his difficulty in getting support staff, Dan was able to organize 5 workshops around the country to bring regional AHEC leaders together, share experiences, and help them better understand how the program works. Here he is with several AHEC leaders at a workshop in South Carolina, mid 1970s.*

The 1976 Act that recentralized AHEC also increased funding for AHECs and added several new provisions, including new urban AHECs to meet special needs of inner cities, as well as AHECs for rural areas and statewide programs. A new RFP was announced, and responses were to be received by August 12, 1977, with contracts to be awarded for the fiscal year beginning October 1. Again, it was a huge undertaking for my small staff.

A study on AHEC conducted in 1979 by the investigative staff of the House Appropriations Committee noted that, throughout much of fiscal year 1977, "the National AHEC Coordinator [me] was the only full-time professional staff member on the Central Office AHEC Staff" and "During the initial period following recentralization (October 1977-January 1978) the program operated at about 35 percent of authorized professional staff."[49] In short, we had much more to do and nowhere near enough staff to help do it!

At some point during this time, Ms. Reese was approved for a trip to Hawaii on government business by her new boss, Dr. Robert (Bob) Graham. Like Ms. Reese, he was a member of the Commissioned Corps, the uniformed service of the U.S. Public Health Service. Members of the Corps were often called the "yellow beret" by others because they had uniforms and military perks but were not expected or required to engage in direct military combat. Dr. Graham had previously served at HEW from 1970 to 1973 and returned in 1976 as Deputy Director of the Bureau of Health Manpower Education, Health Resources Administration.

## MY PERSONAL CIVIL RIGHTS BATTLE

When Ms. Reese returned from Hawaii, Dr. Graham appointed a new supervisor to replace her as Director, Office of Special Programs. Dr. John Mather, a foreign medical graduate from England, walked in with his little black doctor's bag and bragged that he was the only physician in the Bureau who had passed his medical boards. It was soon obvious to me that he was brought in to be the "hatchet man" to remove me as head of the AHEC program.

"I'm here to help you," he said at my first meeting with him. He asked if there was anything he could do for me. I noted that I was without a full-time secretary and indicated that I had drafted a document to go to him, as my supervisor, but it needed to be typed. He volunteered to have his secretary type it for me, and so I gave it to her. She typed and returned it to me. I signed it and put it in Dr. Mather's in-box, since it was due to him by close of business that day, and no one was in his office. The next morning, I received a scathing memo from him, stating that he would not tolerate my producing documents that were not on time. He did not acknowledge that no one was in his office at the time to receive it nor that his secretary had typed the letter for me because I had no secretary of my own to do it.

There were many similar incidents that Dr. Mather documented against me. The worst was a lengthy memorandum dated June 10, 1977, declaring a notice of a possible unsatisfactory rating and giving me 90 days to improve my performance. It was an astonishing litany of minor infractions. The cited performance levels ("job requirements" or "performance standards") were created by him and had never been discussed with me. I had never been given notice that they would be used to judge my performance. He even complained that I was once 30 minutes late for an internal staff meeting, one for which he previously knew I would be late!

No recognition was given for the many extra hours I worked daily and on weekends nor my many and noted accomplishments in developing and implementing such a huge program with such a miniscule staff. His claims were ludicrous.

## Survival Mode

My philosophy in life had always been that in a disagreement, I would give my opponent 75 percent of the argument, to my 25 percent, but I would never give 76 percent to my 24 percent. I stuck to that position and still do. So, I went into a personal survival, battle mode. I figured I was in a war between the system and me. I developed a strategy and took several steps in preparation for battle.

The first step was to deal with Dr. Mather himself. I knew he was tracking my actions and every decision. I needed to know what he was reporting about me. I also knew that he loved new furniture, flags, and windows. His office was directly behind mine, and he ordered new furniture, including a new desk. When his desk arrived, he then went on a one-week vacation. Meanwhile, I was working night and day on the AHEC program. I realized drastic action was needed to protect my good reputation, my position, and my income, on which my family was dependent.

One night about 11 p.m., lock and key were removed from my old desk and were put on his new desk, and a duplicate key given to me. Then the lock from his new desk was put into my desk and a key was given to me. This enabled me to use my old keys to open his desk any time I wanted. As a result, I found that he had developed an extensive dossier on me, with self-serving memos and related information.

Mather also brought in as his aide someone I viewed as an "Uncle Tom," a "token" Black, to demonstrate that the system was not prejudiced. He had worked somewhere else in the Public Health Service and knew nothing about the AHEC program or its history. Because of his attitude of indifference to our heavy workload, he was immediately disliked by the AHEC staff.

At the same time, Dr. Graham was also creating his own rationale against me – for example, asking me questions that I should not have been expected to answer off the top of my head on technical, complicated matters that were being handled by my small staff, particularly my able assistant, Marcy Gross. He nitpicked typos in my correspondence, largely due to my lack of clerical support. This was long before computers made it easy to correct mistakes. If one word was misspelled in a letter, the clerk would have to retype the whole letter.

The situation became very tense. Then, on October 28, 1977, Dr. Graham filed an adverse action suit against me, covering two months of the period during which he had been my supervisor. It came as quite a surprise. His stated rationale was that I could not plan or organize and that I lacked command of the English language! He listed a litany of bureaucratic infractions he perceived that I had made. None reached the level that I felt merited this action.

The adverse action, if effective, would have reduced me from a grade GS-14, and Chief of the AHEC Program and National AHEC Coordinator, to a grade GS-12 and Program Analyst on the AHEC staff. It would have meant that, although I had successfully managed the program for five years and was frequently acknowledged as the "Father" of the AHEC program, if the suit were effective, I would have to report to the very people that I had hired.

The battles that I had faced before were now turning into a real war!

## CHAPTER 15

# AHEC Part II –
# Saving the Program and Me!

Following Dr. Graham's filing of the adverse action against me, I knew that in addition to saving my job, I had to make certain that the AHEC Program would continue and move in a positive direction even if I were not successful with my case.

So, I consulted with two non-federal AHEC project directors - Dr. Eugene (Gene) Mayer, University of North Carolina School of Medicine, and Dr. Edward G. Haskell, Jr., at the Medical University of South Carolina.* They were both white and we had become close friends as well as colleagues. They had established exceptionally effective AHEC programs and had strong ties with Members of Congress. We developed a long-term plan with congressional staffers and others to ensure the future support for the AHEC. (It worked, and 50 years later AHECs in modified forms exist in almost every state.)

---

* Dr. Eugene S. Mayer was a University of North Carolina (UNC) School of Medicine faculty member from 1971-1994. He held faculty positions as Professor of Family Medicine and Medicine. He served as Associate Dean of the UNC School of Medicine and Director of the North Carolina Area Health Education Center Program from 1978-1994. He died November 2, 1994 (age 56). Dr. Edward G. Haskell, Jr., became involved with AHEC as an associate professor at the Medical University of South Carolina. He continued his advocacy of AHEC for many years, even when he moved to Virginia Beach, VA in 1980. At Eastern Virginia Medical School, he was a professor in the Department of Family Medicine as well as the Project Director for AHEC. He died February 1, 2011 (age 81).

Next, I elicited the help of others outside the government, starting with my good friend, the Reverend John Walker, the first African American Bishop of the Episcopal Diocese of Washington, D.C. He also presided as the Dean of the Washington National Cathedral. Bishop Walker contacted Maryland Republican Senator Charles "Mac" Mathias, an Episcopalian, to see if he could intercede on my behalf. Senator Mathias arranged for a meeting with me at his office, and I explained my situation.

"I'm willing to investigate," he said. "But if I do, you know the system will put a check mark on your file indicating you are a problem."

"They already have two or three checks against me for my blackness," I responded. "That's nothing new to me." I left feeling confident of his support. It was, however, the last time I heard from the Senator. He never got back to me or Bishop Walker.

## CONGRESSIONAL AND OTHER SUPPORT

I then decided to contact the Congressional Black Caucus. It had been recently established in 1971, "committed to using the full Constitutional power, statutory authority, and financial resources of the federal government to ensure that African Americans and other marginalized communities in the United States have the opportunity to achieve the American Dream."

I started initially through a friend, Shirley Downs, whom I had met when I was employed at OEO developing Neighborhood Health Centers. A young white woman, she was administrative assistant to Democratic Congresswoman Shirley Chisholm of New York, who, in 1968, was the first Black woman elected to the U.S. Congress and, in 1972, the first to run for president of the United States. She was one of the founders of the Congressional Black Caucus.

Shirley Downs and I often had lunch together, and I explained my situation. I pressured her several times, hoping to get the congresswoman to take up my cause.

"Mrs. Chisholm doesn't have time," she exclaimed. "I've talked to her frequently about you. She's fighting for her survival and respect after the beating she took during the presidential primary."

I pleaded again. "Okay, I'll ask Mrs. Chisholm to phone you directly," she said. When I arrived back at my office, I was not there more than 10 minutes when the phone rang. To my surprise, it was Congresswoman Chisholm. She indicated that she knew about my problems.

"I'd like to help," she said, "but I'm overloaded and I'm having similar racial issues myself on the Hill." She suggested that I seek assistance from another member of the Congressional Black Caucus. I was dismayed but I understood her problem and hence did not push further for her help.

Later that day, I phoned another friend, a Miss Green, whom I had met in Oakland, California, while on a trip working to develop OEO Neighborhood Health Centers. She was a constituent of Congresswoman Yvonne Brathwaite Burke of California, who was also a member of the Black Caucus. Ms. Green immediately phoned the congresswoman and told her my situation.

The next day, I received a call from the congresswoman's administrative assistant, Frank Cowan, who was very knowledgeable about how the "system" works. I gave him more information about my situation, and he invited me to meet at his office that Saturday, which I did. To my surprise, he had a memo written by Congresswoman Braithwaite Burke and Congressman Louis Stokes of Ohio to the members of the Black Caucus. They requested their intervention and signatures on a letter to Secretary of Health, Education, and Welfare Joseph Califano, Jr.

The letter noted, among other things, that I had received a satisfactory performance rating from my departing supervisor, quoting in part:

"Mr. Smith is undoubtedly one of the hardest working and dedicated employees in the Bureau of Health Manpower. In his role as National AHEC Coordinator, he has worked tirelessly with minimal staff support to carry out the purposes of the program."

She described my situation and the adverse action I faced, further noting:

"Management has not identified any one issue of action that Mr. Smith took or failed to take that adversely affected the AHEC program or was not made in the best interests of the Nation. The circumstance surrounding this apparently systematic effort first to build a record against and then to replace Mr. Smith raises a very strong inference of institutional racism within the Public Health Service.

"...There are a pathetically small number of Blacks holding significant positions of executive responsibility or authority for decision making within the Public Health Service or the Bureau of Health Manpower.

"In summary, Mr. Smith's case represents the classic situation of allowing Blacks to move up to a certain level in the system and then denies them true top management positions which represent power and authority."[50]

Frank invited me to "walk the halls" with him the following week. I did not know what he meant by walking the halls, but I agreed. So, several days later, Frank and I walked through the House of Representatives from office to office, gathering signatures of members of the Black Caucus on the letter to Secretary Califano. The letter said they "consider the case against Mr. Smith to be without merit and request your personal intervention on his behalf."

The letter also urged a halt to the adverse action; personal recognition, including the promotion recommended in 1973; and that "the AHEC office be given the staff, administrative support and upgrading recognition that it obviously merits." It was signed by 14 Members of the House of Representatives.[51]

## More Support and Letters

Senator Edward William Brooke of Massachusetts, the first Black Senator since Reconstruction, wrote a telegram to Secretary Califano stating that he was "deeply disturbed at the official actions being taken to demote Mr. Daniel R. Smith," adding that "Mr. Smith has been a dedicated manager of a growing, important program despite the fact that he has been given few, if any, professionals to assist him in the performance of his job. I also am concerned about Mr. Smith's status because of the implications of the actions against him for other minority professionals within the Public Health Service of HEW."[52] Senator Edward (Ted) Kennedy from Massachusetts joined in the appeal with a similar letter.

A host of professional consultants, project directors, and others who had worked with me in the past on the AHEC Program also sent letters that were very supportive of me.[53] I have retained all the letters because of what they mean to me, but also because I think they have historic significance.

For example, Dr. Marilyn Gravink, Deputy Commissioner, Department of Mental Retardation for the State of Connecticut, who served on the original review panel for the first AHEC programs and later the consultants panel, wrote: "I know that much of the time that Mr. Smith has been directing the program he was without staff assistance, including full-time office staff. It would seem that whatever respect and success has been demonstrated by AHEC must be directly related to Mr. Smith's knowledge of the program and ability to administer it."[54]

Dr. Donald R. Korst, Professor of Medicine, University of Wisconsin, wrote: "I would find it very difficult to understand anything that would reflect in a negative sense on the performance and dedication of this individual. He has stuck with a new federal program under difficult circumstances as it has grown to significant status. He should be recognized for his efforts over the past six years with the AHEC program."[55]

Around the same time, I filed a discrimination complaint with the Equal Employment Opportunity (EEO) Commission against Drs. John Mather, Robert Graham, and Graham's supervisor, Dr. Daniel Whiteside, DDS, associate director of the Bureau of Health Manpower Education, who became part of the discussion. It is important to remember that the problems I faced came at a time in the early to mid-1970s when the racial tensions of the 1960s were still not resolved. I had many examples of how I had been mistreated due to racial discrimination. Indeed, no program chief who was white (and the others all were white) was unable to get the staff and supplies they needed to run their programs.

Much to my regret now, I dropped the EEO complaint after the adverse action case was completed. I was simply exhausted and not ready for another battle with the system, which would have required even more time away from my neglected family.

## ANOTHER MOVE

Meanwhile, the AHEC program had been moved from the Office of Special Programs to the Division of Medicine, also in the Bureau of Health Manpower Education -- which was a downgrade. As one can imagine, I was more than frustrated. It was at this point that Dr. Robert (Bob)

Knouss, another member of the Public Health Service Commissioned Corps, became my immediate supervisor as the head of the Division of Medicine. A "boy wonder," he had been first in his class at the University of Pennsylvania Medical School. He was what I called "a good company man," meaning he did what the Public Health Service wanted him to do.

During the turmoil of my adverse action case, Dr. Knouss came into my office one day and acted as if he did not know anything about what I was going through.

"The AHEC program is doing fine," he said, "but I'm afraid that your responsibility to run the program while dealing with the adverse action will give you an ulcer."

"No, no, no, Bob, you don't understand. I DON'T GET UL-CERS, I GIVE THEM," I responded. "You must make a decision, to be neutral in this situation or to support my position." He was startled and quickly left my office. Knouss shortly thereafter accepted a staff position with the U.S. Senate.

Subsequently, I got a new supervisor, George R. Halter, Ed.D, Chief, Professional Education and Development Branch, Division of Medicine. We got along well. Indeed, much later, in response to a request from Van R. Olsen, a friend of mine who was considering me for a position in another outside organization, Dr. Halter had only good things to say about me.

"I would expect and predict that Mr. Smith would be a valuable asset to your Association," he concluded. "As to whether or not I would rehire Mr. Smith again, the answer is categorically yes."[56]

## ENTER THE ATTORNEYS

Facing the adverse action initiated by Bob Graham, I knew that I needed legal help, which I could not afford. About the same time, my wife Sandy and I had hosted a neighborhood social at our home. Fortunately, among my neighbors in Bethesda were several lawyers. This gave me the opportunity to discuss my plight with one of our guests, James (Jim) Robertson, senior partner in the DC-based international law firm of Wilmer, Cutler & Pickering (now known as Wilmer Hale).†

*Attorney James Robertson.*

Jim Robertson had previously worked in the south as Director of the Lawyers' Committee for Civil Rights Under Law in Jackson, Mississippi, so he understood my plight. He was able to get his firm to take up my cause on a pro-bono basis. In addition, attorney William (Bill) Richardson had recently joined Wilmer, Cutler & Pickering, and he worked with Robertson on this case.

Robertson and Richardson soon met with Henry Foley, Ph.D., Administrator of the Health Resources Administration, to discuss the situation. Dr. Foley, as head of the agency, oversaw both the Bureau of Health Manpower Education and Division of Medicine. My lawyers learned that federal regulations required the government to have a hearing

---

† James Robertson remained a partner at Wilmer, Cutler, & Pickering until 1994, when he was appointed by President Clinton as Senior Judge of the United States District Court for the District of Columbia. He served until December 31, 2008 and died September 7, 2019 (age 81). William R. Richardson became a partner of Wilmer Cutler Pickering Hale and Dorr LLP in 2004. He is an expert in Federal communications law.

examiner handle the adverse action case and make findings, conclusions, and recommendations. It would be conducted like a civil court suit. Dr. Foley would be the official who would make the final decision on my case after the hearing.

*Attorney William Richardson with Dan, 2006.*
*Photo by David Hamilton.*

In addition to having attorneys, I received support from all the AHEC project participants and my AHEC Advisory Council, which I had set up in 1972 as consultants for the AHEC Program. As part of my strategy, I also contacted my associates in the government bureaucracy to keep me up to date on what they heard about my situation. Because of this, I learned that the system had pre-selected the man who would be the hearing examiner and that the decision was a *fait accompli*, although the government would go through the motions.

A three-day hearing was held on March 29-31, 1978,[57] presided over by Joseph Doneghy, a Black man who was the government's hand-picked hearing examiner. Timothy White, a government attorney, represented the agency. My attorneys, James Robertson and William Richardson, were aided by Dr. Dolph Hatfield, a brilliant molecular scientist at

NIH and a friend of mine from Bethesda, who was serving as my EEO counselor.[‡] Dr. Hatfield had obtained, and submitted, numerous letters of support from high-level physicians and medical educators who had worked directly with me from the beginning of the AHEC program. My wife Sandy attended along with her mother, Amy Hawkins, and Clarence Parks, the husband of my deceased younger sister Margaret.

The first two days involved testimony of government witnesses. It began with attorney White calling on Dr. Graham and Dr. Mather. They repeated their complaints about me, which were, for the most part, as my attorneys later described them, petty: my typos in draft letters; unwritten memos; tardiness at meetings; a "pert chart" of time and staffing needs that I prepared at Dr. Mather's request, which they did not approve of, etc. It was both tedious and grueling. Although there was some recognition of the complex nature of the AHEC program, they did not acknowledge my major achievements in setting it up and directing it for the previous five years.

## Government Witnesses Defend Me

The first bright spot was the testimony of Joanne Van Vechten, my secretary from February 1977 to January 1978. Joanne stressed our extremely limited support staff, including some teenagers in a work-study program who did not serve continuously. She described her complex responsibilities – taking dictation and typing reports, congressional letters, filing, handling tickler systems, date and calendar keeping. She noted that this was during

---

[†] Dolph Hatfield, PhD, spent his entire career at NIH and became Chief, Molecular Biology Section of the National Cancer Institute. He published almost 300 scientific articles and numerous non-scientific works. He also holds 71 medals from the Senior Olympics and a black belt in Tae Kwon Do. His adventures have included spelunking and skydiving; Formula 2000 auto racing and off-road racing. He celebrated his 80th birthday in 2017 by leaping off the Macau Tower in China, the world's tallest bungee jump.

the contract-renewal process, a period of high workload at the AHEC office. At the same time, regulations were being drafted to implement the new legislation.

"It was a crunch period, "she said. "Everything kept on piling up." My attorney, Richardson, asked her if my work weeks at AHEC were normal or excessive.

"Excessive," she answered, "…oftentimes we were there until 6:00, and then on weekends. In the evenings I would stay over, and he would, of course, be there. Other times, there would be work in the morning that he would bring in from the weekend…work that he had been doing at home."

When asked how her workload compared to others in the Bureau, she said she kept longer hours.

"How do you know that?" Richardson asked.

"Because it got to the point where my husband had to pick me up from work because I could never get home. I could never get out of the office or leave because I felt as though I should stay there and complete the heavy workload that we had."

Asked about my workload, she agreed that I was "not working a normal work week" and devoted more time to my job than was required to make up a 40-hour work week.

More testimony was given by David Rost, chief of the Contract Operations Branch of the Health Resources Administration, who, among other things, testified that he had agreed to my recommendation about not accelerating the due date for the 11 existing AHEC projects to submit their reports for projects during 1977. It was a very technical matter, but important because this was during the time that the program was being recentralized back to my office. The regional offices had corroborated my position on the due date and, as a result, Rost had changed his position, which he acknowledged at the hearing.

My attorney also called Marcy Gross, the program officer who served as my top assistant. She worked only part-time, three days a week. Marcy verified everything I had said about our huge and complex workload and the lack of staff support. She noted that, given the fluctuations in our work, a pert chart such as the one Dr. Mather requested would be a waste of time.

"We have more to do than we have staff to do it, which doesn't take a chart to show." She explained how the Bureau's priorities kept changing. For example, during her AHEC activities, she was required to work for the Director of the Division of Medicine on other matters, which "have been imposed on us that interfere with the [AHEC] projected schedule."

Marcy also described issues related to the funding of the AHEC projects. There were many intense negotiations. She confirmed that the Senate Appropriations Committee had increased the funding "from $14 million to $16 million, as Mr. Smith had originally recommended."

*Others to the Rescue*

On the third day of the hearing, several representatives from AHEC programs around the country testified. They consistently spoke to the fact that my office was hardworking and capable, but very understaffed. Some examples:

*Edith D. Leyasmeyer, PhD, Director of the AHEC program in Minnesota.* When asked if she believed "Dan Smith has been operating with an adequate staff to handle his responsibilities," she replied: "Under no circumstances could I agree with that statement. From telephone conversations, from attempting to make contact to people in the Bureau, there has never been enough people, whether secretarial or professional staff, to be available."

*Carlton Paul Menge, PhD, University of New Hampshire.*[§] Dr. Menge served as a consultant to AHEC in several capacities, from participating on the team reviewing 25 AHEC proposals to advising on the design of urban AHECs that I had championed and helping with workshops we held in Cleveland, Cherry Hill, and Los Angeles. "Mr. Smith has called me nights for consultation, in New Hampshire, and I have observed him working weekends." Asked how he knew about my working weekends, he responded, "Because I was there on weekends, and he made sure I was working there myself. Frequently we had night sessions – and on Saturdays and Sundays."

Some of the most powerful testimony came from *Dr. Paul Cornely, MD, Professor Emeritus at Howard University.* A medical doctor, he also had a doctorate in public health.[**] Dr. Cornely and I had worked at OEO on the Neighborhood Health Centers program, which he described as "one of the important innovations in this country in terms of health-care delivery."

When I went to NIH, I had brought Dr. Cornely in as a consultant to the AHEC program. He testified at my hearing that, as a non-physician heading a new medical program, I recognized that I needed the help of physicians, economists, and health educators and that I had put together a group of consultants to provide me with advice. He described the importance and magnitude of the program and my work.

"I was amazed," he said, "that here was a man doing this kind of work with half of a secretary who was not a very adequate secretary, and with a part-time associate, trying to run a $90-million business...we

[§] Dr. Carlton Menge, PhD, a graduate of Springfield College Mass, and the University of Chicago, was a professor of educational psychology at the University of New Hampshire, retiring in 1990. In addition to serving as a consultant to AHEC, he was a consultant to the anti-poverty program I directed in Alabama in the 1960s. He died February 16, 2010 (age 92).
[**] Dr. Paul Cornely was the first African American to earn a doctoral degree in public health, at the University of Michigan. He was elected President of the American Public Health Association in 1970. He died February 9, 2002 (age 95).

brought this to the attention of Dr. Mather, who became his supervisor...
and told Dr. Mather in order for Dan Smith to do a job that he needed
the personnel to do it...Yet what did we get? We got a lot of criticism, we
got a lot of statements about his inadequacies, inefficiencies, and so forth,
and I firmly believe at the bottom of all this is the racism that existed in
the [Department of] Health, Education and Welfare.

"The Civil Rights Commission actually called the Health, Education and Welfare the most racist agency in the government, and I believe
that at the bottom of all this is this kind of approach: If Dan Smith were
a white person he would not be subjected to this kind of humiliation."

Richardson concluded by asking Dr. Cornely if "in the course of your
experience dealing with other federal programs, have you had occasion to note
what the GS rating is of the people who are serving with program responsibilities like Dan Smith's? Do you concern yourself with matters like that?"

"I don't concern myself with matters like the one you mentioned, but
I have had some ideas to the kinds of levels that individuals of Dan's position
and responsibility carry, and they carry anywhere from 15, 16, 17." When asked
if he knew what my GS level was (14), Dr. Cornely said, "I really don't know."

Dr. Cornely's testimony was reinforced by Dr. Harold B. Haley,
Associate Dean and Professor of Surgery, University of Virginia, and Director of the Remote Site Clinical Education Center. He was first asked if
he had come to the hearing at his own expense.

"Yes," he replied. "Sadly. But intensely." Dr. Haley explained that
he was involved with AHEC from its beginnings in 1972, and he described the team of consultants that I had put together.

"We had a very wide range of backgrounds and personalities, and
it was a very open group. We fought and we argued, and we went off in
corners with each other. At one time Dan set up subteams so that we

wouldn't all have to come to Washington. We did a lot of these things, but when it was all over, Dan had put it together and synthesized what we said and [took] our conflicting viewpoints [to] establish the policy--and then [went] through and did an excellent job of getting consensus out of these differing people."

Dr. Haley noted that in 1972, he had seen my tiny first office, which he described as "miserable," and then the one in Building 31, and that "when I called this time, he answered the phone because he didn't have any help." Then the office was moved again, "finally out to Hyattsville, and every time I go to the office, at most there has been a full-time secretary, sometimes not that," he said.

"I have never seen a time when Dan has been left in a stable situation, where his office has been in the same place, where he has had consistency of help, and had the opportunity of carrying out things the way he would want to do it. I think that is important, but I think it is the second importance. The first importance is that the Federal AHEC Program is a successful program. It is a good program. It is effective."

Dr. Haley emphasized that he was an expert on medical education and had done extensive evaluations of both AHEC and non-AHEC programs, with many on-site visits. He wrote a professional paper and gave a presentation on AHEC requested by the Association of American Medical Colleges at their national convention. From that background, he was willing to come out and state his opinion that the federal AHEC program had been well run and was a good program.

"I don't think things like that happen by accident," he testified. "Somewhere there was good leadership, and there is only one identified leader, and when I see the combination of what has been accomplished in the programs and the lack of resources to do it, I think we are very fortunate that we have the quality of work that we have done."

*Summations*

The summary statements by the Bureau's attorney, Timothy White, and my attorney, James Robertson, could not have been more different. White simply reiterated the accusations that my supervisor Bob Graham and former supervisor John Mather had made – five bureaucratic issues that were inconsequential to the success of the AHEC program.

In contrast, Robertson methodically rebutted the agency testimony on every point and stressed that none rose to the level of requiring a demotion from a grade GS-14 to a grade GS-12.

"This is deadly serious business," he said. He concluded by highlighting the testimony of the AHEC leaders, medical doctors, and educators who had praised my job performance. They spoke "on the level at which one would hope that his supervisors would evaluate him," he said.

"These are senior established professionals. They have shown in considerable detail that the AHEC program is not a mechanical bureaucratic program in which the manager's job is to constantly keep his supervisors satisfied with the paper flow. It is an innovative, intellectual program of major concern to the public at large."

Robertson stressed the youth and inexperience of Dr. Graham and Dr. Mather "who are concerned about covering their own backsides, who are concerned about ripples that make their life a bit more difficult for them, and who primarily want someone in that job who will keep feeding the paperwork up to them, who will keep giving them cost-accounting matrices, and keep giving them their management information systems and ignoring the really fundamental job that Dan Smith is doing, not at a Grade 14 level, Mr. Doneghy, but at a 15 or 16 or 17 level, being paid as a 14."

## HOW IT ENDED

Not unexpectedly, Doneghy, the hearing examiner, ruled against me and recommended that the adverse action should be effected. His written report, dated July 11, 1978, was a joke. He just parroted the bureaucratic claims of Mather and Graham, declaring in each case that the "preponderance of the evidence" (the major test to render a decision under the regulations) sustained the cited specifications. He never mentioned the statements of Graham and Mather that were challenged by my attorneys. Nor did he acknowledge the laudatory testimony of the expert outside professionals – all of whom had direct knowledge of the AHEC program spanning many years and were top professionals in their field – who spoke so eloquently and, I thought, persuasively on my behalf.

Before my lawyers received the hearing examiner's decision, Dr. Foley called me to his office. He had received Doneghy's letter, and he read the findings from the report. Dr. Foley told me what the hearing examiner's recommendation had been – to demote me.

To put it mildly, **I LOST IT**! I remember that I was so angry, I really did not know where I was. I literally could not see. I was very emotional. Anything could have happened!

"Don't leave your seat," Dr. Foley said. He then went into his outer office complex, shut his office door with me alone inside, and told the staff to leave right away. All the secretaries and others of his immediate staff left for home. Dr. Foley returned. He was a mild-mannered man, whom I considered to be very fair-minded. He calmed me down.

"Take the remainder of the day off and go home and rest," he said. Which I did.

Once home, I quickly called my attorneys to inform them of the situation. They had just received their copy of the hearing examiner's letter and decision. Attorney Robertson wrote to Dr. Foley on July 14 and requested a meeting with him. He noted that it was Dr. Foley's duty, as the deciding official, to review the hearing examiner's report "and to determine whether or not to give effect to the Notice of Proposal to Demote Mr. Smith."

He wrote that they had not had the opportunity to study Doneghy's report in detail, but upon a very quick initial reading, "we must say that we are shocked, not only by Mr. Doneghy's conclusions, but by obvious errors of fact, procedure and logic that appear even on a first reading." He pointed out to Dr. Foley the omissions in the decision and exhibits and other issues that Doneghy should have considered before he ruled.[58]

A month later, on August 24, 1978, my attorneys wrote a 20-page letter to Dr. Foley detailing their extensive review of the hearing examiner's decision.

"Our reading of the decision led us to conclude that Mr. Doneghy's decision not only contained errors of judgment but also evidenced a failure to consider substantial parts of the record compiled in the three-day hearing required in this case…

"Our comments are extensive. This is because Mr. Doneghy's decision is, quite frankly, an unusual document – not so much for what it says as for what it simply dismisses without mention. Despite its frequent observations that each charge at each specification is 'sustained by a preponderance of the evidence,' the decision affords absolutely no clue for determining why Mr. Doneghy has reached conclusions so critical to Mr. Smith's future as the head of the AHEC program."

Then they methodically reviewed and debunked virtually every allegation that had been made against me. In conclusion, they emphasized that their letter "is not an ideal vehicle for addressing, in a complete fashion, all the flaws and omissions in Mr. Doneghy's report. What we have intended to do here is simply to point out that the report simply fails to deal with virtually any of the critical issues adduced at the hearing in this case; with all due respect, such a report has rendered the opportunity for a hearing virtually meaningless. Testimony has little value if it is never considered," they stated.

"Without virtually any explanation, Mr. Doneghy credited the uncorroborated assertions of a single individual who sought to demote Mr. Smith after having supervised him, on a part-time basis, for some two months. Contrasted with these assertions is the testimony of Mr. Smith's coworkers, his AHEC project directors, and the AHEC consultants, as well as a study by neutral investigators from the House [of Representatives] Subcommittee staff.

"That Mr. Doneghy has dismissed the combined weight of these views is itself enough to suggest error, since it is the agency which must supply the preponderance of proof. That he has done so with virtually no explanation simply makes a mockery of the hearing process. We submit that Mr. Doneghy's report is entitled to no weight in your decision concerning Mr. Smith's abilities as AHEC national coordinator, and that Dr. Graham's notice should be withdrawn or overruled." [59]

Subsequently, on September 1, my attorneys met with Dr. Foley and followed with another letter two weeks later, rebutting more claims made against me by Dr. Graham and the Bureau's attorney, Timothy White. They closed by stressing that the "Bureau's administrative difficulties, if any, are a matter quite distinct from the specific charges against Dan Smith. These charges are, and should be, insufficient to deprive a devoted civil servant of his opportunity to continue his supervision of a program that under his direction has made a major contribution toward solving distributional problems of the health professions in this country."[60]

## Decision Rendered

To his credit, Dr. Foley took home all the documents - the transcripts, letters, and exhibits – and studied them. Shortly thereafter, he called me to his office. I did not know what to expect. Although confident that I would be exonerated, I was not sure what my mind would let me do.

"Following a careful review," he said, "I do not agree with the examiner's position. I am going to reverse his recommendation to demote you." To say that I was relieved would be a gross understatement of my feelings, but my gut had indicated that he would support the truth. Leaving me alone in my hyperventilated state in his office that afternoon in July and sending his staff home without calling the police showed him to be a fair-minded and honorable man.

Dr. Foley further told me that he was going to restore me as head of AHEC and as the National AHEC Program Coordinator. He would also increase my grade to GS-15 as my previous supervisor, Dr. Fenderson, had twice recommended several years earlier. Then, on October 4, 1978, nearly a year after the initiation of the adverse action against me, Administrator Foley officially made his decision in a memorandum entitled "Cancellation of Proposed Adverse Action."

"I have now reviewed with considerable care and thought the verbatim transcript of the hearing and the Report of Findings, Conclusions, and Recommendations of July 11 issued by Mr. Joseph W Doneghy, the employee appeals examiner. Mr. Doneghy's recommendation is that 'the proposed demotion be effected.' However, I disagree with his findings and recommendations."

Dr. Foley stressed that the cancellation of the Notice to Demote "carries with it the corollary that your performance is in fact satisfactory. You will be receiving in the near future a performance evaluation form completed by Dr. George Halter, Ph.D., your immediate supervisor over the past months, and approved by Robert Knouss, M.D. Your within-grade step increase will be signed by your supervisor and will become effective in January 1979. I look forward to receiving a copy of your satisfactory performance evaluation and to your continued service in the programmatic mission of the agency."[61]

Sometime later, I was given a victory celebration in a downtown hotel with Dr. Foley and my staff, project directors, consultants, attorneys, family, and many others who had supported me. It was truly joyful.

## EPILOGUE TO AHEC

I loved my work on AHEC, but I found the whole ordeal of the adverse action extremely exhausting. I continued diligently to direct the AHEC program for almost another three years. I obtained additional staff; my supervisor Dr. George Halter and I worked well together; and the AHEC projects flourished. Although I was not burned out, I knew I needed to prepare myself for another adventure. Hence, I began discussions with Georgetown University Medical School for the possibility of receiving an IPA (Intergovernmental Personnel Act) position. A type of sabbatical, it would provide me with new opportunities in the medical field while allowing me to retain my federal government status.

I left AHEC at the end of January 1981. Once again, I was feted with an event, this time at the annual AHEC Directors Meeting held at

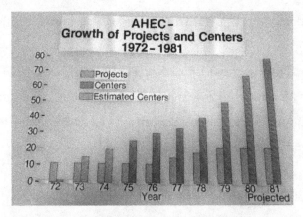

*Chart shows the growth of AHEC under Dan's leadership from 1972 to 1981.*

the Marriott Hotel in Arlington, Virginia. It was truly bittersweet, but I was happy knowing what AHEC had accomplished.

Now, after nearly 50 years since I started the program, AHEC remains in existence in a modified form with the same name in nearly every state. It is administered by the federal Health Resources and Services Administration, an agency of the U.S. Department of Health and Human Services. Despite attempts by the Trump Administration to gut the program, Congress has continued to provide bi-partisan, bi-cameral support for it. Funding in Fiscal Year 2020 was $41.3 million, an increase of $2 million from the year before; in 2021, it was raised again to $43.3. million.

In 1988, the nonprofit, non-federal National AHEC Organization (NAO) was incorporated to support the national network of AHEC and Health Education Training Centers programs. According to NAO, today there are 46 AHEC programs with more than 261 centers that operate in almost every state and the District of Columbia. Approximately 120 medical schools and 600 nursing and allied health schools work collaboratively with AHECs to improve health for underserved and under-represented populations. The national AHEC network consists of more than 300 AHEC program offices and centers, serving over 85 percent of the counties in the United States.

In short, I won both the battle and the war!

## Original Support

I do not want to end this chapter without showing a few of the original Letters, telegram and a memo that aided my cause. There were many, many more.

IC ON APPROPRIATIONS
SUBCOMMITTEES
STATE, JUSTICE, COMMERCE,
JUDICIARY AND RELATED AGENCIES
DISTRICT OF COLUMBIA
FOREIGN OPERATIONS

PLEASE RESPOND TO
OFFICE CHECKED
☐ WASHINGTON
☐ CALIFORNIA

Congress of the United States
House of Representatives
Washington, D.C. 20515

December 1, 1977

ADMINISTRATIVE ASSISTANT

DISTRICT OFFICES
INGLEWOOD CITY HALL
1 MANCHESTER BOULEVARD
INGLEWOOD, CALIFORNIA 90301
(213) 674-5474

9842 CULVER BOULEVARD
CULVER CITY, CALIFORNIA 90230
(213) 838-7201

MARGUENITE J. ARCHIE
DISTRICT ADMINISTRATIVE ASSISTANT

MEMORANDUM

TO: Members of the Congressional
    Black Caucus

FR: Yvonne Brathwaite Burke
    Louis Stokes

RE: Adverse Action Against HEW Employee

We are taking this opportunity to call your attention to
the case of Daniel R. Smith, National Coordinator of the Area
Health Education Center (AHEC) at DHEW and to request your support and signature to a letter (copy attached) we wish to send
to Secretary Califano requesting his intervention in the case.

Mr. Smith's superiors in the Public Health Service have
proposed to demote him from his current Civil Service rating
of G.S.14 (Chief of the AHEC Staff and National AHEC Coordinator
to a new rating of G.S.12 (AHEC Program Analyst), and in the pro
cess to strip him of responsibility for the direct management
of an important National Public Health Service program. This
situation raises serious DHEW racial discrimination questions
and may represent only the tip of an iceberg.

For the past five years (1972 to the present), Mr. Smith,
who is Black, has been National Coordinator of the Bureau of
Health Manpower's Area Health Education Center (AHEC) program.
The program operates within the Health Resources Administration,
Public Health Service, DHEW. The AHEC program is essentially a
contact program, the purpose of which is to attract and train
qualified health professionals (with an emphasis on the training
of primary care physicians) to practice in underserved areas of
the country.

Mr. Smith came to DHEW to start the AHEC program from OEO,
where he worked in the Office of Health Affairs and developed
neighborhood health centers. He is 45 years old and has a
Bachelor of Science Degree from Springfield College, Massachuset
(he is currently a member of the Board of Trustees at Springfie
He has done graduate work at the University of Hartford and
Tuskegee Institute.

Your immediate attention to correct this situation is
urgently requested.

Sincerely,

285

| VC. | PD. OR COLL | CASH NO. | CHARGE TO THE ACCOUNT OF | THIS MESSAGE WILL BE SENT AS A TELEGRAM UNLESS IT IS OTHERWISE INDICATED. | PRESS | | OVER NIGHT TELEGRAM |
|---|---|---|---|---|---|---|---|
| | | | GWA 038 185 | | DPR | NPR | |

ge. subject to the Telegraph Company's conditions, rules and regulations, which are on file with regulatory authorities.

orable Joseph A. Califano
retary
artment of Health, Education
d Welfare
Independence Avenue, S.W.
hington, D.C.  20201

r Mr. Secretary:

I am deeply disturbed at the offical actions being taken
demote Mr. Daniel R. Smith, Chief and National Coordinator of
Area Health Education Centers program and to downgrade the
gram itself.  My review of this matter shows that Mr. Smith
been a dedicated manager of a growing, important program
pite the fact that he has been given few, if any, professionals
assist him in the performance of his job.  I also am
cerned about Mr. Smith's status because of the implications
the actions against him for other minority professionals within
Public Health Service of HEW.

I urge that you immediately order a halt to all adverse
ions against Mr. Smith, including those related to
rganization and physical relocation of his office.  At the
e time I request a report from you within the next week
ating to future plans for the AHEC program, including staffing
ources needed, appropriate organizational placement of the
gram and your plans for assuring that Mr. Smith will be
ated fairly in the future by those in supervisory positions
ve him.

Your attention to this is appreciated.  Both the Labor-HEW
ropriations Subcommittee and I look forward to receiving
ir report.

Edward W. Brooke
Ranking Minority Member
Labor-HEW Appropriations Subcommittee
Senate Appropriations Committee
Washington, D.C.  20510

286

... UNA THWAITE BURKE
24th DISTRICT CALIFORNIA

COMMITTEE ON APPROPRIATIONS
SUBCOMMITTEES
STATE JUSTICE COMMERCE
THE JUDICIARY AND RELATED AGENCIES
DISTRICT OF COLUMBIA
FOREIGN OPERATIONS

PLEASE RESPOND TO
OFFICE CHECKED

☐ WASHINGTON
☐ CALIFORNIA

# Congress of the United States
## House of Representatives
### Washington, D.C. 20515

December 2, 1977

236 CANNON HOUSE OFFICE BUILDING
WASHINGTON, D.C. 20515
(202) 225-7064

FRANK COWAN
ADMINISTRATIVE ASSISTANT

DISTRICT OFFICES
INGLEWOOD CITY HALL
1 MANCHESTER BOULEVARD
INGLEWOOD, CALIFORNIA 90301
(213) 678-1424

8942 CULVER BOULEVARD
CULVER CITY, CALIFORNIA 92030
(213) 836-7301

MARGUERITE J. ARCHIE
DISTRICT ADMINISTRATIVE ASSISTANT

The Honorable Joseph A. Califano, Jr.
Department of Health, Education and
  Welfare
330 Independence Avenue. S.W.
Washington, D.C. 20201

Dear Mr. Secretary:

We Wish to bring to your attention the adverse personnel
actions recently taken by your agency against one of the
Department of Health, Education and Welfare's most valuable and experienced program administrators, Mr. Daniel
R. Smith.

We are concerned about Mr. Smith's situation both because
of its implications for the welfare and status of other
minority professions within the Department and because
we feel these actions are jeopardizing the future of an
innovative and important health manpower initiative.

During the last five (5) years, Mr. Smith has been the
Chief and National Coordinator for the Health Resources
Administration's Area Health Education Centers Program.
In the five (5) years that he has provided leadership and
direction for the program, it has grown from a small research and developmental effort to one of the agencies
most promising initiatives fully supported by Congress and
now provided with specific legislative authority (P.L.
94-484, Sections 781 and 802).  During this period, Mr.
Smith has had significantly little administrative support,
at times forced to operate without even a secretary.

Following more than a year of unrelenting harrassment and
systematic attempts at intimidation, his supervisors now
have taken steps to demote him from a G.S. 14 to a G.S. 12.
At the same time, it is proposed to subject him to the further
humilitation of working as a program analyst in the office

7

THE SECRETARY OF HEALTH, EDUCATION, AND WELFARE
WASHINGTON, D.C. 20201

JAN 24 1978

The Honorable Yvonne Burke
House of Representatives
Washington, D.C.    20515

Dear Mrs. Burke:

Thank you for bringing the situation involving Daniel R.
Smith and the Area Health Education Center Program to my
attention.

First, let me assure you that no attempt is being made to
downgrade the Area Health Education Center (AHEC) Program.
As you know, the AHEC Program is primarily designed to
provide decentralized education for health professionals.
Its new organizational placement within the Professional
Education and Development Branch of the Division of Medicine
will tie it more closely to the direct operating components
of the Bureau of Health Manpower in order to give it more
professional visibility.  We are also increasing the AHEC
staff by seven full-time positions in order to operate the
program more effectively.  All of these steps are designed to
provide the Program with as much administrative support as
possible.

With respect to the situation involving Daniel Smith, I can
assure you that I have been and will continue to monitor this
case to insure that Mr. Smith is fairly treated.  At the
present time, two actions are pending: in July, Mr. Smith
lodged an EEO complaint against his supervisors; in October,
Mr. Smith filed a statement contesting an adverse action
involving a notice of proposal for his demotion.  Currently,
the Administrator of the Health Resources Administration is
responsible for making a determination about this case. He
recently requested an independent hearing examiner to review
the case and make a recommendation for final action.  In
addition, I have asked my Assistant Secretary for Personnel,
Thomas McFee, to personally review the hearing examiner's
report before a final determination is made.  Mr. Smith's
grade will not be affected until these proceedings are
completed.

I appreciate your deep concern, especially about the implications of these proceedings for other minority professionals.
I, too, am aware of the hardships faced by minorities as they
try to move into more responsible positions, and I am firmly
committed to providing every opportunity for capable minority
men and women to reach the highest levels in the bureaucracy.
I believe, however, that the best course of action for me in
this case is to await the results of the hearing examiner's
report and the review by Mr. McFee. As a Civil Service
employee, Mr. Smith has the full protection of the Civil
Service System behind him, including his right to appeal any
final decision.

I realize this situation is difficult for all concerned, but
I trust this information has been helpful.

Sincerely,

Joseph A. Califano, Jr.

WILMER, CUTLER & PICKERING
1666 K STREET, N.W.
WASHINGTON, D.C. 20006

CABLE ADDRESS: WICRING WASH., D. C.
INTERNATIONAL TELEX: 440-239
TELEX: 89-2402
TELEPHONE 202 872-6000

EUROPEAN OFFICE
5 CHEAPSIDE
LONDON, EC2V 6AX, ENGLAND
TELEPHONE 01-236-2401
TELEX: 851 883242
CABLE ADDRESS: WICRING LONDON

July 14, 1978

Henry A. Foley, Ph.D.
Administrator
Health Resources Administration
Center Building - Room 10-37
3700 East-West Highway
Hyattsville, Maryland 20782

Re: Daniel R. Smith

Dear Dr. Foley:

We have today received the Report of Findings,
Conclusions and Recommendations submitted to you by Hearing
Examiner Joseph W. Doneghy in Mr. Smith's case. We understand that it is now your duty, as the deciding official,
to review that report and to determine whether or not to
give effect to the Notice of Proposal to Demote Mr. Smith.
We have not yet had the opportunity to study Mr. Doneghy's
Report in detail, but upon a very quick initial reading we
must say that we are shocked, not only by Mr. Doneghy's
conclusions, but by obvious errors of fact, procedure and
logic that appear even on a first reading. We request the
opportunity of a conference with you at the earliest
practicable date, and in any event prior to your determination. Of course, we do expect that opposing counsel would
be present for any such conference, if he wishes to be.
Kindly confirm to me at the earliest possible time, by letter
or telephone, that we will indeed have the opportunity for
such a conference.

Sincerely yours,

James Robertson

cc: Timothy M. White
    Daniel R. Smith

WILMER, CUTLER & PICKERING
1666 K STREET, N.W.
WASHINGTON, D. C. 20006
———
CABLE ADDRESS: WICRING WASH., D. C.
INTERNATIONAL TELEX: 440-239
TELEX: 89-2402
TELEPHONE 202 872-6000
———
EUROPEAN OFFICE
5 CHEAPSIDE
LONDON, EC2V 6AA, ENGLAND
TELEPHONE 01-236-2401
TELEX: 851 883242
CABLE ADDRESS: WICRING LONDON

September 14, 1978

HAND DELIVERY

Henry A. Foley, Ph.D.
Administrator
Health Resources Administration
Center Building -- Room 10-37
3700 East-West Highway
Hyattsville, Maryland  20782

Re:  Daniel R. Smith

Dear Dr. Foley:

We appreciated your meeting with us on September 1.
We have given considerable thought to the questions about AHEC
funding that you raised in the meeting, and in this letter we
deal with that area in more detail than we did at the meeting.
We think your decision to go back to the actual evidence in the
transcript is a sound one -- necessary, indeed, because of the
Hearing Examiner's failure to provide analysis of any sort --
and for your convenience we have prepared and enclose a simple
index of the transcript, organized according to the six
specific allegations contained in the notice.*/

_____

*/        The six issues are listed in the index.  During the
hearing, we referred to them as five issues -- generally
combining the last two into one.

TO    : Daniel R. Smith                                      DATE: 10-4-78
        Health Manpower Education Officer, BHM

                                                              G

FROM  : Administrator

SUBJECT: Cancellation of Proposed Adverse Action

This memorandum serves to cancel the Notice of Proposal to Demote, issued
you on October 28, 1977, by Robert Graham, M.D.

As I pointed out to your representative, Mr. James Robertson, in my letter
to him of February 21, I found at that time that there was sufficient con-
flict in the information presented by the parties involved to warrent a
formal hearing.

I have now reviewed with considerable care and thought the verbatim transcript of the hearing and the Report of Findings, Conclusions, and Recommendations of July 11 issued by Mr. Joseph W. Doneghy, the Employee Appeals
Examiner.  Mr. Doneghy's recommendation is that "the proposed demotion be
effected."  However, I disagree with his findings and recommendations.

This cancellation of the Notice to Demote, mentioned above, carries with it
the corollary that your performance is in fact satisfactory.  You will be
receiving in the near future a performance evaluation form completed by
Dr. George Halter, Ph.D., your immediate supervisor over the past months, and
approved by Robert Knouss, M.D.  Your within-grade step increase will be
signed by your supervisor and will become effective in January 1979.

I look forward to receiving a copy of your satisfactory performance evaluation and to your continued service in the programmatic mission of the agency.

                            Henry A. Foley

                            Henry A. Foley, Ph.D.

cc:
James Robertson, Esq.
William R. Richardson, Jr., Esq.
Timothy White, Esq.
Director, BHM
Acting Deputy Administrator, HRA
Associate Administrator for
 Operations and Management, HRA
Director, OEEO, HRA
Assistant Secretary for Personnel
 Administration

## CHAPTER 16

# Experiencing More Life Changes

## GEORGETOWN MEDICAL SCHOOL

After leaving the AHEC program in 1981, my life took on several new professional and personal turns. It started with my three-year IPA assignment at the Georgetown University School of Medicine in Washington DC.* What a reprieve after the tension and turmoil I experienced with the AHEC program! Even the location and architecture were refreshingly different. Located high on a hill overlooking the Potomac River, the old Gothic and Georgian brick buildings of the university could not have been more different from the mostly bland, modern structures in which I worked for the federal government. It was a pleasure to drive to Georgetown every day and a joy to walk around the campus and along the streets of the historic community surrounding it.

The Georgetown doctors, administrators, and staff were incredibly supportive. I met and became good friends with many of them, including two Black professionals, Earnest (Ernie) Middleton, PhD, and Harvard grad Arthur Hoyte, MD. Dr. Middleton was mentoring Black medical students and Dr. Hoyte, as I recall, had a position with the chancellor and his administration. I shared an office and worked with a Georgetown consultant, Dr. Ted Howard, who was working on a special long-range project.

---

* Georgetown University School of Medicine opened its doors to students in May 1851 as a department of Georgetown College, precursor of Georgetown University. It was the second medical school established in Washington, DC, and the first Catholic medical school in the country.

I found my stay at Georgetown to be a welcoming, restful experience, especially with no direct program or staff responsibilities. I was able to teach, do research, and help design future hospital programs. I had time for some long lunches and interesting conversations with my colleagues. Plus, they have a great library, which I put to good use.

## END OF THE MARRIAGE

During the 1980s there was a huge "women's liberation" movement in our neighborhood, with which my wife Sandy got involved. I recall that she read the book, *Open Marriage*. Then, after 19 years of marriage, when the children were in their teens and right after the death of her father, she decided to leave the family, and did so. It came as quite a surprise to me because I thought we had a good marriage, indeed one of the better marriages among our friends. We went to counseling together, but she had made her decision some time before and didn't change it. I, on the other hand, did not try to dissuade her. I figured if that was what she wanted, I would not stand in her way.

So, on Valentine's Day of that year, a truck arrived to take her belongings to an apartment she had rented. We agreed to evenly divide the contents of our home. Her departure put an extraordinary strain on the family and on me, since I was left with the responsibility of securing funds for one child entering college and the other already in college. Sandy decided that she could not help supporting them in college because she needed her funds to attend law school. This caused a great hardship on me because we had planned on providing for the children's education with two salaries. Nevertheless, I assured April and Rob that I would do my best to make sure they finished college.

Legally, we had to stay apart for a year before filing for divorce. Meanwhile I had to get reestablished. The children chose to stay with me, and I couldn't afford to stay in our home with only one income. I worked through the dilemma under an enormous amount of stress. At the same time, I faced the loss of my beloved and faithful Airedale rescue dog, Rex. He was hit and killed by a bus while we were walking together. It was extremely hard on me, especially with all the other trying things that were going on in my life.

Despite all of this, I was very proud that both April and Rob were able to graduate from college and get advanced degrees.

## INTERNATIONAL PROGRAMS – SOUTH AFRICA

In 1984, I returned to my federal agency, Health Resources Services Administration, in its international programs' office in Hyattsville, Md. I was appointed director of Bilateral and Sub-Saharan African Programs, working with William (Bill) Gemma, PhD. It was a fascinating experience, interacting with foreign ministers of health about their medical needs and assisting in developing several Emergency Medical Services programs in Lebanon, Morocco, and Saudi Arabia. I worked extensively with several high-ranking officials, including Ambassadors and Ministers of Health, in a myriad of countries and provided guidance for health models in Angola, Zimbabwe, and the Seychelles, like those designed for the Republic of South Africa.

One major program that I recall was working with health officials in Saudi Arabia to develop a plan to provide Emergency Medical Services first aid to Muslim participants in the annual Hajj (pilgrimage) to Mecca. I cannot recall if the plans were ever implemented.

It took a circuitous route for me to reach South Africa. For several years, while I was Senior Warden at St. Luke's Episcopal Church in Bethesda, my family was seated in front of or behind Admiral John Poindexter, National Security Advisor for President Reagan, his wife Linda, and their family. We became social friends with them and several others who attended the church and regularly sat in adjoining pews, including our close friends Van and Myrna Olsen. Van Olsen, originally from North Dakota, served as chief of staff for Sen. Mark Andrews (R-ND).

I talked to John about the AHEC program that I had directed and my idea of developing a similar program to train primary medical doctors in South Africa. He took an interest in it. At that time, Blacks in the United States and South Africa were angry at President Reagan's unwillingness to oppose apartheid. I thought this program could be a politically safe way to do something positive to help South African Blacks.

John and I agreed to have a meeting in his West Wing office to plan for my upcoming trip to South Africa. The security at the White House was much looser at that time (pre-9/11). I walked to the gated entrance on Pennsylvania Avenue, was cleared by the uniformed guard, and proceeded into the White House.

A very disgruntled security officer escorted me to John's office. I recall that he sat in a chair with his back to the wall, between the President's Chief of Staff and John's office. I was surprised to find such an unhappy white employee in such a position at the White House. As he and I chatted, however, he unloaded to me his issues, including being overworked, receiving low wages for his responsibilities, working long hours, and having problems with his supervisors. He could have been in any office anywhere with his complaints!

When I entered John's office, he was engrossed with completing a report. His desk was piled with paperwork. I noted that his secretary was busy doing some form of typing. John gave me a friendly greeting, and we finally discussed the issues at hand, including plans for a sponsor for my trip to South Africa.

## Meeting Bishop Desmond Tutu

Earlier, I had become friends with Rev. John Thomas Walker, Suffragan Bishop and Dean of the Washington National Cathedral and then Bishop of the Washington Diocese. We met through our children – his son Carlie was the same age as my son Rob. The two boys attended the Saint Columba Church pre-school program in Washington, D.C. In addition, I had been recently elected Senior Warden at St. Luke's Episcopal Church in Bethesda, Md.

*Bishop John Walker, protesting apartheid at South African Embassy, Washington DC. The Archives of the Episcopal Church.*

Then, in December 1984, South African Anglican Bishop Desmond Tutu was awarded the Nobel Peace Prize for assisting the peace process between the South African National Congress and the Apartheid-led government. Sometime during the next year, Bishop Walker invited me to lunch with Bishop Tutu at Germaine's, a popular restaurant on Wisconsin Avenue in Georgetown, D.C. The three of us had a lengthy conversation regarding the racial injustice and other issues of the day. Bishop Tutu and I became friends.

When Bishop Tutu had his installation as the first Black Anglican Archbishop of South Africa in 1986, he and his wife Leah sent me a formal invitation. Because of my international work and the African health initiative, John Poindexter put me in contact with officials who aided in the financial expenses for my journey to South Africa. My sponsor and I had breakfast at the Four Seasons Hotel in Georgetown. He requested that I bring a travel budget for my trip, which should include travel days, lodging needs, air, and taxi costs, etc. Because I was trained as a federal official to keep the budget low, I spent considerable time negotiating with myself over the total cost of the planned 10-day trip.

For our breakfast meeting, we were seated at what appeared to be the sponsor's regular table. I recall he ordered a bowl of oatmeal, coffee, and toast. I ordered eggs, bacon, hot chocolate, and toast. He was interested in my relationship with John Poindexter, a former Admiral who had graduated first in his class at the Navy Academy. Then we talked about my trip to South Africa. I gave him the $12,000 trip budget that I had developed. He reached in his vest pocket, produced a check book, and wrote me a $12,000 check.

"I had budgeted $25,000 for this trip," he said, smiling while writing the check. He said I should submit a report on my return, which is the normal procedure.

I did not meet my sponsor again until several months later, after I returned from giving my report to John Poindexter's staff in the Old Executive Office Building next to the White House. I was waiting for the elevator and when the door opened, out stepped my sponsor. We chatted for a moment. He said that although he was retired, his former boss, William Joseph Casey, Director of the Central Intelligence Agency (CIA), had asked him to return and assist with some tasks.

## *Attending Bishop Tutu's Installation*

For Bishop Tutu's installation service as Archbishop, I flew into Johannesburg International Airport and was surprised to be met by Bishop Tutu himself and other officials. I was then driven to Cape Town with an entourage, and while I enjoyed the beautiful, verdant countryside, I was petrified at the speed of the drivers.

Bishop Tutu's installation was held on September 7, 1986, a day-long event of ceremonies, starting in the beautiful St. George's Cathedral with about 2000 Black and white religious leaders and invited guests. Many luminaries had come from throughout the world and the United States, including Coretta Scott King, national news correspondent Renee Poussaint, Mayor Coleman Young of Detroit, and several senators and congressmen.

The cathedral was magnificently decorated with flowers and religious symbols. The music was a mix of traditional Anglican songs and traditional African hymns. It was a solemn yet festive setting. In his sermon, Archbishop Tutu spoke about his commitment to nonviolence and opposition to apartheid, a system of racial segregation even more intense than Blacks in the United States had faced following Reconstruction after the Civil War.[†]

"It is important when talking about violence to note that the primary violence in this country is the violence of apartheid," he said. [62]

---

[†] Apartheid was an acute form of racial segregation established in 1948 by the National Party under F.W. De Klerk (1989-1994). It separated whites from Blacks in all systems of South Africa – jobs, education, health, living conditions and authority. The whites in power incarcerated Nelson Mandela on Robben Island for 27 years and killed countless numbers of Black South Africans during their reign under Prime Minister Hendrik Verwoerd (1958-1966).

The service moved in the afternoon to a large stadium in an area where many of the city's Blacks lived. About 10,000 people attended. Prayers were conducted in English and several African languages. A huge reception was held afterwards, resembling a big family reunion with those close to Bishop Tutu extolling his peaceful approach to problem solving in South Africa. Among others, I had an opportunity to meet and converse with the Mayor of Cape Town and several members of the African National Congress (ANC).

While in South Africa, I also stayed for a time with a Mrs. Corvilla. She was married to an Iranian and was classified as "coloured"[‡] under the brutal apartheid system of government. Mrs. Corvilla was the owner of a taxicab company business. In one of our conversations, she told me that her company had a contract with the South African government. It called for her in the evenings to cruise the streets in Cape Town collecting the dead, picking up derelicts and "others" from the streets, and delivering them to various hospitals and the coroner's office. She indicated that a representative of Dr. Christian Barnard (who developed the first human heart transplant) requested that she bring to the hospital derelicts who were still living but probably would soon die.

On several evenings I met with members of the African National Congress and members of their staff. We discussed the ANC's so-called South African Traitors (those Africans who cooperated with the South African Police). We talked at length about the tire necktie as a deterrent for Blacks working with the Police. It was the act of putting an old tire around the neck of a suspected apartheid collaborator, filling the tire with gasoline, and lighting the tire on fire. They accused Winnie Mandela of such atrocities.

---

[†] There were four racial classifications of people in South Africa: 'native', 'coloured', 'Asian' or 'white.'

*Recruited by the CIA*

Sometime after returning from my trip to South Africa, I was contacted by a CIA staffer, who asked me to meet with him for breakfast and select the location. Again, as a budget-conscientious "fed," I disappointed him by selecting the Hot Shoppe restaurant in Bethesda instead of the plush Four Seasons Hotel in Georgetown.

Over breakfast, he and I discussed the CIA's needs. They wanted me to infiltrate the African National Congress and spy on them for the Reagan Administration. I had a wife and two children and thought of Nelson Mandela's wife Winnie who was deeply involved in fighting the African apartheid system, one that I had marched against in Washington.

I did not accept the CIA's offer. In addition to possibly losing my life to espionage, I did not want to spy against the ANC since that would be repeating the historical syndrome of pitting Blacks against Blacks.

## SECOND TRIP TO SOUTH AFRICA

I subsequently developed a new entity called the Korean War Veterans Foundation and established a Board of Directors. I elicited the help of Stephen Winchell, a Republican fundraiser who raised about $50 million dollars for the Reagan presidential campaign. He and I had met at a Parents' Night event, where our sons attended the same private elementary school.

In 1987, Stephen and I, as Board members of the veterans foundation, journeyed back to South Africa to continue the quest for a modified Area Health Service and Education Program (AHSE). Our visits were coordinated by the African Forum, a South African government-sponsored organization responsible for guest visits to South Africa. We were escorted by two women, Julia LeRouch and another young woman whose name I cannot recall. We had back-to-back meetings with several

high-level leaders, including the
owner of Pick n Pay, one of the largest grocery store chains in South Africa. I met with health officials at the
Medunsa Medical School (now the
Sefako Makgatho Health Sciences
University) and visited Bophuthat-
swana[§] in the northeast, which was
in the process of developing a medical school.

We also toured Soweto, the
racially segregated township for non-
whites near Johannesburg. It is
known for the student uprising
against apartheid on June 16, 1976,

*Photo of Hector Pieterson at the memorial
of the Soweto uprising in 1976.*

triggered by the students being forced to speak the Afrikaans language in
their schools. About 20,000 students participated, and estimates range from
175 to 700 who were shot and killed. Among the dead was 13-year-old
Hector Pieterson who became the iconic image of the Soweto uprising when
a newspaper photo of him being carried by a fellow student was published
around the world. We visited the memorial erected there in his honor.

Soweto was still in the throes of apartheid during our visit. While
we were touring the township, people were in panic and started running
around, here and there.

---

[§]Bophuthatswana was a Bantustan (also known as "Homeland"; an area set aside for members
of a specific ethnicity) which was declared nominally independent by the apartheid regime of
South Africa in 1977. With the end of apartheid after the first multi-racial elections and the
coming into force of the Interim Constitution of South Africa on 27 April 1994, Bophuthat-
swana ceased to exist and once again became part of South Africa.

"The Hippos are coming!" they screamed.

I did not know what the Hippos were and thought they were animals. I was led away in haste to a safer location in the area. My guides explained that these Hippos were giant armored and weaponized tanks with huge tires that could run over and smash any house in Soweto. I had not yet seen the 1987 film "Cry Freedom," starring Denzel Washington, that vividly shows the destructive force of the Hippos in destroying a Black shantytown in South Africa.

In the midst of our busy schedule of meetings, we did get to have some recreation along the way. The African Forum arranged for Stephen and me to visit the home of a white, private business owner who lived on a 120-acre farm outside Johannesburg. We were treated with a traditional African dinner, including antelope and ostrich. In addition, we were able to visit a resort called Sun City, like a "little Las Vegas," about a two-hour drive from Pretoria.

When we returned from South Africa to America, it was our understanding that we would have a photo op with President Reagan and be introduced to corporate leaders who would likely be interested in financially contributing to assist our group in developing the modified AHEC program. However, we soon learned about the Iran-Contra scandal that was in progress. It involved the sale of arms to Iran in exchange for money to support the Contras in Nicaragua. Congressional hearings were held, and both Colonel Oliver North and John Poindexter were involved. This activity resulted in the termination of our efforts in South Africa.

## THOUSAND POINTS OF LIGHT AND COMBINED FEDERAL CAMPAIGN

In 1990 I had the honor of being tapped to help launch President George H. W. Bush's Thousand Points of Light (TPOL) initiative in the Health Resources and Services Administration. The TPOL was created to promote the spirit of volunteerism that the President described in his 1989 inau-

*Dan with Acting Surgeon General Dr. Audrey Manley who served as Judge for the Halloween Costume Contest.*

gural address: "I have spoken of a thousand points of light, of all the community organizations that are spread like stars throughout the Nation, doing good." The goal was to motivate individuals and organizations across the nation to help others through service.

As part of the TPOL activities, I came up with a creative way to engage employees to kick off the giving season for the Combined Federal Campaign (CFC) – a Halloween Costume Contest. The CFC is the world's largest annual workplace charity campaign, with almost 200 CFC campaigns throughout the country and overseas raising millions of dollars each year to support eligible nonprofit organizations. At that time, several different federal agencies were located in the 18-story Parklawn Building in Rockville, Md. With over 5000 employees, it was a great opportunity to raise funds for CHC charities and other organizations serving underserved people in Maryland and Washington, D.C.

I met a new federal employee in the building's cafeteria named Sherilyn Pruitt. She was a recent graduate with a master's degree from University of Michigan and was working for HRSA. I recruited her to chair the Halloween Contest. She took the lead and assigned people to obtain prizes, get judges, identify local charities, and coordinate with the facilities management to secure space and refreshments.

*Sherilyn Pruitt, chair of the CFC Halloween Contest.*

On the day of the event, Sherilyn showed up in a drum major's uniform that she borrowed from Howard University. She led a parade of costumed federal employees throughout the building, through the day-care center, and around the neighborhood immediately adjacent to the Parklawn building, much to the delight of neighbors, businesses, and motorists. Some of the characters included a mother-daughter duo who were the front and back end of a cow (complete with milk squirts and milk duds), a house that was in a hurricane, a pregnant nun, and a group of medics from the television show MASH.

Judges included Rear Admiral Dr. Audrey Manley, Acting Surgeon General who later served as the eighth president of Spelman College, and Dr. Donald Weaver, who became the U.S. Surgeon General. Prizes were awarded to the Funniest, Scariest, Most Creative, and Most Mission Oriented costumes. This event led to the most successful CFC season ever led by federal employees in the Parklawn Building.

## CHAPTER 17

# Ushering: Washington National Cathedral

I want to share my experiences from more than two decades of involvement with the Washington National Cathedral. At 301 feet high, the Washington National Cathedral is the tallest building in the nation's capital, sixth-largest cathedral in the world, and second largest cathedral in the United States.* Located near the corner of Wisconsin and Massachusetts Avenues, it is more than 500 feet long from west to east. The Washington National Monument, laying down, could nearly fit within

*Dan at National Cathedral, Oct. 2006. Photo by Loretta Neumann.*

---

* The largest church in the world is St. Peter's Basilica in Rome. The largest cathedral in the United States is Saint John the Divine in New York City. The official name of the Washington National Cathedral is the Cathedral Church of Saint Peter and Saint Paul. It was completed 83 years to the day after it was begun (September 29, 1907-September 29, 1990). It sits on 51 acres of landscaping.

it. It took more than 80 years to be built, and the grounds were designed by the noted landscape architect Frederick Law Olmsted, Jr.

Although Episcopalian, the Washington National Cathedral serves as the nation's church, especially in times of both national celebration and mourning. Besides its beauty and majesty, however, the Cathedral has many other charms and tales to tell. For example, I recall that when I first became acquainted with the Cathedral, there was a rumor that at one point in its history, a couple made their home inside for a period of time. They and their living arrangements were discovered when the Cathedral police did a safety inspection, which prompted new security and fire arrangements.

## BISHOP JOHN THOMAS WALKER

In 1976, the Protestant Episcopal Cathedral Foundation was in the process of selecting a new bishop for the Washington Diocese. Bishop William Creighton, who had served as the bishop for 15 years, was retiring. The Cathedral Foundation had a search committee to identify a new bishop, and it was considering, Rev. John Thomas Walker, then the current Suffragan Bishop.[†] He was well known for his social and humanitarian activism and for forging the way for Blacks and women within the Episcopal Church.

My wife Sandy and I had previously become good friends with John and his wife Maria. We discussed at length with the Walkers whether a Black bishop would be accepted for the whole Diocese.[‡] Subsequently, however, the search committee nominated John, and on June 12, 1976, he

---

[†] A Suffragan Bishop is a bishop appointed to assist a diocesan bishop. Walker had served in that capacity from 1971 to 1976.

[‡] The Washington Diocese includes the District of Columbia and the Maryland counties of Montgomery, Prince George's, Charles, and St. Mary's.

was elected by the Episcopal Convention on the first ballot to serve as the Bishop Coadjutor until installed as bishop. He received nearly twice the number of votes as his three competitors combined. There was instantly much jubilation within the Episcopal community. As the Cathedral's newspaper described it:

> Delegates and spectators jumped to their feet. They filled Epiphany with spontaneous and enthusiastic applause. They hugged each other. Some cried happy tears...As Bishop Walker was escorted toward the front of the church, a crush of delegates spilled into the aisle to greet him and express their joy.[63]

Bishop John Walker became the first Black bishop for the Washington Diocese and only the second Episcopal Black bishop in the United States. He was installed on September 24, 1977, in the great nave of the Washington National Cathedral with the usual fanfare and grandeur of the Episcopal Church. Immediately afterward, my wife Sandy and I hosted a luncheon at our home for Bishop Walker and Mrs. Walker. Many of his friends and Cathedral

*Bishop John Walker.*

members and leaders attended. It was truly a joyous day.

After he was installed, Bishop Walker appointed me to the Committee of Homosexuality and the Church and also as Lay Servant to visit, inspect, and nurture relationships with the Episcopal Churches in the Diocese. In 1978, he appointed himself also to be Dean of the Cathedral, following the retirement of Francis Sayer, Jr. A grandson of President Woodrow Wilson, Sayer had served as Dean for 27 years. Bishop of Washington Mariann Budde later wrote that Walker "poured himself into the hard work of fundraising for the Cathedral, while at the same time leading the diocese and providing moral leadership during one of the most volatile periods of our society."[64]

Then unexpectedly on September 30, 1989, my good friend John – Bishop Walker – died of a heart attack. I was devastated. The funeral, of course, was held at the Washington National Cathedral. It was fitting and beautiful. Archbishop Tutu and other dignitaries attended and provided remarks at the service. There was a significant reception at the Cathedral and in Bishop Walker's home, where I again had a chance to converse with Bishop Tutu and to introduce my children to him.

Bishop Walker is still remembered and revered. He served as president of the board of Africare from 1975 to his death. A nonprofit organization based in Washington DC, it has provided development aid for Africa since 1970 and annually presents the Bishop John T. Walker Distinguished Humanitarian Service Award in his honor. In 2008, the Bishop John T. Walker School for Boys in Southeast Washington opened as a tuition-free Episcopal school for boys from underserved communities. It is supported and administered by the Washington Diocese.

## SERVING AS HEAD USHER

Several years earlier, Bishop Walker had suggested that I consider ushering at the Cathedral. So, in 1991 or thereabouts, I became an usher. It started another adventure in my life. Indeed, the Cathedral was so imposing, I had always felt in awe of it. I recall that Derrick Humphries, who had been appointed Head Usher by Bishop Walker, was an attorney and the first Black Head Usher. Afterwards, Sara Maddox, a State Department official, replaced Derrick, and I believe she was the first female Head Usher. Later, she left to concentrate on her position at the State Department.

*Dean Nathan Baxter installing Dan as Head
Usher of the Washington National Cathedral.*

The Cathedral administration then sent out an announcement inviting ushers to apply for the position. The talk around the Cathedral was that the two most sought-after head ushering positions in Washington, D.C., were at the National Cathedral and the Cosmos Club, a prestigious private club, on the corner of Massachusetts Avenue and 21st Street, which at the time, I was told, did not accept Black clientele and had restrictions as to what rooms women were allowed to enter.

I initially was not going to apply at the Cathedral, but was encouraged by fellow ushers, so I did, along with several others. The selection was made, and Dr. Alfred Muller, MD, became Head Usher. I was selected Assistant Head Usher, a two-year term for both positions. When our terms were completed, I was appointed to the Head Usher position. The week after my appointment, the former Head Usher became involved in a profoundly serious situation in the basement restroom with a young man who had arrived with a bus tour group. It was widely publicized.

## Working with the Ushers

As I assumed my Head Usher responsibilities, I learned more about the operation and the dynamics of the Cathedral. Specifically, the cast of characters of the 95-member usher corps and the five chapels that required usher assistance, especially on Sundays and special services. The head usher was identified by a red-square badge, which was generally worn on the right lapel of his or her suit jacket. The other ushers had elongated name tags that they wore while ushering.

One of my major roles as Head Usher was to assign ushers to their duties in the chapels. Their jobs involved meeting, greeting, and seating Cathedral guests and looking after their safety and welfare. I remember a time when assigning ushers, I asked an usher if he would work with another usher in one of the chapels for that service. He looked at me with distain.

"Well," he said, "I was a colonel in the Army, and he was just a captain. I would like to be with someone of similar stature."

This seemed silly and it happened only occasionally, but it happened enough to be disturbing. Most of the ushers held important positions in private corporations, government, or the military. We were all volunteers. It was often difficult, however, for some of those who held high-level positions to leave their egos outside the cathedral. It became challenging at times to work with them. Of the 95-odd ushers, five were Black. Yet for the most part, we had a very enlightened, cohesive, and congenial

311

religious contingent of men and women who enjoyed ushering at the Cathedral. I was also pleased that they did not have to be of the Protestant Episcopal faith to be an usher.

*Collections*

One of my other major responsibilities was overseeing the ushers with the passing of the collection plates, the securing of the funds in a safe until counted, and the placement of the money in the Cathedral steel chest to be taken by an armored vehicle to the bank. This activity involved thousands of dollars, and we felt the huge responsibility this placed on us.

I learned that at one point in the Cathedral's history, the collection plates were handled by the purple-robed vergers. They are staff employees who escort speakers to the pulpit or readers to the lay pulpit. At one Easter, however, during the biggest service of the year, when the vergers were busy collecting the plates and making certain the collected funds went to the bank, the money was not deposited, and the Cathedral lost a significant amount. As a result, the ushers became responsible for collecting and securing the funds.

As I indicated earlier, the ushers are or were mostly high-level, active or retired professionals from the DC area. A prominent member of the Cathedral, however, had a son with a slight mental disability who wanted to be an usher. Following a discussion with his parents, I agreed that he could become one.

It should be noted that ushers in religious institutions are generally seen as much as the minister by parishioners. When an usher does something or is involved in something in a negative way, it is reflected on all the ushers. An incident happened at a major service while the ushers passed the collection plates. When the plate came from the aisle to the

*Dan with some of the ushers of the Washington National Cathedral, 2006.*
*Photo by Loretta Neumann.*

usher with the mental disability, he took some money from the plate and put it in his pocket. I just happened to be on the opposite side of the aisle and observed his action. Several nearby congregants also noticed. The service ended, and his parents, who had been seated in the front of the Cathedral, approached me while I was speaking with other people.

"We are so glad that our son is enjoying ushering," his mother said.

"Let's move over to the Lincoln statue in the corner and talk," I replied. We walked over by the statue in the Cathedral, and I shared with them how their son had handled the plate. They were mortified. I assured them that their son had likely seen others put money in the collection and sometimes made change from it.

"I believe your son was probably doing what he thought others did," I said. In any event, they banned him from ushering for a while. He later was allowed to return, after promising not to do it again. He subsequently became one of our most faithful and conscientious ushers.

## Dealing with Disruptions

As indicated earlier, the Cathedral staff and the Dean spend considerable time planning to make sure that the services go as smoothly and timely as possible, starting with the procession at the beginning to the recession at the end. At the start of one service, the procession had begun, as usual, with the choir in the lead. Standing in the middle of the aisle was a woman looking up at the stained-glass windows, blocking the procession. I approached her and asked if I could help her find a seat.

"GOD WANTS ME TO MAKE SURE THE STAINED-GLASS WINDOWS DON'T FALL ON THE CONGREGATION," she proclaimed. "Therefore, I have to stand here."

"Right now," I responded, "the Lord wants me to guide you to a seat, so that you can check the stained-glass windows while seated." I showed her to a seat, and she promptly sat down.

At another service, a different woman was standing in the aisle just when the procession was about to start. She would not move when approached by an usher, who then brought her to my attention. I immediately went to speak with her.

"I can't move," she stated, "because the LORD SAID THAT JESUS WANTS ME TO STAND HERE UNTIL HE COMES." The procession was moving closer and closer.

"Right now," I explained, "the Lord wants me to tell you that Jesus, if he has time, will come and sit next to you." So, she sat throughout the service. After it was over and people filed out, she remained there. I informed security that the woman who was seated needed some type of help. I never learned what happened to her.

## Services

The main service on Sundays started at 11 a.m. and usually lasted for about an hour and a half. "State Day" was the celebration of one of the states in the Union, often accompanied by visitors from that state, with someone among them selected for a special reading. My sister Marion and her Episcopalian friends from Hartford and West Hartford would take a bus to come to the service for Connecticut's day. Other times, we also had morning services in different chapels. At 4 p.m. the "Sunday Evensong" featured an hour of beautiful hymns and prayers.

Especially interesting were the activities for a major event with the President of the United States in attendance. The Cathedral would be locked down at midnight. Then, very early in the morning the Secret Service with their sniffer dogs would arrive to further secure the building, and the Secret Service SWAT team would assemble. The building would remain in lockdown until around 6 a.m., at which time a larger contingency of Secret Service and the Head Usher would arrive.

The Cathedral has four main entrances at the ground level. The west entrance, facing Connecticut Avenue, serves as the main entrance; the north entrance is used for the President and other selected dignitaries; the south entrance is where members of the President's Cabinet usually arrived by bus. There is a balcony above the north, south, and west entrances. Members of the press were seated in the south balcony. The west balcony was considered a prime site because of its great view of the Nave.

With such a major event, tickets were required, and people would line up to at the west entrance as early as 7 a.m. (rain, sun, or snow), waiting for the doors to open. At 9 a.m., the Cathedral Police would open the heavy glass doors, and visitors passed through a metal detector operated by Security Police or the Secret Service. Then they were directed to their seats by the ushers, who would hand them printed programs.

When the President, Vice President, and some dignitaries arrived at the north entrance, it was my role to greet and escort them into the holding room (the "Slype"). The service started with a long procession led by the Cathedral Dean, who followed the Cathedral Choir and other participants. With colorful robes and majestic music, it was always awesome to behold. Below are just a few examples of my experiences.

## MEETING AND ESCORTING DIGNITARIES

### *President William Jefferson (Bill) Clinton*

President and Mrs. Clinton attended several services at the Cathedral. I remember one in particular, which was following Clinton's incident with a White House intern. Prior to the Clintons attending the Sunday service, there was a lot of negative chatter, especially among the female staff and ushers regarding the President's involvement with the intern.

However, when President Clinton, his wife Hillary, and daughter Chelsea arrived and were seated, he acted totally presidential throughout the service. Upon his departure, the entire chit-chat climate had changed. The same people who had been critical of him changed to "oohs and aahs." It was amazing to see that even their body language improved as he departed.

*President Clinton with Dan after a service in the Washington National Cathedral.*

Another service I remember fondly with President and Mrs. Clinton was in December 2000, the Clintons' last Christmas Eve service at the Cathedral. As always, it was one of the most beautiful services of the year. At the end, the Secret Service delayed the congregation from leaving the Cathedral until the President left the grounds. In fact, in the past you could see that when the President moved the Secret Service was directly with him, and the crowd moved accordingly.

My daughter April, her husband Andrew, and my son Rob were present at that service. They had always wanted to meet President Clinton. When the Christmas Eve service was over, I was escorting President Clinton to the north side exit. I told him that my daughter and family always wanted to meet him. He stopped in his tracks.

"Where are they?" he asked. "I will wait here until you get them." A very gracious gesture, but it meant that everyone moving from the Cathedral had to stop, because the President had not left. I located my family and brought them to the Secret Service line. They delayed me for a minute because I was walking through their secured corridor. But because they knew I was the Head Usher, they allowed us to pass through, and my children met President Clinton.

"I would love to invite you to dinner," my recently married young daughter said to the President. He placed his right hand on her shoulder.

"God bless you," he replied.

## Hillary Rodham Clinton

The Clinton family usually attended the Christmas Eve services at the Cathedral. As a result, we had become familiar with each other. I always enjoyed helping Chelsea with her overcoat. Hillary was gracious, friendly, and easy to talk to when we discussed issues of the day. I was struck by her penetrating blue eyes, which she used very effectively. I felt comfortable enough to ask her, at the last Christmas Eve service they attended, if she would autograph her recently published book, *An Invitation to the White House, At Home with History.*

*Hillary Rodham Clinton and Dan, 2007.*
*Photo by Loretta Neumann.*

"Yes," she said, "I'd be pleased to autograph it." I asked if she would sign three copies, and again she said, "of course."

"May I draft a few comments for you to include?" I asked.

"I'd be glad for you to do that," she replied. She gave me a card with the name of a staffer to contact, which I did.

The Clintons were scheduled to vacate the White House on January 20, 2001. Before she left, Hillary personally signed the books at the White House on January 17. I was, of course, extremely pleased to receive them. I presented copies to my daughter April and son Rob, and I kept one for myself.

### President George W. Bush

In January 2001, before President George W. Bush arrived for his Inaugural Prayer Service the morning after his inauguration, Vice President Dick Cheney and his wife Lynne were escorted into the Slype. Soon after, President Bush and his wife Laura arrived, and I escorted them there. The door was closed, probably for 10 minutes, and I was alone with the Bushes and the Cheneys, without the Secret Service or sniffer dogs. We chatted about various issues, and they discussed the inaugural balls the prior evening. The President continued to walk around and exhibited understandable nervousness about the event.

As soon as all the guests were seated, which was around five minutes before 11 a.m., Assistant Head Usher Mike Heide escorted the Vice President and his wife to their seats on the north side of the front row. Seated in the same row, from left to right facing the altar, were President Clinton and Hillary, former President H.W. Bush and his wife Barbara, and seated next to him would be Laura Bush and the President, who sat next to the center aisle. I was about to escort President Bush and his wife to their seats when I was approached by an official who walked up to me, staring in my face. His nose was about three centimeters from my nose.

"DO NOT SHAKE HANDS WITH THE CLINTONS!" he declared.

I was taken aback. My normal approach was to greet the honored guests seated in the front row, shake hands, and make sure they were comfortable and had a program. As for the Clintons, who were seated at the end of the front row, we had always chatted for a couple of minutes before they were seated. I was doubly annoyed to be stopped from greeting them, because there was so much going on with the Bush staff in and around the Cathedral, moving things around, which at the time somewhat disrupted the normal flow of the pre-service. However, I escorted President Bush and his wife to their seats, and instead of going down the line of the first row and shaking hands and welcoming the front row, I just waved to the Clintons, and they waved back. As I knew, one must be attuned to a lot of unwritten protocols while employed or volunteering at the Cathedral. Politics are always a factor.

*Seating a Special Guest*

One of the best reasons for being attuned when interacting with people at the Cathedral is that you never know with whom you are speaking. At President Bush's Inaugural Prayer Service, it was winter, and time for the service to begin. I had already seated President and Mrs. Bush. The Secret Service sat directly behind them, and the seats going back toward the main entrance were filled by his family members. Cabinet officials followed them along with some Supreme Court justices. Ninety-eight percent of the ticketed seats were filled, with the exception on the outer north aisle next to the wall. A few seats were deliberately not filled in case someone important arrived late.

I was walking up on the north side aisle of the Cathedral, going west to the front entrance, when I saw an elderly woman by herself, wearing a long mink coat down to her ankles, coming toward me. She was looking around.

"Can I help you find a seat?" I asked.

"I see an empty seat four rows behind the President," she replied. "I wish to sit there." I explained to her that those were selected seats designated for the President's guests.

"BUT I GAVE HIM $10 MILLION DOLLARS," she declared. Of course, I seated her in an empty seat behind the President.

*Post 9/11 Prayer and Remembrance Service*

On September 11, 2001, I was living in the Takoma neighborhood of Washington, D.C., and about to have my breakfast. I usually do not watch television until evening, but I had turned it on for the news. It was a clear, bright day, and on the screen, I saw a plane flying and suddenly crashing into one of the Twin Towers in New York City. I did not understand what had happened, but felt it was strange that a plane would be flying over Manhattan that low. Suddenly a second plane crashed into the other tower. Since my son Rob was living in New York, I immediately tried to reach him on his cell phone. The phones in New York, however, were either out or busy, and I was unable to reach him.

A few minutes later, my phone rang. It was my niece Ebonie from California, who said that she had just spoken to Rob. She then connected us together. He was okay. Fortunately, he lived quite a distance away from where it had happened. We quickly discussed his safety and our immediate plans if there were more terrorist attacks. Soon I also learned of the plane that crashed into the Pentagon and the other that ended up in a field in Pennsylvania.

THE WASHINGTON NATIONAL CATHEDRAL
NATIONAL DAY OF PRAYER AND REMEMBRANCE
SEPTEMBER 14, 2001

*Dan escorting President and Mrs. George Bush at 9-11 Service, Washington National Cathedral, September 14, 2001. Signed photo, gift of the White House.*

Following those terrorist attacks, the staff and ushers at the National Cathedral swung into action. President Bush had called for a Day of Prayer and Remembrance to address the nation and calm fears. As Head Usher, I was busy organizing the ushers for locations and placement for the large service which was held only three days later, on September 14. Attending were most of the Bush Administration's cabinet heads and other officials, Congressional leaders, religious leaders, and dignitaries, domestic and international. Past Presidents Ford, Carter, George H.W. Bush, and Clinton attended.

The morning started rainy and gloomy, and guests arrived at the Cathedral carrying umbrellas. The program was very solemn and subdued, but the music was beautiful and calming. Cathedral and military choirs sang, and mezzo soprano Denyce Graves sang "America the Beautiful." Speakers included Muslim, Catholic, Protestant, and Jewish leaders. Rev. Billy Graham gave a major talk and proclaimed, "This event can give a message of hope for the future." President Bush said, "Grief and tragedy and hatred are only for a time." By the time people left, the sun came out and the sky was blue again, which did give us all of us some measure of consolation.

As usual, I had escorted the President and Mrs. Bush to and from their seats. A few weeks later, they gave me a photograph of us walking down the aisle from the north nave. Both signed the photograph, and I treasure it.

## Justice Sandra Day O'Connor

For services at 9 a.m., Supreme Court Justice Sandra Day O'Connor often was a reader. Justice O'Connor would drive herself to the Cathedral, robe into her church garments, participate in the procession, and do her assigned reading. She enjoyed the break from her regular duties as a Court Justice.

Initially, I did not know how to address her. She and I came up with the term "Justice O'Connor." We became extraordinarily strong acquaintances. We discussed upbringing, education, and her learning to ride a horse among other things. She told me about her not being hired in some positions when she was a younger female attorney.

After the 9 a.m. service, I would walk her from the Cathedral to her car. One time I asked where her driver or bodyguard parked. I could not believe it when she said she had none.

"You really need a bodyguard," I replied. I persevered and insisted that she should have one. We bantered back and forth on that issue as we stood by her car. Finally, as only a self-assured dignitary can do, she looked at me square in the eye.

"Dan, I do not need a bodyguard," she firmly said. That ended our discussion.

Two months later, at the National Cathedral's service following the 9/11 airplane attack on the United States, when President George W. Bush addressed the nation, the Cathedral was packed, with all forms of dignitaries. It was a very tense time. I had been working with the Secret Service, making sure the ushers were in their proper locations, and waiting to escort President and Mrs. Bush to their front row seats. Justice O'Connor was seated several rows back from the President's chair on the outside center aisle, and I did not see her. She grabbed my arm as I walked by.

"Dan, I have security now," she said. We both smiled and talked for a minute or two. She noted that she had received several threats. Then I continued walking to the west entrance to discuss issues with the ushers.

*Condoleezza Rice*

One of the duties of a Cathedral usher besides meeting, greeting, and seating visitors is to be non-partisan with guests who enter the Cathedral. It is doubly important for the Head Usher to set an example for others. There was, however, an incident for which I was not proud of, and for which I need to apologize. It was during the Inaugural Prayer Service for President George W. Bush, on January 21, 2005. The President's entourage, Supreme Court justices, and other dignitaries were seated prior to the arrival of the President. The chairs were being filled by selected people on the north side of the Cathedral behind the President.

I had often observed that certain female staff of the President were escorted to their seats by military personnel. In this instance, Dr. Condoleezza Rice, who was to be the next National Security Advisor (and, in Bush's second term, the Secretary of State), was escorted from the north entrance to her seat by a female Bush staffer. Apparently, many of the newly appointed administration personnel had never entered the Cathedral. Consequently, they were unfamiliar with the entering and exiting locations. I observed this was the case with Dr. Rice, especially at the end of the service when it was time for her to depart through the north exit where her transportation was waiting.

After a large State service, high-ranking officials who entered from the north entrance were usually escorted out by an administrative staffer who had escorted them into the Cathedral. This did not happen with Dr. Rice. I observed that the person who had escorted her to her seat was busy speaking to another official. She only gave directions to Dr. Rice for her to find her way by herself. This, of course, was confusing, especially with the crowd gathering around, hoping to speak with the new President. As Dr. Rice left, she went the wrong way to find the north exit. Looking dignified, however, she quickly returned to get further directions from the staffer who brought her in. That staffer still did not walk with her to the exit, but simply gave her directions on how to reach the north exit. Fortunately, despite all this confusion, Dr. Rice was finally able to leave.

One will recall that President Bush's first election was controversial, with "hanging chads" in Florida that resulted in the Supreme Court stopping the count and effectively deciding that George W. Bush had won the election over Al Gore. As a result, my partisanship kicked in. Instead of coming to Dr. Rice's rescue, I let her search by herself for the north entrance. I should have stepped forward and escorted her out. For that, I apologize. I have never before shared this story with anyone. It has, however, been on my mind in my apology bucket list.

## *Jessie Jackson*

The Dean of the Cathedral and others who will be a part of a service spend an enormous amount of time devoted to the sermon and in preparation for a guest speaker. This time-consuming effort and the logistics accompanying it are really a serious undertaking for the Cathedral staff. It is important that the music and procession of the participants are synchronized, which enables the service to begin at a precise time and move smoothly, especially at the 11 a.m. Sunday service.

There was an occasion when the Reverend Jesse Jackson was to give the Sunday sermon. Most speakers arrived at the Cathedral 15 to 30 minutes prior and were held in the holding room, the Slype. Since the procession generally started around 10 minutes before the service began, the Cathedral's handlers and Head Usher waited even earlier to receive Reverend Jackson.

However, 10:30 a.m. arrived and no Jesse; 10:40 no Jesse; 10:45 and still no Jesse. The procession began at 10:50, no Jesse. At 10:55 a.m., Jesse arrived and asked if his aide could use the copy room, from what I gathered was for his sermon. Soon after, I chuckled to myself as people were scurrying around to find a photocopier. I said to myself, I wonder what people of color, who noticed the delay and the staff's concern, would call that.

We finally had to bring the Reverend through the Great Choir section to his seat. He did, however, give a rousing presentation!

## Weddings and Funerals

I was fortunate to have ushered at several beautiful Cathedral weddings. One was for Senator Strom Thurmond's daughter. I had the opportunity to have a lengthy discussion with the Senator while waiting in the bride's chamber for the service to start. Sen. Thurmond, Republican from South Carolina, had been a staunch opponent of civil rights legislation in the 1950s and 1960s. He and I had a dialogue regarding my life. I found it amusing that Sen. Thurmond asked me some personal questions about my life and my family that I had never been asked before.

Another was Vice President Al Gore's daughter Karenna's wedding, held 27 years after her parents had been married at the Cathedral. A lovely private ceremony, it was attended by 300 invited guests. Especially memorable were when Aretha Franklin sang and when the bride's father gave her away.

Also, I recall the wedding of Alexis Herman, Secretary of Labor under President Bill Clinton, the first African American to hold the position. People were surprised when President Clinton attended and provided a Biblical reading at the service. Many dignitaries attended, including Dorothy Height, past president of the National Council of Negro Women.

# WEST WING "TWO CATHEDRALS"

The television series *West Wing* had an episode in May 2001 filmed at the Cathedral regarding the screen death of Mrs. Landingham, the secretary to screen President Bartlett. As I was Head Usher, for the film I continued

*Dan and his son Rob with Martin Sheen after taping of
West Wing "Two Cathedrals" episode.*

my responsibility of escorting the President (portrayed by Martin Sheen) and his wife to their seats.

Martin Sheen and I were at mid-nave in the Cathedral, chatting before the shoot, when they were about to "snap" the clapperboard to start the shoot. Sheen noticed my hands.

"Where did you get those big hands?" he asked.

"We Blacks built this country," I responded. Sheen cracked up.

"I'm not going to go there," he laughed. The director had to restart the shoot.

Then, at the beginning of the episode, I am seen escorting "President Bartlett" to his front row seat and standing (my backside and a bit of profile) while he is seated. It is one of those "blink and you'll miss it" moments.

I did have a chance to have a real influence on the show. When they had the first rehearsal, the people in their seats, including President Bartlett, remained seated as Mrs. Landingham's casket passed by at the end of the service. After the first take, I told the director that it was not what would happen at a funeral in the Cathedral. Everyone would stand when the casket was taken down the aisle. So, they more accurately reshot it.

When the film was shown on television, I received phone calls from my daughter April and others chastising me for my letting Martin Sheen smoke in the Cathedral and put his cigarette out on the floor – as if I could have controlled the script! Nevertheless, the episode was a huge success for the quality of the acting, the setting, and the filming. Several TV critics later proclaimed this episode of West Wing the best in the series.

# EPILOGUE

I served as Head Usher of the Washington National Cathedral until late 2001, following the funeral service for Katharine Graham, former publisher of *The Washington Post*. I resigned after a major clash with the event planners who were paid to handle the service for the Graham family. The Cathedral leadership did not back the ushers, and we were largely shunted aside. It was a major frustration and humiliating for all of us.

Despite my disappointment at the time, however, I continued to serve for many years, with deference given to me for having been Head Usher. I ushered at Christmas and Easter services and at other major events, such as for the installations of new bishops (both for the Diocese and the Episcopal Presiding Bishop) and for the funerals of Presidents Ford and Reagan and other dignitaries, such as Dorothy Height.

In short, it has been an honor and a joy to be part of this wonderful institution.

CHAPTER 18

# Enjoying Post-Retirement

## KOREAN WAR MEMORIAL

Following my retirement from the government in 1994, I became heavily involved in the newly established Korean War Veterans Association (KWVA) in developing the Korean War Veteran's Memorial on the National Mall in Washington, D.C. Called the nation's "Police Action," the Korean War was brutal. It lasted just three years (June 7, 1950, to July 27, 1953) with a loss of nearly 37,000 Americans.

The 1995 celebration of the completion of the memorial was a major Washington event, and KWVA was the main mover behind it. As an active life member of KWVA, I was asked to head a committee to plan and implement a banquet for the 5000 Korean War Veterans attending the

*Dan at Korean War Memorial, 2007.*
*Photo by Loretta Neumann*

329

event. The celebration included members and leaders of the Korean community and all the other 34 nations that had been involved in the fighting. My committee arranged with a contractor (Richard Greene, a CPA) to hold the banquet at the Shoreham Hotel. I hired Delicia Gunn as my assistant.

I also arranged to have a special Korean War memorial service at the Washington National Cathedral, where I had ushered and knew most of its leaders. At that point, Sara Maddox, the Cathedral Head Usher, said the service would be approved if I would continue to usher at the Cathedral, which of course I agreed to do.

The speakers at the ceremony on the National Mall featured President Clinton, Vice President Al Gore, and Secretary of Veterans Affairs Jesse Brown. There were also Medal of Honor recipients, including General Ray Davis. Other Medal of Honor awardees that were acknowledged included Scooter Burke, who was cited by the President and hailed from Arkansas, and Ronald Russor, who passed away in September 2020.

In addition to my other responsibilities, I established my own new video/film corporation and named it "Courage Productions." Along with a post-production company (MVP) out of Virginia, it produced two major videos regarding the events on the National Mall and service at the National Cathedral. I called the videos the "Final Convoy" and the "Forgotten War Remembered."

## SPECIAL FRIENDS

*Senator Vance Hartke*

Sometime following my retirement, I developed an import/export company and, at a business meeting, I had the opportunity to sit next to former

*Sen. Vance Hartke, right, with Dan's daughter April and fiancé Andrew Motaung and, rear, friend and colleague Eric Chavis.*

Senator Vance Hartke from Indiana. We struck up a conversation discussing his heavy involvement in the Medicare/Medicaid legislation and his deep interest in trying to include support for kidney treatments. I discussed with him the AHEC Program that I had directed. I explained its value and the need for the nation to have both such programs.

We became strong associates and good friends over these issues. The senator invited me to lunch at the Senate Office Dining Room and subsequently for birthday parties at his home in Virginia. These were not the usual type of birthday parties that I was accustomed to. Of course, there were plenty of goodies to eat and beverages to drink. But at one of them he had also arranged for a parachute landing near the swimming pool. This was exciting. It was followed by guests swimming in the pool and using his tennis court. There seemed to be several hundred or more people in attendance. Senator Hartke was a gregarious person, and he insisted that we take a picture with him. Unfortunately, a few years later, on July 27, 2003, he passed away and was buried in Arlington National Cemetery.

## Colonel Fred Cherry – A True War Hero

I first met Colonel Fred
Cherry, a former flying ace
in the U.S. Air Force, in
1995. He and I received
awards from the Congres-
sional Black Caucus com-
memorating our service to
the nation in the Korean
War and to the community.

*Dan with Col. Fred Cherry, Vietnam POW.*
*Photo by Loretta Neumann.*

Following that event, Fred and I became very good friends. We shared a
number of social events. He attended my wedding with my second wife,
Loretta Neumann, at the Washington National Cathedral in 2006.
Loretta and I attended his 80th birthday party at his home in Silver Spring
in 2008. Fred and I had lunch together every other Tuesday at the Copper
Canyon Restaurant in Silver Spring, Maryland.

Early in our friendship, I had met with Cherry and his assistant,
Eric Chavis, a member of the Lumbee Indian tribe. The meeting, at Howard University, was to try to develop a joint venture arrangement between
Fred's company, the Cherry Group, and mine, Takoma Enterprises, with
the Howard University Department of Engineering. The project was to develop for the U.S. Government a system to track, investigate, and evaluate
the emission of the air trails of commercial jet planes as they fly overhead.

Colonel Cherry was not just an ordinary pilot. He was from Suffolk, Virginia, grew up under the typical segregated southern system, and
went to one of the Rosenwald high schools built for rural Black communities. He had to fight the system, kicking down a military officer's door

because he was being denied the opportunity to compete for flying, on which he had excelled in all areas of Air Force training.

Colonel Cherry was a fighter pilot who saw action in both Korea and Vietnam* and flew the most advanced planes. On his last mission in Vietnam, he was shot down by the Viet Cong, captured, tortured, and put in prison (the "Hanoi Hilton") for seven and a half years. At the same time, future Senator John McCain was there for five and a half years. Both were treated harshly, starved, and endured months of isolation.

Fred's cellmate was the Navy pilot Porter Halyburton, a privileged white man from Virginia. The Viet Cong deliberately put them together on the assumption that a Black and a white southerner would not get along. Instead, Halyburton nursed Col. Cherry back to health amid his many wounds, fractured shoulder, and other broken body parts. I believe that Porter and Fred deserve to receive the U.S. Congressional Medal of Freedom, and I strongly urge people to read the book *Two Souls Indivisible* by James S. Hirsh. It tells the story of the two imprisoned pilots, one Black and one white, who became friends for life.[65]

In 2015, Fred arranged with the Pentagon for Loretta and me to have a tour at Andrews Air Force Base in Maryland of the President's plane (Air Force One when the President is flying). Unfortunately, Fred became ill and was unable to go with us. He passed away at the Walter Reed Medical Center in Bethesda on February 16, 2016. I believe I may have been the last of his friends to see him alive after an operation. He was buried in Arlington National Cemetery that summer, with full military honors, including a military fly-over at his interment. Afterward, I was

---

* Col. Fred Cherry received the Air Force Cross, Silver Star, Legion of Merit (2), Distinguished Flying Cross (2), Bronze Star Medal (2), Purple Heart (2), Meritorious Service Medal, and Air Medal (3). There is a commissioned picture of him placed in a prominent location in the Pentagon.

asked by his family to provide remarks at his memorial service, held in Suffolk, Virginia. In the fall of 2018, the Col. Fred Cherry Middle School in Suffolk opened its doors to students and staff. Loretta and I attended its ceremonial opening along with Fred's family, Porter Halyburton, and a mutual friend, Robert Stevens.

## Afghan Kobir Kohistany

The purpose of the company I formed after retirement was to trade in imports and exports of all forms of commodities, including intellectual properties. It would not hold products, but would serve as a middleman (broker), bringing buyers and sellers together and collecting a fee for that service. At some point while doing this, around 1995-1996, I met a man from Afghanistan named Kobir Kohistany. He was a member of the Mujahideen, a rebel group that was fighting the Soviets. At one point he said he was Afghanistan's Minister of Economics.

We became close associates, even friends. I visited his home in DC on several occasions and met his wife and children. He invited me to the Afghanistan Embassy for one of its ceremonies, which included a huge social with both Afghan and western food. Of all the embassy socials I attended, this was by far the most elaborate. My daughter April went with me so that she would have some exposure to these types of events.

Later, Kohistany and I had a meeting, and we discussed specific trade issues. Among them was the purchase of Afghan goat skins. (Afghanistan has a huge population of goats, one of its main revenue-producing products.) Subsequently, we arranged for a meeting at my house with one of the Afghan Sikhs who resided in the United States. We discussed the pros and cons of travel to Afghanistan.

The decision was made that the Sikh and Kohistany would return to Afghanistan, set up the necessary arrangements for the transaction of goat skins, and inform me when I should arrive. Then I would fly to meet them and sign the necessary papers. However, when they returned to Afghanistan, both were soon assassinated on a rural road by a rival tribe. I was shocked. But, of course, I knew it was fortunate that I was not with them.

## MOVING TO TAKOMA
## AND NEW MARRIAGE

In the late 1990s, I moved into a large old house in Takoma, an historic, tree-lined, integrated neighborhood in northwest Washington, D.C. I liked its old-fashioned charm – like a small town in the midst of the city, with the bonus of a Metrorail station nearby. I also greatly appreciated the Trinity Episcopal Church just a block away. A small Gothic-looking edifice with rugged stones, it was designed by Philip H. Frohman, the architect of the Washington National Cathedral. It soon became my church.

My daughter April was married to Andrew Motaung in Trinity Church in 1998. It was a big family event, including a cook-out the night before in my back yard. The wedding itself was beautiful. April was glowing and Andrew was gleaming. They looked so happy. The reception was at Mrs. K's Tollhouse restaurant in nearby Silver Spring, Maryland, at the time one of the oldest and loveliest restaurants in the Washington area.

Then In July 2002, I was invited to a neighborhood backyard party at the home of Loretta Neumann, who lived two houses down from me. She and friends had owned the house as a group since 1978. Although I had lived so close for several years, I had never met them. I was initially hesitant to attend, as I always expected to be directly invited to a party by the host but was assured by a neighbor that everyone who lived around us was invited.

The event was in honor of Neighbors Inc., an organization founded in 1958 during the "white flight" from the city. The purpose was to combat racial segregation and maintain integrated neighborhoods in the area, including Takoma. Loretta was a past president of Neighbors Inc. The party turned out to be fun, and I met many other neighbors. The food was delicious too. One of the treats was a huge bowl of mussels in a garlicky white wine broth that another neighbor, a professional chef, had donated.

A couple months later, Sara Green and Richard Holzsager, a married couple who lived two houses away on the other side of Loretta, hosted a party for Phil Mendelson, a friend running for re-election to the District Council, the governing body of Washington, D.C. I attended it, as Loretta did, separately. Once again, our neighborhood chef attended, and he donated a bowl of his mussels. I was standing nearby when Loretta asked Sara if she could have what was left of the broth after the party.

"I froze the leftover broth from my party," Loretta said. "I'll add yours and save it to make bouillabaisse." She noted that it is a fish stew from the south of France, where she had visited several years earlier.

"I like bouillabaisse," I said. Loretta looked at me and smiled.

"Okay," she responded. "I'll invite you when I make it for a dinner party." Two months later she had the party, which I attended along with a few other neighbors. Of course, the bouillabaisse was delicious.

Then at Christmas I invited her to help me decorate my tree, and later I attended her New Year's Eve party. We saw each other frequently after that. Winter brought heavy snow, and our neighbors could see the path Loretta and I forged between our homes.

In February 2003, we traveled to California to attend a memorial service for a close friend of Loretta's, Susan Nelson, with whom she helped with legislation to establish the Santa Monica Mountains National Recreation Area. On that trip we also visited my brother Abe and his wife Ruth in Palm Springs, California. In July 2003 Loretta was with my family when my daughter April gave birth to my granddaughter Tselane. That November we flew to Dallas for Thanksgiving, and I met more of Loretta's relatives. In December, we went to Connecticut for my sister Marion's 80th birthday celebration, and Loretta met the rest of my family.

What is special about all of this is that my family accepted her and hers accepted me. Soon we were living together, first at my house and then at hers. And anytime we saw a couple who appeared to be flirting together, we would laugh and say, "Bet they like bouillabaisse!"

## Loretta's Background

Although Loretta is white and I am Black, our life stories have many similarities. These include losing one of our parents at a young age (her mother died when she was nine, my father when I was six); being very independent (both of us got through college on our own); having a variety of experiences (many different jobs); and moving to Washington DC in the late 1960s from our home states (hers Oklahoma, mine Connecticut).

*Loetta's senior yearbook photo,
Oklahoma State University, 1965.*

Ironically, our first marriages were both in August 1965, a few days apart. She married a white man in

Oklahoma, and I married a Black woman in Connecticut. Because state laws prohibiting interracial marriages were not ruled unconstitutional by the Supreme Court until the *Loving v. Virginia* case two years later, we could not have legally married each other at the time in Oklahoma. (Connecticut, however, had never enacted anti-misogyny laws.)

## Wedding at the National Cathedral

In June 2006, I proposed to Loretta. She said yes, and we then had to decide where and when to get married. The next Sunday, we attended service at the Washington National Cathedral. As former head usher, I was able to show her around the chapels available for weddings. They were beautiful but not quite large enough. Then I took her in the side entrance of the Great Choir, at the Cathedral's main altar. A majestic sight, Loretta was awed.

"You mean, we could get married here?" she asked. I said yes, if a date were available. Afterwards I checked, and Saturday, October 28, was open. We grabbed it! Loretta also checked with her congregation, the Washington Ethical Society, about having the reception there, and it was also available. I will not describe all the endless details of organizing such an event, but like most weddings it was mind numbing.

But it turned out perfectly. Many of the ushers I had worked with at the Cathedral came to help. The service itself was a blending of our families, one white and the other predominately Black. We also merged two very different religious affiliations, Episcopal and Ethical Culture, and had officiants from both – Cathedral Canon Rev. Eugene Sutton, later appointed the first Black Bishop of the Episcopal Diocese of Maryland, who led me in my vows, and Adjunct Washington Ethical Society Leader Donald Spears who led Loretta in hers. As for music, there were traditional Episcopal hymns and also the Negro National Anthem, "Lift Every

Voice and Sing," which brought me to tears. And, unexpectedly, Rev. Sutton sang a cappella, in his deep baritone, "How Can I Keep from Singing?"

Afterward, our reception at the Washington Ethical Society was a delight, with help from more than a dozen friends. Special toasts were said, first by my brother, Abe. He started by joking, "It was a dark and stormy night when Dan looked in Loretta's eyes and said, 'Deal or no deal.' Loretta just smiled and said, 'Deal!' So, we welcome our own Heidi Klum and Seal." (Loretta and I did not even know who they were – Heidi, a beautiful blond model and Seal a famous Black singer who were married at the time.)

*Dan and Loretta's wedding at the Washington National Cathedral with officiants, Washington Ethical Society Adjunct Leader Donald Spears and Cathedral Canon Rev. Eugene Sutton, Oct. 28, 2006. Photo by Donovan Marks.*

Loretta's nephew, Dr. Christopher (Chris) Putman, was very touching in his toast. "I was immensely honored when Loretta asked me to escort her down the aisle. It is the role that would traditionally be reserved for her father, my grandfather. It's my greatest honor to stand in for him on this day. He was extremely proud of Loretta, and I can assure you that my grandfather would be very proud of his new son-in-law." In turn,

I was very proud to hear what he said. Chris was clearly sending a message to everyone that Loretta's family was welcoming me.

Another treat was hearing a special song composed for us and performed by Joshua Rich, "Love Only Knows." He stressed that while we may have come from different worlds, love is what brought us together.

To summarize: it is hard to describe the joy of that day and evening. One of the best parts was just seeing so many old friends: My high-school buddy Alfred Youmatz; my college girlfriend Diane McCambridge; my early Bethesda neighbor Christine Haire; a friend from my HRSA days, Jim Walsh; one of my lawyers in the AHEC battle, Bill Richardson; and my dear and heroic friend Col. Fred Cherry, among others.

## Families – Connecticut, Oklahoma, and Texas

It has been a pleasure for Loretta and me to meet our respective families. We have blended well. I recall early on when Loretta's sister Marilyn Bows with her son Chris Putman and family came to dinner one evening. I cooked ribs outside on our barbeque grill and, to my chagrin, I burned them. I was mortified, but Loretta insisted on serving the ribs.

"They are just a little charred," Loretta claimed. She was being polite. I know that my family would have berated me for overcooking the ribs.

"These are delicious," her sister Marilyn said. The others agreed. I did not believe them, as I thought the ribs were awful. But as I learned, Loretta's family is very gracious.

In turn, Loretta said she always felt very welcomed by my family. We visited them often. I remember, before we were married, the first time we stayed at my oldest sister Marion's house in West Hartford. Marion was old fashioned. I had to sleep on the couch in her living room and not with Loretta in the guest room. On the other hand, when we visited my younger sister Hennie, she always let us be together. Both, however, were equally friendly to Loretta before and after we were married.

We also visited Loretta's families in Oklahoma and Texas, and I have always felt their friendship. They have a tradition of family gatherings at Thanksgiving, rotating among their homes. We hosted two Thanksgiving dinners in our home in Washington, D.C., and we attended several of theirs in Dallas and Houston. In short, our families and the communities we grew up in, Black and white, have enriched both of us.

## BACK TO SOUTH AFRICA

In July 2004, Loretta and I flew to South Africa to celebrate the first birthday of my granddaughter, Tselane. It was my third trip to South Africa and Loretta's first. The family of Andrew Motaung -- my daughter April's husband and Tselane's father -- had not yet met Tselane, and we had not met all his family. We stayed in and toured Pretoria, seat of the executive branch of government of South Africa. We were especially surprised and impressed at how comfortable we felt there as a bi-racial couple.

Several times, Loretta and I visited Andrew's sister and brother-in-law who live outside the city in one of the nearby townships, Mamelodi. During apartheid, Blacks in South Africa had to leave the cities at the end of the day. Many lived in squalid townships, although some of the townships were more middle class. When we visited post-apartheid, Andrew's family's home was quite nice and the neighborhood well-tended.

Andrew took us on a tour of Attridgeville, the township he had lived in when he was a boy during apartheid. We heard some hair-raising tales. One was about how boys sometimes hid at night to avoid the white police who prowled the neighborhood and might abduct them. Fortunately, Andrew was later able to leave South Africa and go to college in the United States on a scholarship. He earned an undergraduate degree at Montreat College, a private liberal arts college in North Carolina, and a master's degree in theology from the University of Princeton in New Jersey. Later, after he married April, he earned a second master's degree, in education, from Notre Dame University in Baltimore. He became a teacher and then an assistant principal in the Baltimore school system.

We also toured Soweto, which I had visited in the mid-1980s. What a difference. No Hippos – security tank police vehicles – to be afraid of! But still, the signs of the previous sad story of the 1976 student uprising and the killing of student Peterson were there, including some plaques and stark photos. We visited the home of Nelson Mandela, a truly sobering experience.

*Smith and Motaung families, Fouriesburg,*
*South Africa, July 2004.*

For Tselane's birthday, we were driven to the home of Andrew's father, Morbudi Motaung, in Fouriesburg, a pleasant, small town situated near the Maluti Mountains in the province of Free State. It was a four-hour drive from Pretoria through beautiful countryside. While there, Loretta and I were driven up to Lesotho, a separate, high-altitude, land-locked country encircled by South Africa, like a hole in a donut. We only had a few hours, so we did not see much. What we saw was some stark poverty amidst a gorgeous landscape.

But, of course, our main purpose was to celebrate my granddaughter Tselane's first birthday. It was quite a festive occasion. Andrew's family came, about 16 of us in all. It was a beautiful, sunny day, and Andrew's stepmother, Maphumotsa, welcomed everyone into the home. She wore a colorful South African dress, as did April. Outside, Maphumotsa cooked "pap," a South African staple made of a type of finely crushed white cornmeal, slowly stirred and thickened in a huge pot of hot water over an open fire. It is like the corn meal mush of the American South that Loretta was familiar with. Maphumotsa taught Loretta how to prepare it and the accompanying sauce made of tomatoes, peppers, and onions.

Inside the Motaung home, gifts were shared, and toasts were made. Andrew paid honor to his father, who gave me a tribal ceremonial hat. April wore a traditional African blanket. The party ended with a group photo of us, the beautiful mountains in the distance. A fitting way to celebrate Tselane's birthday!

## INDIA

I feel fortunate to have traveled to countries so different from the United States and meet many people very different from me. I think if more white Americans had similar experiences, there would be less hate and more understanding of those who are different from them.

A special example is my friend Suresh Dutia, from India, who lives in northern Virginia. He and I first became friends in 1987, introduced by a mutual business acquaintance. Mr. Dutia (we always call each other by our surnames) was a businessman who traveled a great deal internationally. We worked on some business deals and trusted each other. I also think we both seemed to have smiles that appealed to each other, impish but sincere.

Soon Mr. Dutia and I became social friends. He invited me to his home to meet his wife Aruna and their children. At the time, Mrs. Dutia was pregnant with Raj, her youngest and the last of three sons. A couple of years later I visited them again. I remember Raj hanging onto the skirt of his mother's sari and peaking around at me. She picked him up and brought him to me.

"Mr. Smith is our friend," she told him. Raj and I smiled at each other. We developed an instant bond, one that we have maintained. I also met Mr. Dutia's father, who lived with them. When he died, I was asked to be present with them for his father's cremation. As part of their Hindu ritual, before the cremation the men walked around the casket seven times. It was somber, and for me a very moving and educational experience.

"You are part of our family," Mr. Dutia said.

## Traveling to India

Several years later, the Dutias met Loretta, and they were also very welcoming to her. Although all three of their sons were born in the United States, when the oldest – Ketu – got engaged, he and his fiancé Lavanya Prakash wanted to fly back to India to be married. In June 2012, we attended their engagement ceremony at the Hindu temple in Potomac, Maryland. It was a solemn yet colorful and musical event. Later, to our delight, Mr. and Mrs. Dutia invited us to attend the wedding in Delhi, and they paid all the expenses for our travel, including airfare, hotel, and meals. We truly felt part of their family!

Our trip began on November 26, 2012, at Dulles Airport, where we met up with Mr. Dutia for our flight. When we arrived the following afternoon in Delhi, the weather was sunny and warm, but the air was extremely polluted, to the point where Loretta was choking.

"I can hardly breathe," she said. "I hope this doesn't last the whole time we're here!"

From the airport, we were driven to our accommodations at the Gujarati Sumaj Guesthouse, a facility operated primarily for visiting residents of Gujarat, the Dutia's home state in India. It has many motel-like rooms, and we obviously were given a special one. The guesthouse also had a huge open courtyard in the middle of the ground floor, with food service. That evening, we were feted at a communal dinner with most of the older members of the Dutia family. The air pollution was still heavy, but the conversation was delightful, and the food was delicious.

The next morning, Loretta and I woke to a breeze and much cleaner air. We were driven further into the city to see some of the sights. The Delhi National Capital Territory is comprised of nine districts. With a population of nearly 17 million, it is the eighth most populous metropolis in the world. The city of New Delhi, built by the British in early 1920s, is the capital of India. Of course, we only saw a small segment of it.

We stopped and walked around for many blocks with Raj Dutia and a friend. Quite an eye opener! Some areas were quite nice but in others, many buildings were in shambles, as if they had been bombed. Sidewalks were often crumbled, with huge cracks and holes, making it difficult to walk. Children played in the rubble, emaciated men squatted, and unleashed dogs roamed unattended. There were, however, many outdoor vegetable markets and food stores. Women, even the poorest, wore colorful saris, and male Sikhs wore vivid turbans.

That evening, we traveled on the subway with eight members of Mrs. Dutia's family to visit the beautiful Lotus Temple, a Baha'i House of

Worship that was dedicated in 1986 and is notable for its flowerlike shape. Unfortunately, it was closed. But we walked past it for the equivalent of several blocks into the entrance of an old Hindu temple, through a dark corridor lined with stalls and impoverished beggars who lived in squalor in the caves beyond.

"I don't feel comfortable taking pictures here," Loretta said. She is an inveterate photographer, so this was unusual. We both walked quietly by, shaken by what we saw. Once inside, however, we encountered a brightly lit and colorful array of altars and stalls, with dozens of people strolling along. People were smiling, and the vendors were happy to see us.

## Ketu and Lavanya's Wedding Ceremonies

The next morning, the three days of wedding ceremonies began. We and many family members were taken by bus to a temple where Ketu, the groom, was escorted to a room and a priest performed Puja, a prayer service with a small pit of fire. That night was the Sangeet ceremony, traditionally held the night before a wedding. It started with Mehndi, when henna, a dye, was applied decoratively to the hands or arms of women and men. After an elaborate dinner, music and dancing started. A vibrant blur of swirling, brilliant colors that lasted for hours.

The following day, we were driven to meet with Mr. Dutia and his family for the actual wedding. All the men wore orange turbans, and I was presented with one. Again, they made me feel a part of their family. We gathered at the ISKCON Temple, one of the largest temple complexes in India. With music and dancing, we walked together, accompanying the groom to the wedding ceremony. A grand procession!

*Dan and Loretta with Dutia family after the wedding
of Ketu and Lavanya (seated).*

The wedding itself was held next to the temple under a tent fes-
tooned with colorful, striped banners. The parents, bride, groom, and
priest sat under the "Mandap," a four-pillared canopy decorated with flowers. Loretta and I sat near them on cushioned chairs, along with family
members and other honored guests. At the end of the ceremony, the new-
lyweds asked for blessings from their elders by touching their feet, including mine. I was very moved to be included in this ritual.

The next night was the reception honoring the wedding. It was
breathtaking. A huge gathering, with tables of food that stretched along
both sides of a long hall. No meat and no alcohol. But delicious! Plus, once
again, much music and dancing, lasting until 3 a.m. We finally made it
back to our lodgings totally exhausted.

The following days we were on our own. We walked around the
neighborhood and found a majestic old British hotel, the Oberoi Maidens.
We reserved a suite for the following night, and the staff ordered a driver to
take us to the town of Agra to see the Taj Mahal. We left Delhi early in the

morning. It was a harrowing three-hour drive, down a crowded two-lane highway often facing huge trucks in between motorcycles, ox-driven carts and small, swerving cars.

Once there, we found Agra charming and the Taj Mahal truly majestic. We arranged for a special tour and sat on the "Princess Diana Bench" for a photo. Returning to Delhi late in the evening, we had dinner at the hotel – our first with meat

*Dan and Loretta on the "Princess Diana Bench" at the Taj Mahal.*

and a glass of wine for Loretta. We slept well that night!

## Visiting Dubai

Our trip home included a two-day stop in Dubai, the most populous city in the United Arab Emirates. It was the first time for either of us in an Arab country. We hired a driver to show us the city. Quite an eye-opener after India. The buildings, streets, and sidewalks were all new and pristine. The people were an eclectic mix, with Arab women in full black burkas and female European tourists in colorful short skirts.

We toured the old part of Dubai, established in the 18th century as a small fishing village, then spent the evening downtown and viewed the Burj Khalifa, the tallest building in the world. We ate dinner around a man-made lake that displayed what were claimed to be the world's tallest fountains, with jets and lights choreographed to music. It was magical.

Loretta was disturbed, however, to watch a young Arab couple seated across from us. The man and his son ate readily, while his wife had to quickly pull back the black fabric covering her face to furtively eat a small morsel. Very sad to see, an image that we have both long remembered.

# CHAPTER 19
# Engaging in Politics

I cannot end this book without stressing my strong feelings about the need for people, especially Blacks in America, to be involved in the political process at all levels, local and national. I worked hard during my life to enable Blacks to vote, starting in the 1960s in Alabama. This effort must continue. Too many people, Black and white, died for us to have this right, and we must exercise it. Now, with "white supremacists" pushing to reduce the ability of Blacks to vote, it is even more important that we double down on our efforts to be heard.

*Muriel Bowser, then candidate for District Council and later Mayor of Washington D.C. with Dan and Loretta at their backyard birthday party for her, July 2006.*

As for Loretta and me, we are both Democrats. Although we have Republican friends, we feel strongly that the Democratic Party has more empathy and concern for the issues we care about, especially protecting rights for women and minorities and for saving the environment and preventing the catastrophes from climate change. But we also believe that everyone, including Republicans and Independents or members of any other party, should be active on issues they care about so long as they fight fair. In a democracy, everyone eligible to vote should be encouraged – indeed helped – to vote.

Loretta and I live in Ward 4, in upper northwest Washington D.C. We have campaigned on behalf of local candidates for mayor and members of the District Council. We have circulated petitions for candidates to get on the ballot and held many fundraisers in our back yard. I also served for several years as financial secretary of the Ward 4 Democrats. As residents of the nation's capital, however, we do not have representatives who can vote in the U.S. Congress, so we also promote candidates in other states, in congressional as well as Presidential elections. Following are a few highlights of our activities for Presidential candidates.

## JOHN KERRY AND THE DNC

We started campaigning together in 2004 for John Kerry's Presidential campaign. Loretta was a volunteer working a couple of days a week with the Women's Leadership Forum of the Democratic National Committee (DNC). We both spent many hours there stuffing envelopes and making phone calls. As a result, we received credentials for the Democratic Convention that was held in Boston, the first either of us had attended. It was spectacular. Later, we attended many DNC events, held a large fundraiser for Kerry in our backyard, and traveled to Harrisburg, Pennsylvania, both for Kerry and to support a Democratic woman running for the House of Represent- atives. We walked the streets, knocked on doors, and talked to many people to encourage them to vote. Needless to say, we were very disappointed when Kerry lost.

*Dan with Senator Kerry at a Congressional Black Caucus reception, May 2004.*

## HILLARY CLINTON

In 2008, we agreed to support Hillary Clinton in the Democratic primary. While I respected Barack Obama, I did not think at the time that a Black man had a chance of being elected President. Also, both Loretta and I knew and admired Senator Clinton and felt strongly that she would make a fine President, the first woman to hold the position.

Our most memorable political trip was a bus ride we took with her campaign to New Hampshire in January 2008. Three busloads were

*Hillary Clinton with Loretta and Dan at breakfast reception, Feb. 2008.*

packed with mostly much younger Democrats – we and a few others were among the oldest. Our group ended up high in the mountains in Berlin (pro- nounced Burr-lun, empha- sis on the first syllable), a depressed town of about

10,000 where hundreds of people had lost their jobs when the major employer, a paper mill, closed the previous year.

*Dan and Loretta, campaigning in Berlin NH, January 2008.*

Hillary's staff was very well organized, and they kept us working for 10-12 hours a day in frigid weather, walking door to door. Many residents agreed that Sen. Clinton had the desire and ability to help them. Former President Bill Clinton spoke at a large rally in City Hall. He wowed them with a strong message about Hillary's past experience and future plans. Several times we stood on busy street corners with totem-pole style Hillary signs and waved at the passersby. On the day of the New Hampshire primary election, at "our" polling place, we noticed right away that most Democrats said they were for Sen. Clinton.

"She's GOT to win," an elderly woman exclaimed, and her husband nodded in agreement. Several people stressed her knowledge and experience. A Republican man said he would vote for Hillary in the general election.

After the polls closed that night, we got back on our bus and headed slowly down the mountain in the dark, stopping to pick up volunteers in other towns along the way. Cell phone coverage was sparse, and we initially thought Barack Obama was in the lead. We heard the results as we arrived at the Clinton headquarters in Manchester around 11 p.m. It was filled with people—young and old, Black and white—watching one small television set. We all cheered mightily as Hillary made her New Hampshire victory speech.

We continued to work for Hillary's campaign until Barack Obama surged ahead of her in the later Democratic primaries, and she finally conceded to him. Then we immediately switched to working for Obama.

*Dan casts his ballot for Obama on Nov. 4, 2008. Photo by Loretta Neumann.*

## BARACK OBAMA

After Obama won the primary, we spent our time working for him, mainly in northern Virginia. We knocked on doors to talk to voters and delivered campaign literature. Loretta and I cooked many meals that we delivered to volunteers working at local Democratic headquarters. We attended several rallies, including Obama's last one the night before election day in Manassas, Virginia, a truly exciting event held in an open-air arena. Casting my vote for Obama the next day was truly a very moving moment for me. And it was, of course, thrilling when the votes came in that night and showed that Obama won.

*Dan and Loretta at President Obama's
inauguration, January 21, 2009.*

Then in January, the inauguration of President Obama was truly one the highlights of my life. Loretta and I were fortunate to receive tickets from Rachel Kennedy, a dear friend of ours and close friend of Michelle Obama's mother, Marian Robinson. Because of the extremely frigid weather (the high was only 16 degrees), we bundled up and were elated to sit in the middle near the front of the audience, under the Presidential stage. We both cried when Obama took his oath of office.

I truly never believed that I would see America elect a Black man as President. That night we attended several parties and an Inaugural Ball, and the next morning I ushered at the Inaugural Prayer Service at the Washington National Cathedral. Again, because of our friend Rachel Kennedy, Loretta was able to sit in the front row across from the President.

Four years later, we again worked on President Obama's behalf for his re-election, including canvassing around DC and spending several days campaigning with our friends Marianne Smith and Carl Pechman in and around Richmond, Virginia. Both Loretta and I prefer meeting with people in person rather than phoning them.

We were, of course, thrilled that President Obama again won his election. This time my niece Gail (daughter of my sister Henny) and her husband Jim Cody joined us to watch the inaugural parade on special bleachers along Pennsylvania Avenue. The next day, they came with us to the White House for a post-inaugural tour.

*Jim and Gail Cody with Loretta and Dan at White House, Jan. 22, 2013,*
*day after President Obama's second inauguration.*

Again, I was very moved by it all. As the son of a slave, I never thought I would see this happen - a Black man twice elected President of the United States! I thought of what my grandfather and others who came before him must have suffered under slavery; what my father and others endured with Jim Crow laws, lynchings, and segregation; and what Black Americans continue to suffer today with the effects of discriminations and of white supremacy.

# HILLARY CLINTON AGAIN

*Loretta and friend Gueta Mezzetti in Pennsylvania, November 2016.*

In 2016, we volunteered once more to help elect Hillary Clinton for President. Loretta was then working part-time as membership and communications coordinator for the Woman's National Democratic Club. We participated in many campaign activities, especially writing cards and emails to encourage people to vote for her. During the last few days before the election, Loretta spent time canvassing for Hillary in Pennsylvania.

The night of the election, November 9, Loretta and I attended a gala "watch party" at the Woman's National Democratic Club, held in their majestic and historic mansion, the 19th Century Whittemore House. Every room was filled with Democratic women and men, dressed in their finery, and sitting at tables with food and champagne, eagerly awaiting the election results. However, as the returns came in, we were devastated when she lost the electoral votes to Donald Trump, although she won the popular vote by more than two million. We left early and drove home in sadness.

The next four years were extremely difficult, as programs that we care about dealing with civil and women's rights, environmental protection, climate change, education, and many social programs were decimated. Trump had no empathy for people who were not like him. Hispanics and Muslims were vilified, and Black Americans faced extremely troubling times. The riots provoked by white nationalists in Charlottesville VA in 2017 and the horrific death of George Floyd in Minneapolis in 2020 were especially distressing. Trump's mishandling of the Covid outbreak in 2020 lead to the loss of thousands of lives. It was truly a dark four years.

# JOE BIDEN

In 2020, because of the Covid pandemic and my personal health problems, we were not able to get out physically to volunteer on elections. But we donated money, made phone calls, and wrote emails and postcards urging voters to support Joe Biden and Kamala Harris for President and Vice President. Loretta had met Biden when he was a senator, and we both had met and supported Harris when she ran for the Senate in California.

After the election, we were appalled at the efforts of Trump and his Republican followers to use baseless lies to overturn the election. We were especially upset to watch Trump's supporters storm the U.S. Capitol on January 6, 2021. Their threats to our Constitution and our nation's democracy were very real, and they continue as I end my story.

Despite these tribulations, I feel that President Biden is trying his best to do right by all Americans and to undue many of the harms that Trump inflicted. It is unfortunate that most Republican politicians have demonstrated their unwillingness to support policies and programs that help the public. Biden has too often been blamed for things that were out of his control or were caused by others. He has also not been recognized for the many good things he has accomplished.

I tend to be an optimist. My hope is that somehow we can all work together, regardless of our differences and political affiliations, We MUST keep our constitutional democracy intact. There is too much hate today and not enough kindness.

*Dan in front of his home with Biden signs, Nov. 2020.*
*Photo by Loretta Neumann.*

# Learning from the Past

I want to conclude with a few more observations and thoughts about racism in America. It brings me to tears that in the third decade of the 21st century, the nation seems to be regressing rather than progressing in the areas of civil rights—just as it did a hundred years earlier. Apparently, and unfortunately, too many people in our nation still do not agree on eliminating the types of obstacles I and other Black Americans encountered in our lives and careers.

In the historic, systemically racist American tradition, it was the norm for minorities initially to do the dangerous or dirty, heavy work. Then they would be pushed out of sight, hidden, and replaced with white workers who would be given the credit by the media for the success of the project. An example was the construction of the Alaska Highway in 1942. It was built by about 11,000 soldiers in the U.S. Army Corps of Engineers, 95th Regiment, of which one third were Black Americans in three newly formed Negro Regiments. Most of the back-breaking work was accomplished by the Black soldiers. However, the film crews, journalists and photographers who documented the completed project only showed the white regiments. And the Blacks were treated in the Yukon with the same racism they would have faced in the Deep South.[66]

Similar discriminatory treatment was inflicted earlier, during the mid-1800s, on the Chinese immigrants who constructed the Transcontinental Railroad. On May 10, 1869, after the railroad was completed, the celebratory photograph showed two locomotives from East and West meeting at Promontory Summit, Utah. In it are engineers shaking hands and popping champagne, surrounded by a cheering crowd of railroad workers. But none of the 20,000 Chinese immigrants who had risked their lives to blast granite and break through the Sierra Nevada by hand were included.[67]

The term today is "white supremacy," which until recently I had never seen in my old dictionaries. The earliest mention I found was in my 1995 edition of the Random House *Webster's College Dictionary*: "a belief that the white race is superior to other races, esp. the black race." On the Internet I found a more expansive and disturbing definition: "The belief that the white race is *inherently* superior to other races *and that white people should have control over people of other races.*"[68] [Emphasis added.]

Many white people resent the term white supremacy and any discussion of the racism that emanates from it. They confuse bigotry, which they may claim to abhor, with systemic racism, an institutional construct that they do not understand. A white person can genuinely have a Black friend and still support policies that will harm that Black friend's life and opportunities.

I also find very befuddling the current outrage by many conservatives against the study of "critical race theory" in public schools. It is another term that I had never heard of until recently, and I was surprised to find a definition of it that is virtually the same as how I have long felt. A New York Times article stated that the theory "argues that historical patterns of racism are ingrained in law and other modern institutions, and that the legacies of slavery, segregation and Jim Crow still create an uneven playing field for Black people and other people of color. The idea is that racism is not a matter of individual bigotry but is systemic in America."[69]

I frankly cannot imagine how anyone can dispute what that definition says nor the need for a study of it. Systemic racism is simply a truism. Indeed, I feel strongly that everyone in the United States—not just students—should learn about the history of racism in a manner that is appropriate to their ages and abilities including Black, brown, and Asian Americans as well as white. Surely by having a free and open discussion, we can together find solutions to this problem that still plagues us all.

One solution that has been much discussed and often discounted by white Americans is the possible provision of reparations for descendants of enslaved people. The question is how can the United States compensate citizens whose ancestors were treated as mere chattel for nearly 250 years? How to make amends when, even after the Civil War, Blacks continued to face rapes, lynchings, forced labor, and other depredations that stripped them of their dignity, civil rights, and even their lives? How to reimburse them now for the discriminatory actions by federal, state, and local governments that stripped them of the social and economic opportunities afforded white Americans?

The fact is that the ancestors of enslaved Black Americans were ripped from their homes and families in Africa and were forcibly brought to this country against their will. They did not come by choice. Hence, unlike immigrants who came here freely, we were the only ethnic group unable to retain our own native language or culture. And we received no payment for our labor in helping to build the physical and economic wealth of this country.

I do not know what can be done to make suitable reparations for all the harm that has been inflicted. I assume a good economist would find the true cost to be in the multi-trillions of dollars. But I do feel that the time has come for a full examination of the issues and that recommendations should be found for a solution that is both appropriate and fair.

*Dan with Rep. John Lewis, Oct. 2012. Photo by Loretta Neumann.*

In the meantime, we must not allow the discontinuation of studies about slavery and racism in this country. We must not forget our heroes who did so much to further equality for all Americans. Among these I remember my friend, the late Representative John Lewis who wrote, "There is an old African proverb: 'When you pray move your feet.' As a nation, if we care for our beloved community, we must move our feet, our hands, our hearts, our resources to build and not to tear down, to reconcile and not to divide, to love and not to hate, to heal and not to kill. In the final analysis, we are one people, one family, one house— the American house, the American family."[70]

Indeed, as I have often said, with so much hate in the world, what we most need is kindness. We cannot continue in this nation hating each other. Although my father was born into slavery, he never hated anyone. He always said, "Do good things." That is what has guided me throughout my life.

*Daniel R. Smith, Sr.*
October 2022

# Tributes To Dan

ALFRED YOUMATZ
*Dan Smith – My Friend for Life*
April 23, 2021

*Alfred (Al) Youmatz and Dan, 2013.*
*Photo by Loretta Neumann.*

I believe it was the summer of 1948 when I first met Danny in our home town of Winsted, Conn. I was 15 and Dan was 16 or 17. I was out walking, looking for a summer job to earn spending money for my freshman year at Gilbert High School. I had seen Dan around town, but never actually met him before since we attended different schools. We ran into each other on Oak Street and struck up a conversation.

Dan had his dog with him that day, and I remember how impressed I was with the dog's behavior and his ability to respond to hand commands. Dan had worked for Dr. Church, the veterinarian in Winsted, where he learned how to handle animals. I was in awe, and though he was somewhat of a dog "whisperer."

At the time we met, my family lived on North Main Street and Dan's on Chestnut Street. I thought that was odd because Chestnut Street was known as "Little Italy" back then and Dan was black, but it didn't really matter to me. In 1948, there were just a handful of black families in the Winsted area. In high school, I think Dan had just one black friend – he was very much alone in that respect.

Dan and I soon became fast friends. In 1950 he got me a job at Smith's Chicken Farm, affectionately known as "Smitty's". (No relation to Dan.) It was hard work, but also full of fun and shenanigans! Dan was exceptionally strong! He could easily lift a 100-pound bag of feed off the delivery truck and carry it up to the 2nd floor of the chicken coop. No one would dare mess with him!!

In addition to feeding and caring for the chickens, we did a lot of construction work on an additional building Mr. Smith was putting up to expand the farm. I barely had my license but remember driving the dump truck to pick up stone and dirt, and then Dan and I mixing and pouring cement. Unfortunately, the new building was lost in the flood of 1955. Had this not happened, Smitty would have had over 10,000 egg-laying hens!

Dan and I both graduated from Gilbert High in 1952. He was drafted into the Army and sent to Korea; afterwards he went on to Springfield College. I went straight from high school into the Navy, marrying my high school sweetheart in 1954. After completing our respective service obligations, I came back to Winsted where I still reside with my wife of 66 years; Dan went to D.C. where he continues to live an exemplary life of public service.

While we took very different paths, we've managed to stay in touch throughout all these years, updating each other on the comings and goings of life, and sharing fine memories. I still call Dan my best friend and know that when our days on this good earth are done, I will meet him again in Heaven.

VIRGINIA
MCCABE
HOFFMAN
*Tribute to Danny Smith*
June 3, 2021

*Dan and Virginia (Ginny) Hoffman, 2009.*
*Photo by Loretta Neumann.*

There used to be this teen-ager who came to our house, sometimes to do his home-work. I was the pesky little kid who wouldn't leave him alone. But Danny was good to me. He talked to me as though we were equals.

Danny was a member of my father's Boy Scout troop, Troop 18 in Winsted, Conn. He eventually became troop leader, and, I think, assistant Scout Master. Danny loved my father and Dad loved Danny. My father had two daughters and was outnumbered in our family, so I'm sure it was a blessing to him to have a "son."

My memories are not great in quantity, but one thing I do remember is the collecting of newspapers. This was post-WWII, and money was tight. Even I, at about 10 years of age, knew that. We had a dirt cellar into which those newspapers would go. On the weekends, a couple of Scouts would come to the house to bind the papers into bundles they could handle. Pretty soon the cellar would fill up. As I remember, when the cellar was full, there was a ton of newspapers in it. Someone would come with a truck and load them up to be hauled away.

I don't remember how much money the Scouts got for that truck load, but I do remember that it paid for every Scout in the troop to attend Camp Workcoeman for one week, free. And that allowed the Scout Master and his family to stay in the Scout Master's cabin for a week, free. We did that for two or three years. And that's where I learned to swim!

Those are great memories. And where would we be without them.

BILL BABCOCK
April 18, 2021

*Dan with William (Bill) Babcock, 2011*
*Photo by Loretta Neumann.*

I have known Dan Smith for 64 years. We were friends in college and lived in an apartment together with two other students for one year.

Dan is five years my senior and had spent several years at war in Korea. He entered Springfield College the same year I did in 1956. We shared some classes and became friends in a lifesaving swimming class. Dan almost drowned me, and I chased after him. We ended up laughing and afterwards became friends.

"Why did I become friends with a Negro?" I was asked. Negro was the preferred name in those days before the "Black" era. There were other questions, such as, "Do you eat off the same plates?" and "How can you live with someone like him?" I had seen racism in my small town in Branford, Connecticut.

I did not understand it, and I was very ignorant of its impact. Negroes all lived in designated areas close to the railroad factories. Many whites worked there too. All who worked there died in their forties because of massive pollution. My mother was the reason I was somewhat open-minded. She opened our home to all my friends. She seldom had harsh words for anyone.

Dan was involved with various student activities and frequently led those activities. Years later, after graduate school, I began to see how segregated professionalism was. I had several training experiences in D.C. and Dan and I renewed our friendship. I had been best man at Dan's wedding, and he was best man at my wedding. We had children and shared some fine experiences.

Dan has devoted his life to bringing diverse groups together. He has provided leadership to us all. His influence has changed lives and brought many people to a greater understanding of racial equality. It sure has worked for me.

I loved getting to know Dan's children. They are very independent and opinionated. Just like Dan, and it annoys the hell out of him. I loved watching April pound the dickens out of an opponent in a karate class. Dan wrestled at Springfield College but knew very little about the sport. However, his opponents respected his strength and determination.

When Dan was working towards integrating state and federal agencies in Connecticut and Massachusetts, he had a Doberman pincer traveling with him for obvious reasons. When Dan was not at home in our apartment, "Mark" roamed the apartment like a Bengal tiger looking for prey. Dan went out for the football team. Being a Physical Education college, most of the players had been team captains in high school. Dan played Guard. On defense, two players would try and block him to clear the way for the running back. Our coach said Dan was the most difficult guard to move he ever saw. Dan has always been difficult to move on any position. God bless him!

## DIANE HAZARD GREEN MCCAMBRIDGE
*Tribute from "Danni"*
May 9, 2021

I was in college with Dan. He was always polite, respectful, fun, and goal oriented. We had a special connection, and I will treasure that friendship forever.

*Diane (Danni) McCambridge and Dan, August 2017.*
*Photo by Loretta Neumann.*

## SHERILYN PRUITT
*A Tribute to Dan*
May 9, 2011

I met Dan Smith in 1991 through my work with the Federal government and we became fast friends. At that time, he was the lead for President George H.W. Bush's Thousand Points of light Initiative and invited me to get involved in the Combined Federal Campaign Halloween Contest for Charity. I agreed to participate and to my surprise, I was not just involved, Dan appointed me to lead the effort. It was a bit overwhelming for me as I was a brand-new federal employee. But with Dan's support, the event was wildly successful in raising money and boosting employee morale and comradery across the government agencies located in the massive Parklawn building.

Over the years, our friendship flourished inside and outside of the workplace. Dan served as a

*Dan with Sherilyn Pruitt (right) and her children Steven and Shaina, Christmas 2018. Photo by Loretta Neumann*

mentor to me and was always available to discuss workplace issues and career decisions. When I became a mother, he provided guidance on how I could be the best parent I could be. I watched him and learned a great deal about his life choice and how he prioritized family above all else. Dan's caring, generosity, and support was not just limited to his family members – he has also provided financial and emotional support to a wide range of friends and colleagues.

I marvel at the stories of his humble beginnings. Dan and his siblings lost their father to a terrible accident when they were young and grew up in extreme poverty. Despite their early circumstances, Dan and his siblings were all able to overcome adversity and become optimistic, kind, highly successful members of society. Dan has truly inspired me.

I am thrilled that my relationship with Dan has deepened and grown over the years. Our families know each other, and my children and I spend most holidays with Dan and his lovely wife Loretta. We are so close that Dan is the emergency contact for me and my kids. I am thankful to God that my chance encounter in a government cafeteria 30 years ago turned into a life-long blessing in the form of my friendship with Dan Smith – mentor, best friend, emergency contact.

## MORTON LEBOW
May 2021

I first met Dan Smith i
when he was tapped to
the first Area Health E
Centers. These AHE
authorized by Congre
increase the supply
care practitioners in

*rton (Mort) and Eileen Lebow, Jan. 1, 2020.*
*Photo by Loretta Neumann.*

city underserved areas.

Hampered
program going by
day there are more
which owe their

g shortages, Dan managed to get the
ar contracts to 11 medical schools. To-
 organizations in all parts of the country,
art that Dan was able to give them.

## SURESH D            DUTIA) AND FAMILY
August 17, 200

Mr. Daniel                 Smith) has been our Family Friend for over
35 Years; h                 ntegral part us, and we always feel that he has
become a ]                  our Family.

I                          uring a business meeting in 1987, and we continue to                   pportunities in various fields. We developed a
friendsh                    transformed into close family.

Mr. Smith has been a true mentor, guiding us through many challenges in life and providing us valuable assistance whenever situations warranted. Mr. Smith has never failed us; from our experience, we have realized that Mr. Smith is unquestionably truly trustworthy.

*Dan and Mr. Dutia, Delhi, India, November 2012.*
*Photo by Loretta Neumann*

During illness of my parents (both over 80s), Mr. Smith stepped in and provided valuable assistance. He has never failed to deliver, personally, flowers on Easter, Mothers' Day, and Christmas, continually for the last 35 years.

We feel blessed to have Mr. Smith in our life.

*Dan on his 90th birthday with Raj Dutia,*
*March 2022. Photo by Aruna Dutia*

## RAJ DUTIA

When I was young, I was told that Mr. Dan Smith was my Godfather. I did not really understand what that meant; to me he was just Mr. Smith. As I get older those bits of wisdom he shared with me are more useful, and I have a better understanding of what the word means.

APRIL SMITH
MOTAUNG
*Tribute to My Dad*
June 2, 2021

*Dan with his daughter, April Motaung, Thanksgiving 2021. Photo by Loretta Neumann*

My Dad is a very special man. From the first time I can remember he has always been there for me. He has instilled in me the value of hard work, commitment, and dedication to anything I was involved in. He taught me to be proud of being a "Smith," and that that name meant something special. He made sure that I was taught the best social etiquette lessons so that I could navigate any social situation. He had many phrases that helped me along the way as I traveled through life: "Take care of business first," "A place for everything, and everything in its place," and many more. These phrases helped me think what I should do and do it well.

My dad was there for me when I was sick. He always knew how to treat a cold: A dose of Alka Seltzer Plus, Vicks Formula 44 and Vicks VapoRub did the trick . . . but more important was his bedside manner that helped me feel better.

I have so many memories of my Dad taking the time to be an important part of my life: standing on his shoulders saying, "Look at me!", laying tile together in the basement, teaching me to ride a bike, jumping the waves in the ocean, willing to taste my concoction of a disgusting drink that as a 6-year-old I insisted on him drinking, volunteering to have pies thrown at him for my birthday party, having Daddy/daughter movie dates to see *Time After Time* and *The Jerk*, his being at every soccer game even if he had to leave work early, doing the leg work to make sure my tuition for college was paid, helping and teaching me how to train my dog, making Thanksgiving dinner for my students in Baltimore City, and finally walking me down the aisle at my wedding.

My Dad is such a big part of who I am today. He taught me good values and morals that have steered me in the right direction and made me a confident little girl who grew up to be a successful woman. I know that I would not be the woman I am today without the love and guidance of my Dad. The most important thing about my Dad is that I know how much he loves me, because he has shown it in so many ways.

## ROB SMITH (DANIEL ROBERT SMITH, JR.)
*Tribute to My Dad*
May 24, 2021

When I think of my father, I think of him as a man of principles, values, pride, and respect. I view him as the ulti-

*Dan with his son Rob, 2014.*
*Photo by Loretta Neumann.*

mate gentleman, or rugged gentleman as he always likes to be called.

Early on in my childhood, he always taught me and gave me great examples of how a gentleman should act. For example . . . holding doors for women, allowing women to enter or exit the elevator or entrance first, standing up when a woman enters a room, having her walk on the inside of the sidewalk, pulling out her chair to help assist her in sitting down, to always sit facing the door so you can see what's going on and be able to protect your date if any chaos happens, and last, but not least, a gentleman always removes his hat when in the house.

My Dad instilled great values in me such as being kind to people, helping people in need and those less fortunate, always help and respect the elderly, be positive, be determined, be gracious, and most important, always try to give someone you meet a smile.

My father is a family man who loves his children and has made a firm commitment to set his children up in life to win. He has always been in my life 120% and has thoroughly prepared me for this incredible adventurous journey we call life! Onwards and Upwards!

# Acknowledgements

This book is the culmination of more than four years of thinking, planning, researching, and writing on topics that relate to my life growing up in America. It would be inappropriate if I did not mention key figures who played major parts in putting it together – primarily my wife, Loretta Neumann, who began with me by typing up my handwritten and spoken stories. I especially appreciate her photographic talents, tracing our lives together. She also found historian Deborah Harvey and Professor Eileen Scully, who did the extensive research on my family history. Research for other parts of the book was also done by friends Farleigh Earhart and Sherilyn Pruitt.

Loretta then edited and formatted the stories into files that were subsequently organized into a coherent manuscript with a table of contents by Rebecca Maxey, wife of producer Mark Maxey, who is planning a film about me and has given me much support and encouragement. The manuscript was then extensively edited by Amber Jones, a good friend and experienced book editor. It was shared with journalist James Astille, who used it as background information for a December 2021 article in *The Economist*[134] and who introduced us to Natasha Fairweather, a literary agent, who also read it and made many constructive suggestions, most of which we incorporated.

I was also helped because I was lucky to have had the chance to tell my stories for more than 13 years on numerous radio and television programs and in various print media, beginning with an NPR interview in

---

[134] Citations and links for media mentioned herein are provided in this book in "Articles and Interviews with Daniel R. Smith."

2009 by Michel Martin in conjunction with the inauguration of President Barack Obama. I appeared on the front page of the New York Times in an article by Rick Lyman in August 2013, for the 50th anniversary of Martin Luther King's March on Washington and my participation in it. And in commemoration of the 400th anniversary of the arrival of slaves in Jamestown, Virginia in 1619, I was featured in a blog post by Ethical Culture Leader Hugh Taft-Morales.

Then an article was published on Medium.com by Martin Dobrow in June 2020, prompted by the Black Lives Matter protests after the brutal death of George Floyd. It was followed by a featured article in the *Washington Post* by Sydney Trent in July 2020. In turn, Ms. Trent's article led to a wave of television and radio interviews in England, Germany, and Spain; syndicated articles by Virginia Van Zant for Zenger News and by Issam Ahmed for Agence France; a newspaper article in Holland by Dutch Journalist Jan Postma; and even a Sunday sermon by Rev. Lawrence Wood, St. Andrew by the Sea Church in Alabama. In Feb 2022, as part of a series for Black History Month, Jan Crawford interviewed me on a *CBS Mornings* program, "Descended from Slavery," which included an interview of Sana Butler, author of *Sugar of the Crop: My Journey to Find the Children of Slaves.* Subsequently, composer Bruce Adolphe wrote a beautiful song using the words I said at the end of the CBS interview, "We Need More Kindness."

In addition, I greatly appreciate the reviews that other authors I admire wrote for the book: Juan Williams, Joe Davidson, Eugene Meyer, and Martin Dobrow. For legal advice, I want to thank my attorney Steve Bullock and my late and dear friend Jon Hoppe, and for financial advice our CPA Phil Williams. For help in creating this book, formatting it, and designing the cover, I thank Gareth Bentall, manager of Opus at Politics and Prose.

Additional advice on the design of the cover was provided by Sharon Villines, our neighbor and herself a graphic artist. I also thank Carolivia Herron, the best-selling author of *Nappy Hair* and other books, and the owner of Takoma Writers, an imprint of EpicCenter Literary Software. And I don't know how I would have done all this without the help of our cheerful and indefatigable assistant Geneva-Veronica Fields.

I also want to acknowledge and thank my many friends who played an important part in my life and are featured in my stories. And last but not least, I want to acknowledge and thank my family. First, my father and mother, who gave me the early support that I needed, and my siblings, with whom I shared so much of my life – Marion, Abe, Jenny, Hennie, and Margaret. And my daughter April and son Rob, who were with me through so many adventures together when they were young and who stayed with me when our lives changed. They have remained my closest family as we all have grown older.

To summarize, like all books, this one required teamwork, and I was fortunate to have so many great teammates working with me on it. Thank you all!

# Articles and Interviews

1. January 19, 2009 – "Son of Slave Connects Yesterday with Today," Radio interview by Michel Martin, *Tell Me More*, NPR News. *https://www.npr.org/templates/story/story.php?storyId=99549319*

2. August 23, 2013, *NY Times*, front page - "50 Years After March, Views of Fitful Progress," by Rick Lyman. *https://www.ny-times.com/2013/08/24/us/a-time-to-return-to-and-reflect-on-the-march-on-washington.html*

3. Sept. 3, 2019 – Blog #36: "400 Years is Today," Hugh Taft-Morales. *https://www.400years.today/archive/blog-36nbsp400-years-is-today*

4. June 19, 2020 – "Juneteenth: The Son of a Slave Reflects on the America He Sees Today" by Martin Dobrow - Professor of communications, Springfield College, MA. *https://medium.com/@mdo-brow/juneteenth-the-son-of-a-slave-reflects-on-the-america-he-sees-to-day-b45e1ed80c2f*

5. July 13, 2020 – "Springfield College Professor Martin Dobrow Previews Dan Smith '60 Story." Very moving video about Dan's life. *https://www.youtube.com/watch?v=L3DZbmNinfE&t=2s*

6. July 21, 2020 - interview of Dan on Takoma Park radio (WOWD) by Dr. Carolivia Herron about late Rep. John Lewis. *https://www.mixcloud.com/EpicCity/epic-city-july212020-remember-ing-john-lewis-guest-daniel-r-smith/*

7. July 27-28, 2020 - "At 88, he is a historical rarity — the living son of a slave," by Sydney Trent, *Washington Post*. on-line July 27, printed

July 28. *https://www.washingtonpost.com/history/2020/07/27/slave-son-racism-george-floyd/*

8.  Aug 7, 2020 – "The living son of an enslaved Black man," radio interview on BBC British Broadcasting Corp. *https://www.bbc.co.uk/sounds/play/p08mzrv5*

9.  August 15, 2020 - "A son of a slave reflects on his American story," syndicated article by Issam Ahmed, Agence France-Presse. Also, video for AFP's broadcast clients. One of the two text articles in English: Yahoo *https://news.yahoo.com/son-slave-reflects-american-story-022635226.html.* In French: *Le Point, TVS Monde*, and *La Croix - https://www.la-croix.com/L-histoire-americaine-Dan-Smith-fils-esclave-2020-08-15-1301109288*

10. August 28, 2020 – "Black lives matter: Damals und heute," German TV interview at home and Lincoln Memorial, anniversary of MLK 1963 March. Facebook clip: *https://www.facebook.com/watch/?v=3397409110324700*

11. September 8, 2020 – "El sueño de Daniel," Spanish TV interview on Dan and his life story, U.S. since slavery, and Black Lives Matter. *https://www.rtve.es/alacarta/videos/informe-semanal/informe-semanal-sueno-daniel/5657329/*

12. October 15, 2020 – "The Incredible Life of Daniel Smith, Living Son of a Slave," syndicated article by Virginia Van Zandt, Zenger News. *https://www.zenger.news/2020/10/15/the-incredible-life-of-daniel-smith-living-son-of-a-slave/*

13. October 21, 2020 – Powerful TV interview by Dave Fraser for WGBY, Springfield MA. *https://youtu.be/hc0_xCzajik*

14. Jan. 17, 2021 – Sermon by Rev. Lawrence Wood, St. Andrew by the Sea Church, Alabama. *https://www.standrewbythesea.org/recent-services#!/swx/pp/media_archives/3186/episode/84754*

15. Jan. 19, 2021 – Barcelona, Spain, TV interview. *https://www.ccma.cat/tv3/alacarta/telenoticies/dan-smith-fill-desclau-afronta-lera-biden-amb-optimisme/video/6080500/*

16. Dec. 4, 2021 – "Lexington/Son of a Slave "column by James Astill, *The Economist. https://www.economist.com/united-states/2021/12/04/a-racial-history-lesson-from-the-son-of-a-slave*

17. Feb. 16, 2022 –"Descended from Slavery" *CBS Mornings https://www.you tube.com/watch?v=JCWLs8-q4tQ*

18. Feb. 23, 2022 – "Schakel met het verleden," by Jan Postma, *De Telegraaf,* Dutch newspaper. *https://www.telegraaf.nl/nieuws/1098549908/dan-smith-zoon-van-een-slaaf-hielp-amerika-te-veranderen*

19. March 21, 2022 – "We Need More Kindness," song composed by Bruce Adolphe using Dan Smith's words during the *CBS Mornings* program on Feb. 16, 2022.

20. Mar.29, 2022 – "Group seeks to right wrongs at Lincoln Memorial centennial," column by John Kelly, *Washington Post.* Dan is cited. *https://wapo.st/3NG4fxZ*

# Endnotes

## CHAPTER 1

[1] Lynn A. Nelson, *Pharsalia, An Environmental Biography of a Southern Plantation, 1780-1880* (The University of Georgia Press, Athens GA, 2007) 19-22.

[2] Oliver A. Pollard, Jr., *Under the Blue Ledge, Nelson County Virginia* (The Dietz Press, Richmond, VA, 1997) 89.

[3] James Hugo Johnston, *Race Relations in Virginia and Miscegenation in the South, 1776-1860* (University of Massachusetts Press, Amherst, 1970) 161.

[4] Research on Nelson County and Smith family in Virginia provided by Deborah Harvey, Professional Genealogist, Back to Your Roots LLC, Lovingston, VA.

[5] Source: 1860 U.S. census, Buckingham County, Virginia, slave schedule, District 2, p. 46, Robert T. Hubard, owner; image, Ancestry (www.ancestry.com : accessed April 10, 2021). Also, 1860 U.S. census, Nelson County, Virginia, slave schedule, p. 21, R.T. Hubard, owner; image, Ancestry (www.ancestry.com: accessed April 10, 2021).

[6] Census research from Eileen Scully, PhD, Faculty in Society, Culture and Thought, Bennington College, VT.

[7] Pollard, *Under the Blue Ledge*, 218.

## CHAPTER 4

[8] The Gilbert School website at www.gilbertschool.org.

[9] *Winsted Evening Citizen*, March 1950.

[10] Historic Valley Forge, "Boy Scout Jamborees at Valley Forge during the Truman and Eisenhower Administrations" online at www.ushistory.org/valleyforge

## CHAPTER 5

[11] Blanche Saunders, *Training You to Train Your Dog* (Doubleday, Garden City, NJ, June 1952).

[12] Clayton G. Going, *Dogs at War* (The Macmillan Company, New York, NY, 1944).

[13] *Dogs at War*, 34.

[14] *Dogs at War*, 37.

## CHAPTER 6

[15] Interview with Gene Neff, October 12, 2018. Kyle Macy, Interviewer. Louie B. Nunn Center for Oral History, University of Kentucky Libraries. University of Kentucky Athletics: Men's Basketball Oral History Project. Interview Accession Number: 2018oh595_af956. Online at www.kentuckyoralhistory.org.

CHAPTER 7

[16] John Hersey, "A Reporter at Large: Over the Mad River," *The New Yorker,* September 17, 1955: 132.

[17] John Hersey, "Handful of Men Meet Catastrophe with Stirring Epic of Courage," *Boston Advertiser*, August 28, 1955: 10.

[18] Dick Ahles, "Memories of a Flood, 50 Years Later," *The New York Times*, August 14, 2005.

[19] Peter Van Slingerland, "A Connecticut town fights back," *Look*, December 27, 1955.

[20] David Owens and Jesse Leavenworth, "Landscape Changed Forever," *The Hartford Courant*, August 16, 2005.

[21] Dick Ahles, "Memories of a Flood, 50 Years Later," *The New York Times*, August 14, 2005

CHAPTER 9

[22] Rick Lyman, "50 Years After March, Views of Fitful Progress," *The New York Times*, August 23, 2013: 1

[23] Videos explaining the issues and showing clips of Martin Luther King's commencement address are available on www.youtube.com.

CHAPTER 10

[24] Paul Ware, "From the Program Director," *The TISEP Reporter,* September 2, 1965: 10-A.

[25] *The TISEP Reporter* 13-15C, 25-B, 14-A.

[26] Diane Eickhoff, *The TISEP Reporter* 16C.

CHAPTER 11

[27] Michael Lottman, "Poverty War Beings in Old Hayneville Church," *The Southern Courier*, Weekend Edition, February 11-12, 1967.

[28] Kate Harris, "After Turbulent Birth, Lowndes OEO project is quietly under way," *The Birmingham News*, March 12, 1967.

[29] Michael Lottman, "This Is Not the End of the Program," *The Southern Courier*, Weekend Edition, March 18-19, 1967: 1.

[30] Rawles, Lee, "Rosa Parks' attorney: 'If the story would be told, I'd have to tell it'," *ABA Journal*, podcast, August 20, 2013, online at www.americanbar.org.

[31] A.E. Amerson and Lucius Amerson, *Great Courage: The Autobiography of the First Black Sheriff Elected in the South Since Reconstruction* (Amazon Kindle, 2004).

[32] John Hulett, "How the Black Panther Party was Organized," May 22, 1966, Eyes on the Prize Civil Rights Reader: Documents, Speeches, and Firsthand Accounts from the Black Freedom Struggle, edited by Clayborne Carson, et al. (Penguin Books, New York, NY, 1991).

[33] In 1970, John Hulett was elected sheriff of Lowndes County on the LCFO ticket. He served in public office, first as sheriff and later as probate judge, for 22 years.

CHAPTER 12

[34] James W. Loewen, *Sundown Towns: A Hidden Dimension of American Racism* (The New Press, New York, NY, 2018).

[35] Shelley v. Kraemer, 334 U.S. 1 (1948).

[36] Dylan Matthews, "Everything you need to know about the war on poverty," *The Washington Post*, January 8, 2014.

[37] "Dr. Joseph T. English, M.D. Peace Corps Shrink," *Peace Corps Worldwide*, accessed October 20, 2020, www.peacecorpsworldwide.org.

[38] Harbor Health website at www.hhsi.us.

[39] Care STL Health website at www.carestlhealth.org.

[40] Gerald Sparer, George B. Dines and Daniel Smith, "Consumer Participation in OEO-Assisted Neighborhood Health Centers," *American Journal of Public Health*, 60 no. 6 (June 1970), pp. 1091-1102.

[41] *Bill Turque, "In historically Black Tobytown, a 'dilapidated' eternal resting place," The Washington Post, March 7, 2017.*

[42] Parents' Coalition of Montgomery County, "How the Descendants of Freed Slaves Lost their Land in Montgomery County," blog, April 19, 2016 online at www.https://parentscoalitionmc.blogspot.com. Also: "Amid Montgomery's affluence, plight of suburban poor worsens in downturn," *The Washington Post*, November 12, 2010.

[43] National Association of Counties, Brilliant Ideas at Work, "RideOn Route 301— Tobytown Isolated Community," 2017, www.naco.org/brilliant-ideas.

CHAPTER 14

[44] Section 774(a), Comprehensive Health Manpower Training Act of 1971 (PL 92-157, November 18, 1971).

[45] Carnegie Commission on Higher Education. *Higher Education and the Nation's Health: Policies for Medical and Dental Education.* (McGraw-Hill, New York, NY, 1970).

[46] Charles E. Odegaard, *Area Health Education Centers: The Pioneering Years, 1972-1978* (Carnegie Council on Policy Studies in Higher Education, 1979) 22.

[47] Douglas Fenderson, PhD., Director, Office of Special Programs, National Institutes of Health, *Memorandum to Personnel Office*, October 4, 1973.

[48] U.S. Department of Health, Education and Welfare, Public Health Service, Health Resources Administration, Bureau of Health Manpower, *A Supplement to Area Health Education Centers: A Directory of Federal, State, Local and Private Decentralized Health Professional Education Programs,* DHEW Publication No. (HRA) 76-74, Prepared by C.E. Pagan Associates, Inc. Baltimore, MD. March 1976 and *An Evaluation Profile:*

*Summary of the Evaluation Activities of the Individual Area Health Education Centers, Prepared by C.E. Pagan Associates, Inc. Baltimore, MD,* February 25, 1977.

[49] U.S. Congress, House Committee on Appropriations, Survey and Investigations. *A Report on the Area Health Education Centers Program Administered by the Department of Health, Education, and Welfare.* Hearings on Departments of Labor and Health, Education, and Welfare Appropriations for 1979. Part 2. I95th Congress, 2nd session. (Government Printing Office, Washington, DC, 1978).

## CHAPTER 15
[50] Rep. Yvonne Braithwaite Burke and Rep Louis Stokes, Memorandum to Members of the Congressional Black Caucus, December 1, 1977.

[51] Rep. Yvonne Braithwaite Burke et al., letter to Joseph A. Califano, Secretary, Department of Health, Education and Welfare, December 2, 1977.

[52] Sen. Edward William Brooke, telegram to Joseph A. Califano, Secretary, Department of Health, Education and Welfare, December 22, 1977.

[53] Harold B. Haley, M.D, Associate Dean-Roanoke, University of Virginia; Edith D. Leyasmeyer, PhD, Director, Area Health Education Center, University of Minnesota; Carleton P. Menge, Professor of Education, University of New Hampshire; C. Kenneth Proefrock, President, National Association of Health Manpower Education Systems.

[54] Dr. Marilyn Gravink, letter to Dolph Hatfield, MD, National Cancer Institute, National Institute of Health, November 25, 1977.

[55] Dr. Donald R. Korst, letter to Dolph Hatfield, PhD, National Cancer Institute, National Institute of Health, November 29, 1977.

[56] George R. Halter, Ed.D., letter to Van. R. Olsen, Director of Public Affairs, U.S. Beet Sugar Association, September 5, 1978.

[57] U.S. Department of Health, Education, and Welfare, *Transcript of Proceedings, In the Matter of Daniel R. Smith Adverse Action Hearing,* March 29-31, 1978. All quotes are from the original transcript.

[58] James Robertson and William Richardson, letter to Henry A. Foley, PhD, Administrator, Health Resources Administration, July 14, 1978.

[59] James Robertson and William Richardson, letter to Henry A. Foley, PhD, Administrator, Health Resources Administration, August 24, 1978.

[60] James Robertson and William Richardson, letter to Henry A. Foley, PhD, Administrator, Health Resources Administration, September 14, 1978.

[61] Henry A. Foley, Ph.D., Administrator, memorandum to Daniel R. Smith, October 4, 1978.

## CHAPTER 16
[62] Serge Schmemann, "Tutu is Installed in Archbishop's Post," *New York Times,* September 8, 1986, Section A, page 3.

CHAPTER 17
[63] "Bishop Walker Elected," *Washington Diocese*, Summer, 1976.
[64] The Rt. Rev. Mariann Edgar Budde, "Bishop John T. Walker's Lasting Legacy," October 3, 2019, *https://www.edow.org/about/bishop-mariann/writings/2019/10/03/bishop-john-t-walkers-lasting-legacy*

CHAPTER 18
[65] Hirsch, James S., *Two Souls Indivisible* (Houghton Mifflin, Boston, MA, May 10, 2004).

EPILOGUE
[66] Christine and Dennis McClure, *We Fought the Road* (Epicenter Press, Kenmore, WA, 2017).
[67] Vanessa Hua, "Golden Spike Redux," National Parks Conservation Association, Summer 2019, article online at www.npca.org.
[68] Definition of white supremacy, *Webster's College Dictionary* (Random House, New York, NY, 1995 edition).
[69] Lauren Jackson, "What Is Critical Race Theory?" *The New York Times*, July 21, 2021.
[70] John Lewis with Michael D'Orso, *Walking with the Wind: A Memoir of the Movement* (Simon & Schuster, New York, NY, 1998) *503*.